OCR →

D0386482

DISCARD

# Nature, State and Economy

# Nature, State and Economy

## A Political Economy of the Environment

## Second Edition

**R. J. JOHNSTON**
*University of Bristol, UK*

JOHN WILEY & SONS

Chichester · New York · Brisbane · Toronto · Singapore

Published by John Wiley & Sons Ltd, Baffins Lane,
Chichester, West Sussex PO19 1UD, England

National        01243 779777
International    (+44) 1243 779777

First Edition published 1989 by Belhaven Press

*Other Wiley Editorial Offices*

John Wiley & Sons, Inc., 605 Third Avenue,
New York, NY 10158-0012, USA

Jacaranda Wiley Ltd, 33 Park Road, Milton,
Queensland 4064, Australia

John Wiley & Sons (Canada) Ltd, 22 Worcester Road,
Rexdale, Ontario M9W 1L1, Canada

John Wiley & Sons (Asia) Pte Ltd, 37 Jalan Pemimpin #05-04,
Block B, Union Industrial Building, Singapore 2057

*Library of Congress Cataloging-in-Publication Data*

Johnston, R. J. (Ronald John)
    Nature, state and economy : a political economy of the environment
/ R.J. Johnston. -- 2nd ed.
    p.    cm.
    Includes bibliographical references and index.
    ISBN 0-471-96671-1 (pbk. : alk. paper)
    1. Sustainable development.    2. Natural resources.
3. Environmentl policy.    I. Title.
HC79.E5J655    1996
333.7--dc20                                                    96-1060
                                                              CIP

*British Library Cataloguing in Publication Data*

A catalogue record for this book is available from the British Library

ISBN 0 471 96671 1

Typeset in 10/12 pt Times by Mackreth Media Services, Hemel Hempstead
Printed and bound in Great Britain by Biddles Ltd, Guildford, Surrey
This book is printed on acid-free paper responsibly manufactured from sustainable forestation,
for which at least two trees are planted for each one used for paper production.

# Contents

# Preface to the First Edition

> If many environmentalists are guilty of ignoring the importance of political economy and the need to understand the role of state institutions, it is equally evident that most post-industrial theorists give little attention to environmental issues, let alone the political economy of militarism and Third World exploitation. (Frankel, 1987, p. 145)

This book is not a normal study of environmental problems, because its focus is neither the mechanisms of problem generation nor a series of case studies on how such problems can be tackled. Rather it is an essay about the production of such problems and the difficulties we face in tackling them, individually and, especially, collectively. Its goal is to bring some of the central material of social science about the ways in which economies work and politics operates to the attention of students of environmental problems, in a format that is relevant to their major concern.

Why write such a book? In 1979 I published the first edition of a book entitled *Geography and Geographers: Anglo-American Human Geography since 1945*, in which I defended my decision to write about human geography only as follows:

> I find the links between physical and human geography tenuous, as those disciplines are currently practised. The major link between them is a sharing of techniques and research procedures, but these are shared with other disciplines too, and are insufficient foundation for a unified discipline ... To a considerable extent ... human and physical are separate, if not independent, disciplines. (Johnston 1979b, p. 2)

This was attacked by some commentators, though not in published reviews, and some even suggested that I did the discipline of geography a political disservice by hinting that such a split existed. I defended that position in the second (1983, p. 6) and third (1987) editions of the book, however, and will continue to do so in the fourth (1991).

Some of the critics suggested that I was ignoring a large literature which clearly demonstrated the human–physical symbiosis, especially in the fields of resource and environmental management. I responded to this view in a paper that, but for environmental circumstances (heavy snow), would have been delivered at the Institute of British Geographers' annual conference at Southampton in January 1982, and was published in *Progress in Physical*

*Geography* a year later, under the title 'Resource analysis, resource management and the integration of physical and human geography'. This made two major points. Firstly, it demonstrated that neither group of geographers working on issues of resource management – the so-called human–physical interface – took much account of the work of the other, and that indeed some of the human geographers whose work was frequently presented to me as indicative of the richness of that interface (Gilbert White and his co-workers, for example) referenced virtually no work that could be identified as physical geography. Secondly, I argued that human and physical geographers, in their search for accounts of what they observed and described, were increasingly using different conceptions of the nature of science whose epistemologies were mutually incompatible. Integration of the two was thus not feasible (as I had learned to my cost in an earlier published debate – Johnston, 1980b; 1982b; Eyles and Lee, 1982 – on the possibility of eclecticism within human geography). This was not intended as an attempt to separate human and physical geography institutionally, but merely to point out to physical geographers that the two parts of the discipline were philosophically distinct and thus could not be integrated and also that most of their writings at the interface failed to appreciate the nature of research in human geography. David Jones (1983, p. 455) interpreted that as revealing 'such a depth of antipathy towards the "integration ethic", that it is quite possible that *collaborative* research will also be viewed as an unwelcome development'.

The debate continued, and was highlighted at another session at the annual conference of the Institute of British Geographers, at Reading in January 1986 (it snowed again). Four papers were presented in a session organised by Elspeth Graham and these were published, along with her commentary, in the Institute's *Transactions* later that year. In his contribution, Ian Douglas called on geographers to use their detailed research findings and methods to address the 'big issues' – of which he cited the nuclear winter controversy as an example – claiming that when they did 'the unity of geography is obvious' (1986, p. 462; for a similar, more trenchantly stated view see Stoddart, 1987): that unity comes through, he said, 'in the complexity of the problems, the intricacy and ramifications of the interactions' (Douglas, 1986, p. 462). Alongside him, Andrew Goudie (1986b) identified five main arguments for the separation of human and physical geography: human geography is concerned with analysing spatial patterns of human activity and has little need to be concerned with the physical environment; the physical environment is becoming less important as a control on human activity; specialisation in science is necessary to rigorous development; geomorphologists would be better off in geoscience and human geography in social science; and physical geographers have failed to demonstrate the relevance of their work to human affairs because they have not been concerned with human processes. He argued against the fragmentation of the discipline. In my contribution (Johnston, 1986c) I suggested that the physical–human split debate was based on a semantic misunderstanding (an argument that Glick, 1987, at least found 'a revelation'). I suggested that the word geography has two major uses: a *vernacular* use which refers to the discipline's subject matter (so that to speak of physical geography is to speak of the physical environment); and an *academic* use which refers to activity within the discipline (so that physical geography is the study of the processes, and the forms that result from them, within the physical environment). Much writing confuses those usages. Many human geographers writing about physical geography use the latter term in its vernacular sense, for example, because they are not interested in the physical processes: as I put it 'the (human) academic geographer interested in population distributions is no more interested in the causes of the physical environment (such as the operation of jet streams) than in how a television works, and so is not interested in physical (academic) geography, only physical (vernacular) geography' (1986c, p. 450). Each type of geographer needs the vernacular of the other in certain circumstances, I contended, but this does not produce an integration of the two academic concerns: if that point can be accepted, I concluded, 'I don't see the physical:human issue as important, therefore, and I am relatively content with the present accommodation' (1986c, p. 450), and I do not for one moment dissent from Douglas, Goudie and Stoddart pointing us all to the 'big issues'.

I fear, however, that while the debate has not yet erupted again it has not gone away, and I also fear that my position remains misunderstood. Goudie (1986b, p. 457), for example, noted that I 'criticized' (his term, not mine: see Johnston, 1983, pp. 134–5) 'some physical geographers for not taking sufficient cognizance of social factors and processes'. He responded to that by listing a large number of studies – 'an outpouring of material by physical geographers' – which explored the 'highly important interface area between man [sic] and nature'. True; but none of them deal with both academic human geography and academic physical geography – most incorporate vernacular human geography only. I do not criticise them for that. But I do argue that, as a collectivity, physical geographers have yet to come to terms with many of the epistemological issues that human geographers have been tackling in the last two decades. As a consequence, their treatment of why the 'big issues' are present – why we create environmental problems – and why we are apparently not doing very well at solving them, does not address the important issues of causation.

Hence this book, which is an attempt to bring to geographers and all others interested in the creation and potential removal of environmental problems the relevant understanding from human geography and related social sciences. Initially it was to have been written with a physical geographer but, not for the first time in my academic career, a potential co-author and I decided amicably to go our separate ways. (This resulted in the salutary experience of my having to read more contemporary physical geography than I otherwise would have done, which I found extremely stimulating.) Thus the focus here is on two basic question: (1) why do we create so many environmental problems?; and (2) why, despite all our scientific knowledge and a great deal of pressure, are we not very good at solving them? The bulk of the book addresses these questions, the first through the medium of political economy (Chapters 3 and 4) and the second through the study of the state and collective action, at all scales (Chapters 5 and 6). First, however, the need for the approach is set in context by two introductory chapters, one dealing with the nature of the problems as they are currently perceived in vernacular debate and how they reflect the conventional wisdom about the interrelationships between peoples and environments, and the other with a very brief summary of the nature of scientific understanding of the environment, very necessary to an appreciation of the need for, and constraints on, collective action via the state.

The purpose of the book is thus to contribute to the literature on the 'big issues' by bringing together important material from the social sciences, as it relates to the study of environmental problems. It is not meant to present a scenario for the future, my solution to the problems, and so the final chapter, 'Alternative Futures', is relatively brief, setting out the major scenarios currently under discussion and putting them in the context of the material that has gone before. My general pessimism undoubtedly comes through, but I am not (yet) a fatalist.

Why add to the literature? In large part because I believe that the task as I conceived it has not been undertaken before. There are many excellent book that do part of the job, notably that of looking at environmental problems from the political economy standpoint, but none that cover both political economy and the state in the way that is done here. It is thus presented not as an innovative contribution but as a needed overview of some important issues.

This book was written in the first three months of 1989, when I was on study leave from the University of Sheffield, between laying down one large administrative burden and taking up another (potentially larger). I am grateful to the Department of Geography, the Faculty of Social Sciences, and the various university committees for that brief period of relative quiet, and in particular to Alan Hay for all that he did to try to ensure that it was as quiet as possible; at least it meant that I could learn the intricacies of word-processing at home in relative tranquillity. Many people stimulated me to write this book, in a variety of ways; I am especially grateful to Ron Cooke and Steve Trudgill, though they are totally absolved from responsibility for anything I have said, and to Peter Smithson who tried to ensure that I didn't misrepresent the work of physical geographers; he, too, is totally absolved. A particular expression of gratitude is to Iain Stevenson, who was a continual source of encouragement and helped me through more rough passages than probably either he or I care to remember.

This book is dedicated to Rita. That I have now written as many books as the years we have shared is a poor expression of thanks for so much contentment.

# Preface to the Second Edition

The first edition of this book was written in the late 1980s, at a time of relative economic prosperity and political security. Environmental issues were high on political agendas, and there was considerable optimism that, despite the pessimistic views of some scientists and the impending disaster forecast by some ecologists, the many perceived environmental problems would be seriously addressed –locally, nationally and globally. Much of that optimism was naïve, and the expectations were too great. Even among many academics and their students, there was a simplistic faith that, now that those in charge of the state were aware of the problems, solutions would be found; despite a decade of 'New Right' government in the UK, the USA and elsewhere, people were optimistic. This book was conceived to counter that optimism, to illustrate the constraints of political economy and the difficulties that those in charge of the state apparatus face if they want to take radical action to tackle environmental problems.

Much has changed in the intervening few years. The world economy plunged into a major recession, which meant that issues such as unemployment and job security took precedence on political agendas. The communist states of the USSR and eastern Europe collapsed, showing to the world the major difficulties of centralised planning and control of complex economies under 'socialism as practised'; its impact of a half-century on the environment became plain. In the face of such momentous changes, it was not surprising that media attention shifted away from environmental issues so that, although many people remained concerned about the possibility of ecological disaster, this was not the main focus of their attention.

The very considerable exposure given to environmental problems in the 1980s had stirred concern among national and international agencies, however, and this ensured continued attention – culminating in the 'Earth Summit' at Rio de Janeiro in 1992. But by then the sceptics had developed telling cases against what they saw as the 'scare stories' of the 'ecological doom and gloom merchants'; they questioned the scientific findings and their meanings and gave reluctant politicians grounds on which to stall.

So the early 1990s have been difficult years for those promoting the environmental cause. They have won many small battles but the large war is still being waged; there are few national, let alone global, commitments to a blueprint for sustainable development with the environment. The constraints outlined in this book remain very much to the fore.

The main purposes of this second edition are to bring the material up to date and to fill some gaps in the coverage – notably of state policies of regulation and pricing, of international negotiations over environmental issues, and of sustainable development. The structure of the book remains unchanged, and some parts are very little altered. Overall, however, the book is contemporary and more rounded in its coverage – hence the slight change to its title.

I agreed to produce this revised edition more than two years ago, and am grateful to Iain Stevenson for his kind forbearance in waiting for it – and his optimism that it would emerge. And, once again, my thanks to Rita for renewing that contentment as we both come to terms with major career changes.

# Acknowledgements

The author and publishers are grateful to the following for permission to reproduce material:

- Prof R.J. Chorley and Dr B.A. Kennedy for Figures 2.1, 2.3, 2.4, and 2.7
- Dr S.T. Trudgill for Figures 2.2 and 6.3
- Dr R.J. Huggett for Figures 2.5, 2.6, and 2.8
- Prof J.B. Thornes for Figures 2.9, 2.11, and 2.13
- Prof A.G. Wilson for Figure 2.12
- Prof R.U. Cooke for Figure 2.14
- Prof A.S. Goudie for Figures 2.15 and 4.3
- Prof D.W. Harvey for Figure 3.1
- Prof P.R. Gould for Figure 4.1
- Prof P.M. Blaikie for Figure 4.2
- Prof T. O'Riordan for Figure 6.2

Attempts have been made to obtain similar permission from all other authors whose material is reproduced here, but without success.

The work of Simon Godden to reproduce the diagrams is gratefully acknowledged.

# 1 Introduction

The world is dying. What are you going to do about it? (*The Sunday Times Magazine*, cover, 26 February 1989)

Beware of the greens who cry wolf. (Headline in *The Times*, 25 March 1995)

Public and political concern about environmental problems has waxed and waned somewhat in recent decades, at times achieving a very high media profile. This was the case in the UK in the late 1980s: in one week in March 1989, for example, *The Listener* carried the Duke of Edinburgh's Dimbleby Lecture (delivered on BBC TV three days earlier) entitled 'Living off the land'; *Marxism Today* had an article on 'Green times'; and *Living Marxism* followed its lead article of the previous month – 'Can capitalism go green?' – with articles on 'What's gone wrong with the German greens?' and 'An ozone-free zone?'.

Newspapers carried a large number of articles on such issues, many of them carrying messages of impending ecological doom: Lloyd Timberlake's article in *The Independent* (12 September 1988) entitled 'The greatest threat on earth', for example, promoted the thesis that 'ecological disaster will replace nuclear war as the biggest danger in the twenty-first century' (p. 19). Soil erosion; water and atmospheric pollution; global warming; holes in the ozone layer; rapid depletion of fish resources: these and many other issues were commonly discussed topics. The general tenor of the coverage was that the earth is facing impending ecological disaster, and that governments – individually and collectively – must act immediately to forestall it. Furthermore, there was a clear implication in much that was written that human activity was the main cause of most of the problems, and that we were largely unaware of the fact. Thus an article in *The Sunday Times Magazine* (26 February 1989, p. 20) said that:

> You damage the earth just by living on it. You burn fossil fuels – petrol, oil, coal – and huge amounts more are burnt by those who supply you with goods and services. You create waste, which has to be buried, burnt or discharged into the sea. You accept the profits of investments which are trading on Third World poverty and putting further strain on already overstretched resources. You buy goods from farms and factories whose ill-effects from chemical wastes range all the way from dead fish to dead people.

The article continued by calling on people to act, creating political pressure for change:

For decades the health of the planet has been the obsessive concern of a highly vocal and occasionally irritating minority. Now it is at the top of the world's political agenda. . . . . it is your world they are talking about. Your future that is in their hands. If you are concerned about your environment, you will want to know what you can do.

There was a political response, both nationally and internationally. The British government published a White Paper on environmental policy (Department of the Environment, 1990), for example; the Prime Minister promoted the environmental cause in her speech at the 1988 Conservative Party Conference; and a leading environmental economist became a special adviser to the Secretary of State for the Environment. Within a year he produced a major report, *Blueprint for a Green Economy* (Pearce et al, 1989), which made a powerful case for the practice of 'sustainable development', whose theme is that 'future generations should be compensated for reductions in the endowments of resources brought about by the actions of present generations' (1989, p. 3). This calls for policy based on three concepts:

(1) Environmental valuation: natural resources must no longer be treated as free goods to be exploited, but as finite capital which should be properly valued and purchased through market mechanisms.
(2) Long-term horizons: the shape of the future 'to be inherited by our grandchildren, and perhaps beyond' (1989, p. 2) should be in party manifestos and policies, alongside concerns for the short and medium terms.
(3) Equity: emphasis should be placed on meeting the needs of both the disadvantaged today (intra-generational equity) and future generations (inter-generational equity).

Implementation of these goals requires major shifts in the practice of politics, and in particular the measurement of economic growth. But Pearce and his colleagues are certain that, with those shifts, it is possible to achieve the goals of the World Commission on Environment and Development, which involves the commitment

> to leave to future generations a *wealth* inheritance – a stock of knowledge and understanding, a stock of technology, a stock of man-made capital *and* a stock of environmental assets – no less than that inherited by the current generation. (Pearce et al, 1989, p. xiv)

Much of the focus of the present book is on the constraints to achieving that commitment.

One piece of evidence widely cited at the time as indicating a major change in public attitudes in the UK towards environmental concerns came in June

1989, when the Green Party won 15 per cent of the votes cast in the elections for the European Parliament. Most opinion polls and attitude surveys sustained this claim of increasing environmental concern across the population, especially among the professional classes. (Pearce et al, 1989, p. xiii, report that 93 per cent of respondents to a 1988 European Community survey of perceptions of 'very important political problems today' listed 'the environment', which came second only to 'unemployment'.)

Internationally, the same concerns were being voiced throughout the 'developed world' and there was growing anxiety about the perceived 'rape of the earth' in the 'developing world' – with the rapid destruction of tropical forests and the advance of deserts (especially in Africa). A US senator, soon to become vice-president, wrote a book on environmental policy (Gore, 1992). The World Commission on Environment and Development published its report on *Our Common Future* in 1987, which included 'Proposed legal principles for environmental protection and sustainable development', based on the claimed fundamental human right that: 'All human beings have the fundamental right to an environment adequate for their health and well-being' (1987, p. 348). This international concern culminated in a United Nations Conference on Environment and Development, convened in Rio de Janeiro in June 1992, and frequently termed the 'Earth Summit'. Over 178 governments were represented – more than 100 by their head of state or head of government – and most governments submitted reports on their environments and development plans. A large number of other events were staged alongside the inter-governmental conference, many involving non-governmental organisations involved in environmental issues.

The implication is of nearly a decade of debate and action regarding environmental issues, and yet many people remain very pessimistic about the future of global ecosystems and feel that little has been achieved during that period. Public concern remains considerable, even though it gets less media coverage in the mid-1990s than in the late 1980s. Membership of environmental pressure groups has soared in the UK, while membership of some political parties falls rapidly. In England and Wales, for example, membership of the National Trust grew from 278 000 in 1971 to 1 046 000 in 1981 and 2 032 000 in 1990; comparable figures for Scotland were 37 000, 110 000 and 218 000. Over the same two decades, the Royal Society for the Protection of Birds grew from 98 000 to 844 000 members, and the World Wide Fund for Nature from 12 000 to 247 000. Groups with activism high on their agendas similarly exploded: Friends of the Earth had 1000 members in 1971, 18 000 in 1981 and 110 000 in 1990: Greenpeace had none in 1971, 30 000 a decade later, and 372 000 in 1990. (All figures are taken from Department of the Environment, 1992, p. 273). And 1994 saw the rapid growth of public protest against the export of live animals (especially veal calves) from the UK, involving many older, relatively affluent people who had never before participated in such protests.

The British government claims to be responding to these concerns. It estimates that spending on environmental issues increased from £4.8 billion in 1986–7 to £14 billion in 1990–1 (equivalent to 2.5 per cent of GDP); much of that expenditure (£8.8 billion) was on pollution abatement, with 25 per cent from the government and the remainder from private sector concerns (Department of the Environment, 1992, pp. 237–47).

Nevertheless, there is considerable evidence of a reduction in political attention to environmental issues in the face of the economic problems which beset the global economy from 1990 on, accompanied by an unwillingness to commit resources to environmental programmes and claims that the problems are not as severe as was initially agreed. Thus while one journalist produced a book entitled *The End of Nature* (McKibben, 1990), another wrote in *The Times* (25 March 1995) of his

> revulsion at the hijacking of environmental issues by extremists who seem prepared to tell alarming fibs to get attention and market share in the competitive world of green charity . . . regulation, state interference and centralisation are often the problem, not the solution; . . . growth and technology are often the solution, not the problem. (Richard North).

Among the examples of the 'alarming fibs' cited are: hundreds of millions who were to starve to death because of famine in the 1970s, and 65 million Americans in the 1980s; the world would run out of oil by the end of the century; an imminent ice age predicted in the 1970s; a 1983 prediction that one-third of all German trees would die from acid rain pollution; and so on. Slightly more soberly, Beckerman and Malkin (1994, pp. 15–16; see also Beckerman, 1992) have asked 'How much does global warming matter?', concluding that

> it may be a problem, but it is no cause for undue alarm or drastic action. There is plenty of time to improve our understanding of the science and scrap policies that encourage economically inefficient use of fuels. . . . We are not on the edge of an abyss and the human race is not facing destruction from the accumulation of greenhouse gases. . . . Global warming is far more glamorous and telegenic, of course, than the need for better toilets and drains in the Third World. But if we truly care about the welfare of our fellow world citizens, it is these kinds of environmental issues upon which we must focus our attention.

A leader writer for *The Economist* (1 April 1995, p. 13) came to a similar conclusion: 'For all the green clamour, it is far too early to be panicked into Draconian actions to avert global warming; especially when most actions would pose a bigger threat to human wellbeing than does global warming'.

Perhaps unfortunately, there is a secure foundation to some of these claims, because scientific evidence has been overinterpreted and/or overextrapolated in a number of cases. An idealistic view sees politicians take incontrovertible 'scientific facts' and advice – 'scientific consensus tends to generate political consensus' (Litkin, 1994, p.4). But such a simplistic attitude ignores the importance of information to power, and the frequent manipulation of information by those with, or seeking, power. Scientific 'evidence' can be used to legitimate political values, as exemplified by what Thomas and Middleton (1994) call the 'desertification myth'. The evidence of human suffering in African drylands in the 1980s stimulated concern for their plight, which it was believed could only be tackled through international action. A myth was institutionalised by the United Nations, claiming that one-third of the world's land area is threatened by the voracious process of desertification in drylands which are characterised by fragile ecosystems that are highly susceptible to rapid degradation. That process is the cause of much misery and suffering, and so the United Nations must tackle the desertification problem. A major agency was established to mount the fight, based on massive overstatement of the extent of the problem and threat:

> The lack of scientific foundation of early quantification attempts, doubts surrounding the conceptualisation of desertification as the advancing desert front and the lack of clarity of the processes involved have not prevented politicians from using information based on these approaches to indicate the severity of the problem. Scientists have questioned the developing myths, but it is not until now that their voices have begun to be widely heard and increasingly accepted above the clamour created by the UNEP publicity machine. (Thomas and Middleton, 1994, p.66)

It was in the interests of those running the United Nations Environment Programme in Nairobi to promote the myth of rapidly advancing desertification, thereby creating what Thomas and Middleton (1994, p.63) call 'A concept out of hand'.

Such sceptical reactions to the misuse of science appear to have influenced many politicians (although the British Secretary of State for the Environment was reported as saying in March 1995 that he found the scientific evidence for global warming incontrovertible). When the World Climate Conference convened in Berlin in March 1995, as a follow-up to the Convention on Climate Change agreed at Rio de Janeiro three years earlier and ratified by 188 countries since, newspaper reports indicated a waning of resolve to tackle the issue of $CO_2$ emissions. In a story entitled 'Global warming gets cold shoulder', *The Independent* reported (27 March 1995) that Middle Eastern oil-exporting states wanted no commitments to limit the growing use of fossil fuels (because of the potential impacts on their economies) and the largest per capita users (USA, Canada, and Australia) reported that they would not meet their commitment to cut emissions to 1990 levels by the year 2000. Against that, a group of 30 small island states which fear rising sea levels as a consequence of global warming wanted $CO_2$ emissions cut by 20 per cent between 1990 and 2005, but many other politicians and diplomats were influenced by the scientific uncertainties over the rate and amount of warming expected, and by commentators' claims that there are more important problems to tackle. All that the conference eventually decided was that further cuts would be required after 2000, and these would be agreed by 1997.

In other words, we are in a state of uncertainty. There may be a disaster looming, but we are not sure; and if there is, we do not know whether a policy of 'wait and see' might not hasten the disaster. Part of our uncertainty stems from a lack of appreciation of why the disaster may be looming, which calls for an understanding of the operation of both environmental systems and political economy. The first edition of this book was written as a response to that general lack of appreciation among many students and those who taught them. Much of the literature which I reviewed in the late 1980s failed to provide any deep analysis of why we are generating environmental problems and why we do not seem to be tackling them very effectively. Although the situation has changed somewhat in the years since, there is still a need for an approach to the topic which draws on the social sciences and provides the necessary appreciation of how environmental problems are generated and what the socio-political constraints to tackling them are.

## PEOPLE AND ENVIRONMENT

At the heart of the set of issues addressed here is the interrelationship of people and their environment. The nature of that interrelationship and its variations in time and space has produced a substantial scholarly literature (notably the seminal volume by Glacken, 1967). The present situation, and the growth of an environmental consciousness among the population of many countries, suggests a change in the interpretation of that relationship. The rest of this chapter traces the foundations of that change, as an introduction to the rest of the book.

### PEOPLE, ENVIRONMENT AND THE 'HUMAN ASCENDANCY'

At the beginning of his major work, *Traces on the Rhodian Shore*, Glacken (1967, p. vii) identifies three questions that have persistently been posed in human societies:

(1) Was the earth purposefully created for human habitation?
(2) Has the nature of the earth influenced the moulding of individual characteristics and of human cultures?
(3) In what manner have people changed the environment during their long tenure of the earth?

The usual answers provided three ideas: that 'the planet is designed for man alone, as the highest being of the creation, or for the hierarchy of life with man at the apex'; that all life adapts itself to 'the purposefully created harmonious conditions'; and that 'man through his arts and inventions was ... a partner of God, improving upon and cultivating an earth created for him' (p. viii). From these, Glacken (1967, p. viii) argues that

> in Western thought until the end of the eighteenth century, concepts of the relationship of human culture to the natural environment were dominated – but not exclusively so – by these three ideas, sometimes by only one of them, sometimes by two or even the three in combination ... This group of ideas and certain subsidiary ideas which gathered around them were part of the matrix from which in modern times the social sciences have emerged ... In Western civilization these three ideas have played an important role in the attempt to understand man, his culture, and the natural environment in which he lives ...

The remainder of Glacken's book provides a rich series of illustrations and analyses of the changing relative importance of those ideas in Western thought (see also Simmons, 1993). The treatment is largely chronological, and shows how over time the second and third ideas came to dominate, justifying the view of 'man as a controller of nature' and heralding the twentieth century in which 'man has attained a breathtaking anthropocentrism, based on his power over nature, unmatched by anything in the past' (Glacken, 1967, p. 494).

Western thought is dominantly Judaeo-Christian in its origins and content; in its early development, Glacken shows, much of it was concerned with linking the two creations – of humanity and of earth (1967, p. 151). The basic theme to emerge was of a caring God – caring for the earth and all those who occupy it. Within that earth, 'man has a divine mission to control the whole creation. To achieve this, it is God's intention that mankind multiply itself, spread out over the earth, make its domination over the creation secure' (1967, p. 151). This was developed, and in medieval Christianity was formulated into the belief that 'man created in God's image has by God's grace dominion over all nature' (1967, p. 293).

The development of human civilisations was 'virtually synonymous with the conquest of nature' according to Thomas (1984, p. 25) – who illustrates the point by noting that the 30 copies of the Gutenberg Bible printed on vellum in 1456 used the skins of 5000 calves, thereby indicating the dependence of progress on the control of animal resources. That conquest was justified, Thomas argues, by the presentation of the human species as innately different from and superior to all others and, as Glacken had also shown, the justification was sustained through particular readings of the Bible. But, as Thomas shows, acceptance of that view created dilemmas for some people during the eighteenth century, because the treatment of plants and, especially, animals offended their aesthetic and moral sensibilities:

> This was the human dilemma: how to reconcile the physical requirements of civilization with the new feelings and values which that same civilization had generated . . . there had gradually emerged attitudes to the natural world which were essentially incompatible with the direction in which English society was moving. The growth of towns had led to a new longing for the countryside. The progress of cultivation had fostered a taste for weeds, mountains and unsubdued nature. The new-found security from wild animals had generated an increasing concern to protect birds and preserve wild creatures in their natural state. Economic independence of animal power and urban isolation from animal farming had nourished emotional attitudes which were hard, if not impossible, to reconcile with the exploitation of animals by which most people lived. (1984, p.301)

This dilemma continued to develop through the nineteenth and twentieth centuries, until it was overtaken by another which questioned the role of 'man' in 'God's plan' and brought the idea of the 'conquest of nature' into sharp debating focus. Until recently, much of the debate has focused on the relationship between humans and inanimate nature, but the issue of animal rights now occupies a major place on the agenda. Benton (1992, p.79), introducing a series of papers on the topic, points out the paradoxical nature of human–animal relationships: on the one hand, animals are treated as mere commodities (as in factory farming and laboratory experiments); on the other, as in children's literature and with family pet-keeping, 'animals have acquired a quasi-personal status as psychologically sophisticated companions and honorary members of human social groupings'.

## CONQUEST AND CHALLENGE

The nineteenth and twentieth centuries have produced massive changes in the relationships between human societies and the natural environment, with the dominant theme being the conquest of the latter by the former – despite some occasional set-backs. This has been sustained by an ideology in the West founded in the Christian doctrines enunciated above, and advanced through the belief that human creativity and ingenuity is such that it can surmount any difficulties that the environment might place in the way of its search for material advancement – after all, we have now visited the moon, and will soon extend human sovereignty to other planets.

This outlook has been termed *technocentrism* by O'Riordan (1981a) and *technological environmentalism* by Pepper (1984). According to O'Riordan, technocentrism dominates capitalist ideology, and is identified by the values of rationality, managerial efficiency, optimism and faith:

faith in the ability of man to understand and control physical, biological, and social processes for the benefit of present and future generations. Progress, efficiency, rationality, and control – these form the ideology of technocentrism that downplays the sense of wonder, reverence, and moral obligation that are the hallmarks of the ecocentric mode. (1981a, p.11).

Central to this faith is the role of science, which provides the intelligence for the rational control of the environment – not only the physical science which provides the means of manipulating nature but also the social (especially economic) science which evaluates that manipulation in a common metric, money. Thus if, as some argue, manipulation of nature is creating problems and dilemmas, then this calls for greater investment in and application of science in order to advance human desires (Pepper, 1984).

The main opposition to this technocentric ideology until recent years has come from two strands of what Pepper calls ecological environmentalism. The first of these – what Pepper calls the 'non-scientific' strand – grew out of the 'moral and aesthetic sensibilities' to 'the conquest of nature' identified by Thomas. It contains within it a strong romantic element – defined by Pepper as rejecting materialism: 'Romantics noticed and hated the way that industrialisation made previously beautiful places ugly, and they rejected the vulgarity of those who made money in trade' (1984, p.76). To them, nature was independent of people, with its own integrity and ability to survive: respect for that integrity required human 'guardianship' of nature – 'man should be the steward even of those parts of nature for which he has no obvious use or need' (1984, p.89).

Alongside this romantic ecological environmentalism – for which O'Riordan's term is *ecocentrism* – there is a scientific strand which has promoted, in a variety of ways, the view that there are limits to the capacity of the earth to cope with human demands upon it. Pepper identifies its origins with Malthus, traces its development in the concept of environmental systems (see Chapter 2) and the arguments for environmental conservation (of which George Perkins Marsh is frequently presented as an initiator: Lowenthal, 1965), and its culmination in the environmental models predicting ecological disaster, such as *The Limits to Growth* (Meadows et al, 1972). It is that culmination which is crucial here, since it provided the means of bringing together the two strands in a late twentieth-century ecological environmentalism.

## CONTEMPORARY ECOLOGICAL ENVIRONMENTALISM

The ecocentric mode of thinking, drawing on the romantic, non-scientific ecological environmentalism, has five major characteristics, according to O'Riordan:

(1) It identifies a *natural morality*, a set of rules for human behaviour within the limits and constraints of natural ecosystems.
(2) It specifies the existence of *limits* to human activity, and hence to 'progress'.
(3) It promotes the protection of *options*, by maintaining the diversity and stability of ecosystems.
(4) It raises questions about *ends* and *means*, and thus about the political processes through which power is exercised and decisions about environmental use are promulgated.
(5) It preaches *self-reliance* and *self-sufficiency*, with anarchic communities that can respond flexibly to changing circumstances, avoiding the vulnerability of dependence on large corporations and trade. (1981a, pp.10–11)

The five are given different weight by different advocates, leading to a division of ecocentrics into two groups (O'Riordan, 1981b; Pepper, 1984). Both lack faith in technology, elite experts and centralised states as the source of solutions to environmental problems, and criticise materialist growth when pursued for its own sake. But whereas the *deep ecologists* promote the concept of a human society conforming to ecological laws, the *self-reliance, soft technologists* focus more on the anarchist solution. (See also Dobson, 1990; Eckersley, 1992.)

Against these two groups in contemporary society are ranged two types of technocentrist. The *environmental managers* (or accommodators; O'Riordan, 1981a, p.376) believe that growth can continue if properly organised whereas the *cornucopians* (Cotgrove, 1982) are even more optimistic regarding human capabilities, have faith in scientific and technological expertise and believe that 'man can always find a way out of any difficulties whether political, scientific or technological ... all impediments can be overcome given a will, ingenuity and sufficient resources arising out of growth' (Pepper, 1984, p.31).

## THE CONTEMPORARY CONFLICT

There has been conflict between ecocentric and technocentric environmentalists for at least the last hundred years, and both the early 'green politics' (Gould, 1988) and the development of town and country planning (Hall, 1988) owe much to the successes of the romantic ecocentrics. But recent decades have seen an escalation of the conflict to a central place on the international political agenda. The reason for this is somewhat paradoxical, for it is the findings of some scientists which have brought into question the foundations of the technocentric mode of thought, and especially its cornucopian strand. Science is revered in that strand as the source of human conquest of nature, and yet some scientists are now not only producing theories which put the notion of conquest into question but also campaigning for changes within society that will slow, if not halt, the creation and exacerbation of environmental problems. Their concern is aided by enhanced public awareness of those problems, and is taken up by a range of others who, for their own reasons, wish to promote major social change.

Conflicts can be of two types. The first are those which are capable of solution – there is one right answer, and all the rest are wrong. The second are those which can be resolved – with an accommodation accepted by all the parties – but not solved, because there is no right answer. Most of the environmental problems that we face today are treated as in the second category. It may be that in the fullness of time they shift to the first, but at present there is much debate over the scientific findings – within the scientific community itself – and few fully verified theories of how the environment works (perhaps, as laid out in the next chapter, because of its great complexity, if not its inherent mystery). Thus before resolutions can be agreed upon, the existence of a problem has to be accepted (Trudgill, 1990). Increasingly, the latter is taking place but not at sufficient speed, according to many promoting the ecocentric view. Thus we have conflict over whether we are creating environmental problems and how serious they are, and only then over how we may solve (not resolve) them.

Academic contributions to the literature on these conflicts are of three types: those largely supporting the technocentric view; those favouring the ecocentric; and those which do not take a position but seek to analyse both. There are few in the last category, because most analysts, implicitly if not explicitly, are convinced by one of the others. Among them, the ecocentric dominates. Catton, for example, has written widely on the sociological implications of the carrying capacity of the earth being reached (e.g. Catton 1978; 1987) and has concluded that: 'Present human gratification is being achieved at the cost of environmental changes that ensure future human deprivation' (1983, p. 298). He disputes the views of the technocentrics like Simon and Kahn, who believe that because of human ingenuity the term carrying capacity 'has by now no useful meaning' (Simon and Kahn, 1984, p. 45). Catton contends that because of achievements in death control over the last century people received 'a magnificent blessing' but the resulting benefits 'helped us overshoot a permanent carrying capacity' (1985, p. 83); they allowed *Homo sapiens* to become translated into *Homo colossus*, sustained by a 'myth of limitlessness' and leading us to 'rush toward a lemming-like fate without pausing to discern it' (1985, p. 84). We need a clearer definition of carrying capacity which is future-based rather than present-oriented: 'Carrying capacity means, for a given environment, the amount of use that can be exceeded only by impairing that environment's future suitability for that use' (Catton et al, 1986, p. 180).

With that definition, and with the scientific evidence increasingly being made available, we would then conclude that the technocentric view is not sustainable and would promote an ecocentric future:

ecologically realistic sociological analyses could sustain a measure of optimism by helping decision-makers understand the basic forces that shape societal systems, better anticipate impending problems, and more efficiently struggle to preserve and extend the resource base of our own and other societies. (Catton et al, 1986, p.185)

From these premises, Catton seeks to build a new paradigm for his discipline, sociology; his arguments apply equally well to geography and other sciences and social sciences. The dominant paradigm in sociology at the present time, according to Catton and Dunlap (1980), is one of *human exceptionalism* based on the *dominant Western worldview*, which they characterise by four major assumptions:

(1) About the *nature of human beings* – people are fundamentally different from all other creatures on earth, over which they have dominion.
(2) About the *nature of social causation* – people can determine their own destinies, can choose their goals and learn whatever is necessary to achieve them.
(3) About the *context of human society* – the world is vast and provides unlimited opportunities for humans.
(4) About the *constraints on human society* – the history of human society is one of progress; there is a solution to every problem, and progress need never cease. (1980, p.34)

The human exceptionalism paradigm follows these dominant views entirely, by assuming that: both genetically and culturally, humans are quite unlike all other animal species; social and cultural factors are the predominant determinants of human affairs; social and cultural environments provide the major contexts for human affairs, and the biophysical environment is largely irrelevant; and culture is cumulative, so that social and technological progress can continue indefinitely.

Catton and Dunlap promote an opposing, new ecological paradigm, built on the following four assumptions (corresponding again to those of the dominant Western worldview):

(1) Humans have exceptional characteristics but remain one among many in an interdependent global ecosystem.
(2) Human affairs are influenced not only by social and cultural factors but also by the complex interactions in the web of nature, so that human actions can have many unintended consequences.
(3) Humans are dependent on a finite biophysical environment which sets physical and biological limits to human affairs.
(4) 'Although the inventiveness of humans and the power derived therefrom may seem for a while to extend carrying capacity limits, ecological laws cannot be repealed'. (1980, p.34)

If we are convinced by, or at least feel some sympathy with, such arguments regarding the carrying capacity of the earth, and are attracted to the ecocentric set of attitudes, then we need to understand why it is that we continue to press so hard against the carrying capacity constraints and why we do not promote actions which will relieve the strain – or, more accurately, since clearly some actions are being taken, why it is that insufficient action has been taken to ensure that the ecological future of human society is being ensured. O'Riordan argues that there have been considerable advances since the nascent stage in the evolution of environmental strategies in the early 1970s, but continues:

> Whether these reforms have actually altered the basic philosophies of the twentieth-century financial, corporate, trade-union, and political establishment is very much open to doubt, but at least innovations in procedure and analysis have occurred to the benefit of environmentally orientated decision-making. (1981a, p.372)

The media coverage of nearly a decade later reviewed at the start of this chapter suggests some wider appreciation of the issues since, but still indicates a need for deeper analysis of both the reasons for the problems that we have created and continue to create, and the ways forward that are available. With regard to the first of these issues, the argument advanced here is that an understanding of the origins of environmental problems must be found in the discipline of political economy, hence the concentration in Chapters 3 and 4 on modes of economic organisation. Regarding the second issue, most writers accept that individual desires are insufficient and that environmental problems must be tackled collectively – thus Fernie and Pitkethly (1985, p.vii) write that

> all resource problems – overpopulation, hunger, poverty, fuel shortages, deforestation – are fundamentally *institutional* problems which warrant institutional solutions. The success or failure of resource management is intrinsically tied up with institutional structures – the pattern of agencies, laws and policies which pertain to resource issues.

Thus we need to appreciate the nature of collective action, the basis of those institutional structures; this is the focus of Chapters 5 and 6 of the present book.

The heart of this book, therefore, is not environmental problems but rather the conditions that lead to their production and the constraints on collective action in the search both to solve current problems and to ensure that new ones do not appear. Nevertheless, a clear introductory presentation of the environmental context is necessary, to establish the case for collective action, and this is provided in Chapter 2. Finally, although the book does not pretend to offer a blueprint for the future, Chapter 7 briefly reviews the major arguments about how political economy and collective action may be structured in the future, on the assumption that the case against the technocentric view is accepted.

# 2 Environmental Systems

In the world of science emplaced by the eighteenth century in the West, the prevailing model was that of clockwork. After the discovery this century of the uncertainties of the quantum world, the universe takes on more of the aspect of a cosmic lottery. (Simmons, 1993, p.35)

The earth's physical environment is the subject of study by geographers and other environmental scientists. The details of their research findings are not of particular interest here, since this book is concerned not so much with examples of individual environments and how they work as with the generality of their findings. The focus here is on environmental systems (a concept which became increasingly popular with physical geographers from 1970 on: see Gregory, 1985), on the interdependence of all the myriad parts of the environment (its lithosphere, biosphere and atmosphere), on the changes in that interdependence, and on the role of human action in creating such changes. This then allows an appreciation of the nature of most (if not all) environmental issues and on the need for collective action if they are to be countered.

## THE NATURE OF SYSTEMS

Simply defined, a system is a set of linked components. The individual parts need not all be linked directly to each other, but all are connected through indirect links. This can be illustrated by a simple example of an island ecosystem (Figure 2.1; adapted from Bennett and Chorley, 1978, who derived it from Rykiel and Kuenzel, 1971). Initial focus is on the three system components in the central box of the diagram. In this, there is no direct link between the wolf population and the volume of plant biomass on the island, since wolves are carnivores and do not consume plant matter. However, the carnivorous wolves are dependent on the volume of biomass indirectly, since they are predatory on the moose population which is herbivorous. Thus the greater the amount of plant biomass, the greater the moose population that can be supported, and the larger the potential wolf population as a consequence.

This simple example not only illustrates the nature of indirect links but also can be used to indicate the complexity of the interrelationships within even a small ecosystem. Outside the two links isolated in the central box of Figure 2.1 is a large number of others. The amount of plant biomass available

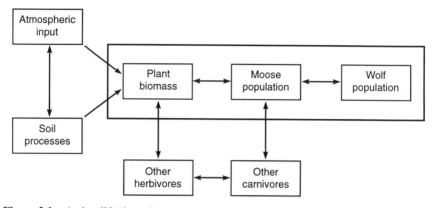

**Figure 2.1**   A simplified model of an ecosystem: Isle Royale (adapted from Bennett and Chorley, 1978, p. 346)

to the moose population is a function both of the amount produced and of the competition with other herbivores. Atmospheric processes influence the production of biomass, both directly through the provision of energy and precipitation and indirectly through the provision of nutrients derived from the soil, whose constitution is partly a function of weathering processes on the local bedrock. Thus the size of the wolf population is indirectly linked to what goes on in both the atmospheric system and the soil system. It is also a function of the competition between the moose population and other herbivores for the available biomass – the more successful the moose in that competition the more wolves that can be supported. It also competes with other carnivores for moose – the more competitors there are, and the more successful they are, the smaller the wolf population.

Figure 2.1 provides a basic illustration of the nature of systems. Most systems are much more complex, but the basic features are the same. It provides a foundation for the remainder of this chapter.

TYPES OF SYSTEM

In the search for the general principles of system structure and operation, much has been done to characterise systems and classify them. As indicated earlier, one way of classifying the systems is according to the part of the environment they occupy, with a basic division between those in the atmosphere, the biosphere and the lithosphere. This division matches the division of physical geography into climatology, biogeography and geomorphology. But there are difficulties of definition here: where does the study of the soil fall – in geomorphology, in biogeography, or in both? The question is largely irrelevant because, as the structure of Trudgill's *Soil and Vegetation Systems* (1988) shows,

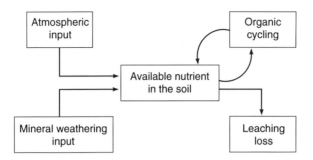

**Figure 2.2**    The system links involved in the study of soil nutrients (redrawn from Trudgill, 1988)

they are all interrelated (Figure 2.2); if one's focus is on the available nutrients in the soil as the support of plant and animal life, one must realise that the volume of nutrients is a function not only of processes within the soil itself (the bottom right link) and between the soil and the vegetation that it supports (top right), but also between the atmosphere and the soil (top left) and the weathering processes that produce the soil's raw materials (bottom left). Furthermore, those external systems are interlinked too; the atmospheric and weathering systems interact, both directly and indirectly, through the soil and the vegetation it supports (the richer the vegetation, for example, the less the direct erosional impact of atmospheric processes).

In brief, a classification of systems according to location within the environment is largely artificial, because all parts are linked to all others in some way. The analyst chooses a particular focus for a study, and defines the system that encompasses it accordingly. It may be confined to the atmosphere only, but it is quite likely that it will not.

A more valuable approach to system classification refers to the nature of the study being undertaken. There are several such classifications (as reviewed, for example, in Bennett and Chorley, 1978; Huggett, 1980; and Wilson, 1981a). One of the more popular among geographers is that proposed by Chorley and Kennedy (1971), reproduced as Figure 2.3. The characteristics of the four types are as follows.

**Morphological systems**

These show the relationships among the various components of a system, and are useful in the description of, for example, the interactions of different elements in a landscape, such as those comprising a slope system, a river channel system, and a drainage basin system. With a slope system, for example, there are relationships among variables such as the angle of slope, the depth of the weathered material on it, the grain size characteristics of the

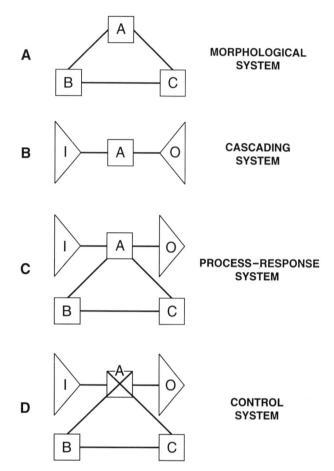

**Figure 2.3**   A typology of systems (redrawn from Chorley and Kennedy, 1971)

soil, the acidity of the soil, and so forth; in a river channel the major
components of the system are discharge, sediment load, velocity, bed
roughness, nature of bed and banks, bedslope, vegetation, and water
temperature (Huggett, 1980, pp. 39–40).

By displaying the various components of a morphological system, the
interrelatedness of the parts is emphasised. This means that when it is
decided to study one component of the system, its place in the morphological
structure is clear and the influences on that component can be readily
identified; for applied work this means that once the relationships among the
components are known, then the impact of change in one on the others can
be identified. Thus Chorley and Kennedy's representation of an interfluve as
a morphological system (Figure 2.4) shows relationships among three groups

of characteristics of that system–the slope itself, the debris on that slope and the vegetation on the slope. The links are shown as either positive or negative, and the strength of the links by the thickness of the lines indicating them. For example, the deeper the soil weathered mantle on the slope, the lower the slope angle and (possibly) the larger the proportion of the area covered by plants (in part also because of a greater volume of moisture available to sustain growth). The steeper the slope, on the other hand, the smaller the proportion of its area covered by plants, which is the strongest relationship in the whole system. So removal of plant cover can lead to increased slope angles and a shallower soil mantle, with the consequence that an even smaller proportion of the area can be covered by plants.

A morphological system is largely a description of the relationships among the components, therefore, and as such is a useful indication of the complexity of the direct and indirect links. It does not account for the relationships, however, and as such must be supplemented by other types of system study if understanding of the environment is to be achieved.

### Cascading systems

These are linked components, through which energy or mass flows. Each component of the system receives inputs and produces outputs, which in turn

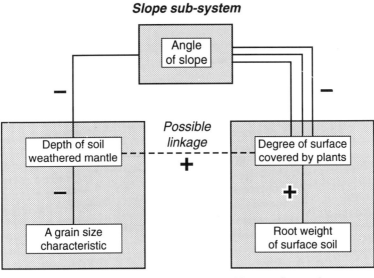

**Figure 2.4**   An example of a morphological system – the relationships among slope angle, debris and vegetation cover (redrawn from Chorley and Kennedy, 1971)

become the inputs of other components; the inputs may be stored in the components, too, perhaps for a substantial period of time. As the mass or energy passes through a component of the system it may be altered in some way, or the component may store some of it. The flow of solar energy is a major example of a cascading system, from the sun itself into the earth's atmosphere, where some is reflected back and the remainder is passed through to the earth's surface, whence it is returned, in an altered state, to the atmosphere and thence to outer space. The hydrological cycle is another example of a major cascading system. The atmosphere receives its water content through evaporation from the oceans (84 per cent) and evapotranspiration from the land surface (16 per cent). Of the moisture content, 77 per cent is returned as precipitation over the oceans and 23 per cent as precipitation on to the land surface; 7 per cent of the latter is transported to the oceans, prior to its return to the atmosphere. (The figures are from More, 1967.)

The study of cascading systems thus involves investigating movements of elements such as energy and water through the components of the environment, as against the description of structures which characterises the study of morphological systems. Again the main purpose of such study is description, but with the goal being to illustrate the workings of environmental systems. Ecosystems, such as that of Isle Royale quoted in Figure 2.1, are clearly cascading systems according to the definitions presented here. Huggett (1980, pp.119–20) uses Milner's (1972) model of ecosystem of the island of Hirta, in the St Kilda group, to illustrate the flows that have to be measured. The island has only one large herbivore (sheep) which has no predators, and the system of which the sheep are at the centre is shown in Figure 2.5; the solar energy that enters the system is received by the vegetation which is grazed by the sheep. As Huggett illustrates, this system (which is only a part of the total ecosystem of the island, since all of the flora are grouped together under one category, vegetation, and none of the other fauna are included) can be translated into a computer model which predicts the sheep population of the island. The predicted and actual numbers are shown in Figure 2.6: Huggett (1980, p.122) argues that 'Agreement with actual fluctuations in population is good, though periods of heavy mortality are slightly out of phase, a deficiency in the model which could be corrected'. What the computer modelling does make clear, however, is that changes in one variable in the system only – the input variable, solar energy – can have substantial impacts on the populations within the ecosystem.

The island of Hirta is a very small ecosystem, and illustrates one of the main problems of much study of cascading systems – defining their boundaries. With an island this is relatively straightforward, and 'system closure' is readily achieved; perhaps that is why much pioneering work on ecosystems was done on islands. (Islands are not closed systems, of course, because of the role of birds in moving seeds, etc.) But with very many

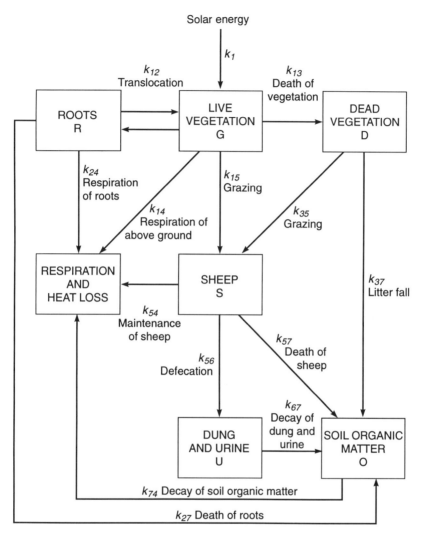

**Figure 2.5** The ecosystem of the island of Hirta (redrawn from Huggett, 1980)

environmental systems, drawing boundaries around them for the purposes of investigation is somewhat artificial, and there is always the danger that important links will be excluded from the study because one of the components involved is outside the system as defined.

Cascading ecosystems are very complex, with a large number of components and links. Even so, they are relatively simple compared with some of the models of the atmosphere that have been developed to study the

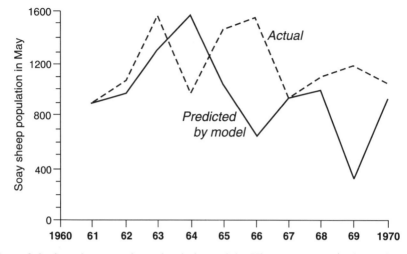

**Figure 2.6**  Sample output from simulations of the Hirta ecosystem (redrawn from Huggett, 1980)

flow of energy through space and time, in the three-dimensional spatial structure within which weather systems are generated. Those cascading models are usually represented as systems of differential equations, and some comprise several thousand such equations. They indicate just how complex the environment is, how much information has to be collected to calibrate the models and provide descriptions of the flows, and how difficult it is to provide detailed enough descriptions from which predictions are possible.

### Process–response systems

These are defined by Chorley and Kennedy as comprising intersections of morphological and cascading systems; the cascading systems provide the processes (i.e. the energy inputs) which produce the morphologies (the structural outputs). As the process input changes, therefore, so the morphological output alters; for example, the slope of a beach alters according to the power of the waves breaking upon it.

An illustration of a process–response system is Chorley and Kennedy's example of the relationships between the characteristics of a valley slope and those of the stream in its central channel (Figure 2.7). On the slope, the amount of erosion is a function of the slope angle: the steeper the slope, the greater the erosion. The output of that process is the weathered sediment that reaches the stream: the greater the amount of erosion, the larger the sediment production, and the greater the volume of sediment entering the stream. Within the stream itself, the greater the sediment load carried, the

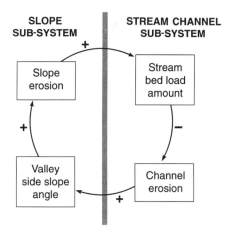

**Figure 2.7** Negative feedback in two linked morphological sub-systems (redrawn from Chorley and Kennedy, 1971)

less the erosive power of the water. The erosion by the stream affects the slope: the greater the channel erosion, the steeper the valley slope. Thus we see the characteristics of the stream responding to those of the slope, and the characteristics of the slope reacting to those of the stream; each is a stimulus to a response by the other.

This interaction among the various components of a process–response system is known as *feedback*, and is a crucial feature of such systems. In the example just quoted, the consequence of the feedback is to 'damp down' the response. For example, if the sediment load of the stream is light, then there will be a high level of channel erosion. This will produce steeper valley slopes and stimulate greater slope erosion. A consequence of this will be greater sediment load for the stream, which will reduce the amount of channel erosion. Thus an indirect consequence of greater channel erosion is less channel erosion, because the output of the channel erosion generates slope erosion, which produces sediment that limits the channel erosion.

Such feedback mechanisms restore equilibrium to a system following some change to its structure, perhaps as a response to an outside influence (i.e. a process operating outside the system defined for investigation), or simply to a change which is inherent in the system itself. The latter can be illustrated by predator–prey models of ecosystems, such as the Isle Royale ecosystem of Figure 2.1. In this there is unlikely to be a precise balance between the numbers of predators (wolves) and prey (moose). At times the predator population will increase somewhat, thereby increasing its demands on the prey. More of the latter will be devoured, which will then mean less food for

24

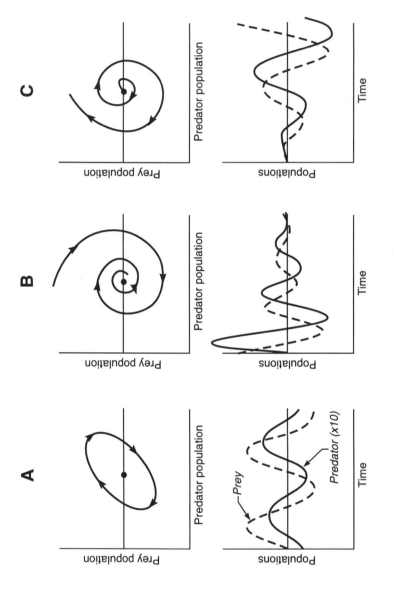

**Figure 2.8** Various types of predator-prey relationship in an ecosystem (redrawn from Huggett, 1980)

the predators. Competition among the wolves will lead to the survival of the fittest, and perhaps a fall in their numbers relative to those of the moose. There will then be an oversupply of prey available, which will encourage the expansion of the predator population. The result is a cyclically stable situation, as shown in Figure 2.8A, in which the variability in the number of prey (the moose) is greater than that of the predators (the wolves). The area within the ellipse of the graph is what Wilson (1981a, p.25) terms the phase space (or state space) of the system; it defines the limits of the two populations.

In the example of Figure 2.8A the relative size of the two populations is always changing; there is no equilibrium situation. This may not always be the case. Instead, there is a steady-state point to which the system will always return after some perturbation, as suggested by Figure 2.8B. Thus there may be a major increase in the size of the moose population, perhaps because of a good summer and a great deal of available biomass; few of the young die. This allows the predator population to increase, and the moose population consequently falls. There is then a consequential decline in the predator population, as fewer wolves can be sustained by the smaller moose population; the latter increases again, but not to its earlier levels, because the wolf population immediately increases again. The cycle continues, but every time the rise and subsequent fall in the populations are less, until the steady-state equilibrium is reached.

There is an equilibrium over the longer term in both of these examples, either with the return to the steady state (as in Figure 2.8B) or with the continued oscillations around the phase state. Of course, those equilibria in all but the simplest of systems will be defined not in two dimensions but in many. For example, in the Isle Royale system (Figure 2.1), as well as the moose and wolves in the central box there is also the biomass, whose volume varies according to the number of moose grazing and the atmospheric conditions which nurture the biomass production. As it falls so the number of moose falls, with consequences for the wolf population; there are fewer wolves and fewer moose, greater biomass production, the ability to support more moose, greater possibilities for the predators, and so forth. The phase space has three dimensions. And then we can bring in the variables outside the narrowly defined system of Figure 2.1 – the atmosphere and the other herbivores and carnivores – to create a much more complicated phase space (or, from the example of Figure 2.8B, a much more complicated spiralling into the steady-state position in the $n$-dimensional space).

In each of these examples there is a return to an equilibrium position. But this need not be so, as suggested in Figure 2.8C. Here we start at a steady-state position from which there is a slight increase in the prey (moose) population. There is then a consequent increase in the size of the predator (wolf) population, which leads to a fall in the moose population greater than the original increase away from the steady state. There is then a consequent fall in the wolf population, which not only allows the moose population to recover its steady-state size, but to exceed it considerably, and then encourages a similar increase in the wolf population. Every period of the cycle shows a greater amplification than the last, until eventually the prey population, which leads in each cycle, become extinct; the predator will soon follow, unless an alternative source of food can be found.

These three examples illustrate the two major types of feedback in a process–response system. The first, exemplified by Figure 2.8B, is termed *negative feedback*, because the consequence of its operation is to return the system to its original state. A system characterised by such feedback is known as *morphostatic* (or *homeostatic*), because the morphological structure is maintained over the long term, even though there may be short-term deviations from it. The slope–channel systems (Figure 2.7) provide an example of such morphostasis; whenever a change from the equilibrium state is stimulated, a consequence of the response to that stimulus is that the system returns to its original state. Clearly the more complex the system, and the larger the number of components it contains, the longer is the likely time before it returns to equilibrium; this is known as the system's 'relaxation time'.

The other type of feedback, illustrated by Figure 2.8C, is *positive feedback*, whereby the system does not return to its equilibrium but moves to a new one as a consequence of the new disposition of forces (in the example, that equilibrium involved the extinction of both species in the ecosystem). Such a system is known as *morphogenetic*, indicating that a change in its morphological structure is a consequence of the positive feedback processes. That morphogenesis may be continual in that no new equilibrium is attained; more likely, however, is a new equilibrium, which in an ecosystem may be different floral composition and/or a different balance of the competing fauna from that which preceded it. The process of desertification is an excellent example of such morphogenesis; a system characterised by certain relationships between the vegetation, fauna and soil is altered – perhaps as a result of climatic change; perhaps because of increased human pressure on the fauna and flora – to one with different relationships, characterised by the lesser ability of the soil to sustain plant and animal life.

**Control systems**

This final category is not distinct from the others in terms of its approach to describing and understanding systems; rather it is characterised by its focus on the practical application of systems understanding to environmental control or engineering. As Chorley and Kennedy (1971, p.9) express it:

> When one examines the structure of physical process–response systems it becomes apparent that certain key variables or *valves*...are those

wherein intelligence can conveniently intervene to produce operational changes in the distribution of energy and mass within cascading systems, and consequently to bring about changes in the equilibrium relationships involving the morphological variables linked with them in the process–response systems.

The importance of this 'instrumental' approach to the study of systems (as criticised, for example, in Gregory, 1980) is made clear in the subtitle of Bennett and Chorley's book, *Environmental Systems: Philosophy, Analysis and Control* (1978), in which the introductory chapter ends by stressing the 'dilemmas which confront man's intervention in natural systems which underlie his "living together with nature" ' (p.22).

The need to understand environmental systems so that societies can come to an accommodation with them is clear whatever the mode of production, so an instrumental approach does not necessarily imply the technocratic attitude described in the preceding chapter. It is as important for 'primitive' tribes to appreciate the way fertility declines in a soil, and thus know when to move on to new lands, as it is for advanced capitalist societies to appreciate the consequences of converting more and more forest to permanent pasture. The difference between the two is that the former recognise the limits of the environment and seek to live within them, whereas the latter, which many (though by no means all) systems analysts seek to serve, wish to alter the environment to serve their interests.

Chorley and Kennedy offer a defence of the need for studying control valves in systems, and the application of the findings, in what they represent as two vital differences between 'human and higher biological' systems and 'physical' systems. The first difference is that the former possess memories, which allow for control to be implemented (if you cannot remember how a system reacted under certain circumstances it is not possible either to reproduce those circumstances – if the reaction was 'good' – or to ensure that the same reaction does not recur). The second is that 'the operation of physical systems is dominated by a tendency for negative feedback, whereas socio-economic systems possess strong positive-feedback loops which make change ongoing' (Chorley and Kennedy, 1971).

In other words, if left to itself the environment would sustain an equilibrium, but human 'interference', with its constant 'demands for more' which characterise growth, will harm that equilibrium. Thus they argue in favour of cybernetics, the science of control, with the study of 'man–environment systems' being seen as a special case of 'man–machine systems'; the environment is a machine to be understood and controlled.

Chorley and Kennedy illustrate their case with reference to atmospheric control systems, terrestrial control systems and ecosystems. Within the terrestrial category they deal separately with drainage basin hydrological systems ('No spatial process–response system has proved so susceptible to human control as the basin hydrological system': 1971, p.317), erosional drainage basin systems, debris cascades, and ground-water systems. They illustrate the role of dams as control valves in drainage basins, regulating the flow of water so as to mitigate the impact of flooding.

## UNDERSTANDING SYSTEMS

Chorley and Kennedy's case for the study of control systems – that the environment is largely in equilibrium as a consequence of negative feedback mechanisms, but that human interference with those mechanisms may destroy the equilibrium – makes a compelling argument for the scientific study of such systems; it provides the information that societies can use to ensure that the changes they induce do not lead to a deterioration in the environment's capability to sustain human life. That information can take two forms. The first is typical of the technocentric view, and states that understanding will bring control which will allow continued demands to be placed on the environment: as long as we know how the environment works, then we can make sure it meets our demands without deteriorating. The other is a more pessimistic, ecocentric view which argues that what we know shows that we are making too many demands on the environment already; we are proving that it cannot cope, and should not increase our pressures on it. Bennett and Chorley present the latter view (apparently sympathetically), in the four-stage argument that if population growth continues, the pressure for control over environmental systems will increase so that 'Ways will therefore be found to subjugate the latter more rapidly, efficiently and completely' (1978, p.543); these ways will in turn make the environment systems more vulnerable to forces 'as yet outside the control and prediction of society', resulting not only in more catastrophes of a Malthusian nature but also in conflicts that will make the practice of democracy increasingly difficult. This leads to the conclusion that

> environmental scientists would place population control at the centre of environmental planning strategies and would regard the present demographic explosion as the main impediment to the application of rational control strategies of systems modelling and control. (p.544)

(For an alternative view see Harvey, 1974).

If the argument just summarised is valid, then it is necessary to produce the evidence to convince societies of the need for population control, at both the individual and the collective level; the products of environmental systems research must be used to educate people about the pressures on nature that they are creating, and even more so about the (probably permanent) damage that could be caused if those pressures are not alleviated. So what is available to educate people with; what do we know about environmental systems and human impact on them?

## ENVIRONMENTAL SYSTEM KNOWLEDGE

At a general level, the adoption of a systems approach by an increasing proportion of the scientific community has provided substantial evidence of: the complexity of the systems that comprise the environment; the interlinking of all parts of the environment; and the fragility of the equilibria states of many of the systems and sub-systems identified and described.

With regard to *complexity*, the work undertaken by atmospheric scientists in their efforts to model the three-dimensional flow of energy through the atmosphere, involving many thousands of differential equations, illustrates the immensity of the task. And yet, as Gleick (1988) argues, even with such complex models climatologists are still unable to forecast weather more than a few days ahead. As he put it, even with models containing as many as 500 000 separate equations, 'beyond two or three days the world's best forecasts were speculative, and beyond six or seven they were worthless' (p.20). The main reason for this is that, despite their size and complexity, the models are insufficiently detailed to capture reality (others would counter that the problem is not the models but the lack of sufficient computing power to make them work properly). In addition, Gleick's thesis is that the task is an impossibility, because the interactions that take place within the atmospheric system (and all other environmental systems too) cannot be predicted by sophisticated mathematical models. We return to this point later.

With regard to the *interlinking* of systems, the effects of events such as the 1986 release of massive amounts of radiation from the nuclear reactor at Chernobyl in stimulating health hazards many thousands of miles away illustrate how what happened at one place in one environmental system (the release of radiation into the atmosphere) affected other systems (local ecosystems) at other places, distant in both time and space, for the radiation once in an ecosystem may remain there for many decades. But the causal links are rarely easy to prove, and there is much scientific controversy – as, for example, over the claims that 'acid rain' in parts of western Europe (such as Norway and Germany) is produced by British coal-burning power stations. And those linked are relatively close in space as well as time. (Park 1987, details the debates over acid rain in Britain during the 1980s, and the position of the government and the Central Electricity Generating Board, as it was then called, that 'there are still too many fundamental research questions as yet unasked or unanswered (1987, p.242) to justify expensive programmes to reduce sulphur emissions from coal-burning power stations'.) Possible links that are distant on one if not both of the parameters of space and time are even more contentious. For example, extreme weather events in the northern hemisphere during the winter of 1988–9, along with more local ones such as a

wet summer in Australia, were linked by some observers to changes in the
sea temperature in the south-east Pacific (*The Sunday Times*, 12 February
1989, p.A16) and it is now generally accepted that the use of CFCs in aerosol
sprays and refrigerators in the northern hemisphere is damaging the ozone
layer over Antarctica. As many users of statistics point out, however,
correlation should not be confused with causation; the latter can only be
proven if the mechanisms underlying the links are understood.

Finally, with regard to the *fragility* of environmental systems, by which is
meant the ease with which an equilibrium state can be disturbed, again there
is much scientific evidence to show that small changes in one variable in a
system can stimulate major alterations to the whole. Both hydrologists and
geomorphologists have become aware of this in their attempts to understand
why some rivers have single channels and others have braided channels; why
one river may have a single channel in one reach and yet be braided in
another; and why in one reach at some times the channel may be braided and
at others not. This has promoted the realisation that a 'threshold' exists
which when crossed leads to a major change in the morphological structure
of the system. In the present context, the critical variables, as described by
Thornes (1987, pp.30–1), are slope and discharge (Figure 2.9). In some
situations, where the slope is shallow relative to the volume of discharge (for
example at *C* in Figure 2.9), there is a single-channel meandering stream,
whereas in others (for example, *D*), where the slope is steep relative to the
discharge, braiding occurs; in some circumstances (such as *E*) the stream is
on the threshold between one state and another, and a slight change in one of
the variables (probably the amount of discharge that it carries) will lead to a

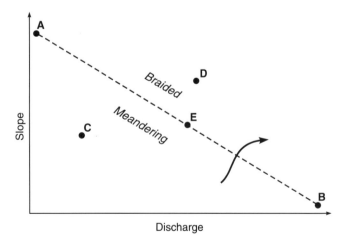

**Figure 2.9**   The threshold between braided and meandering streams (redrawn from
Thornes, 1987)

shift from one morphology to another. Identifying the existence of such thresholds, and modelling them successfully, is crucial to a system, and thus to designing control systems by river engineers (Though properly representing the interlinking aspect of environmental systems means that control of one will almost certainly have a range of consequences for others, as shown by the effects on rivers both upstream and downstream of dams installed to control the flow of water.)

At the larger scale, the impacts of ecosystem changes again illustrate the fragility of the environment, especially when such changes are linked to other systems. In many parts of the world intensification of human occupation is accompanied by major changes in the vegetation cover. In the Amazon basin in recent years, for example, over half of the tropical forest cover has been removed to make way for agriculture. This disappearance of the trees has, according to some, led to a substantial reduction in the amount of carbon dioxide returned to the atmosphere through transpiration. The loss of the store of carbon in the trees, with consequences for the composition of the atmosphere and its ability to absorb some of the incoming solar radiation, and the burning of the trees has accelerated what is known as the 'greenhouse effect' – less energy is leaving the earth's atmosphere because the heat is 'trapped' by the greater concentration of particles and of carbon dioxide in the atmosphere. The result is a process of global warming, it is claimed, which will lead not only to climatic changes but also to melting of glaciers, a consequent rise in sea levels, the drowning of many areas of land (including much that is now densely occupied by people) and adjustments to many morphological systems.

The current debate about global warming and the greenhouse effect suggests that the composition of the atmosphere is being changed by greater burning of wood and fossil fuels, with consequences for climate and thence for other environmental systems. But the composition of the atmosphere can also be altered by 'natural' events, such as major volcanic eruptions. Mount St Helens, Washington, USA, in 1980 provided a graphic illustration of the amount of material that is placed in the atmosphere by one such event, and there have been many larger events in recorded history, notably that of Mt Krakatoa in the East Indies in 1783. These eruptions emit large volumes of dust particles into the atmosphere, which are then carried around the globe by air movements, and so affect cloud formation and weather not only in the immediate area of the volcano itself but also in many other parts of the globe; the impact on weather in other places stimulates further indirect effects. To most people, a volcanic eruption can be understood only as a random event; certainly it is from the point of view of those studying atmospheric systems. Thus weather change, which may precipitate climatic change if the negative feedback chain is broken and the equilibrium destroyed, can be the product of random events. This makes understanding environmental systems very difficult, and their prediction virtually impossible.

Leslie Curry proposed several decades ago that climatic change may be the product of a random series. He argued that within the earth there are two main stores of atmospheric energy – the tropical oceans and the polar glaciers – and attempted 'to show that fluctuations in storage there, resulting purely from random events, can be of the magnitude and duration of the Ice Ages' (1962, p.24). Random year-to-year variation in the amount of energy stored in those two areas was sufficient, he argued, to stimulate major climatic changes.

Curry's argument preceded the mathematical work of Edward Lorenz (e.g. Lorenz, 1963) which provided an alternative case for climatic change as a consequence of small-scale, possibly random, fluctuations in critical variables and relationships. He produced a model of climatic systems, using what we would now recognise as a very primitive computer and representing the vast complexity of the atmosphere by a few equations only. He showed that if you started off his model at the same set of conditions each time, then you produced the same climatic series. But if the starting conditions varied only slightly (at the level of the fourth, fifth and sixth decimal points in the early experiments: one run started with a parameter at 0.506, and the other with only that parameter changed, to 0.506 127) a very different series would develop. Figure 2.10 shows the two series diverging over time (the trace may be of average annual temperature, for example). The original difference was very small – 'A small numerical error was like a small puff of wind – surely the small puffs faded or canceled each other out before they could change important large-scale features of the weather' (Gleick, 1988, pp.16–17) – but sufficient to produce very different weather systems, with presumed consequences for all other atmospheric systems. In Curry's terms, that small change could have been the result of a random event, like a volcanic eruption. The result illustrates the fragility of environmental equilibria.

These three general conclusions regarding complexity, interlinking and fragility have been presented as summaries of what we know about environmental systems without any detailed descriptions, let alone assessment, of the current state of knowledge (which is given in the latest textbooks on the various environmental sciences and in up-to-date reviews

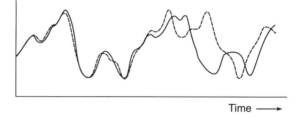

Time ⟶

**Figure 2.10**   Two climatic sequences starting from slightly different configurations (redrawn from Gleick, 1988 p. 17)

such as those in the journal *Progress in Physical Geography*). What is important for the present book is to appreciate the nature of systems, their complexity, their interlinkedness, and their fragility, in order to develop the arguments regarding human 'interference' with those systems. But before turning to that, a brief excursion into how systems are studied is necessary.

## ENVIRONMENTAL SYSTEMS ANALYSIS

How are systems studied, to obtain a full understanding of how they operate? As described earlier, a system can involve a morphology, with relationships between the links; it can be a set of flows through the component parts; or it can be a process–response mechanism, whereby one studies either a morphological change as a response to a particular stimulus or a flow change as a result of morphological alterations. In all of these, what is important is that the system operates as a whole, and its understanding requires an appreciation of that whole; to use a well-worn phrase developed by geographers some decades ago in another context, 'the whole is greater than the sum of parts'.

There are two ways in which a system can be studied, the inductive and the deductive. In the former, empirical investigations are undertaken, which probably involve field measurements of the important parameters of the system (its salient morphological variables and/or flows), allowing a description to be drawn up. In the deductive approach, a model representation of the system is developed (usually, though not necessarily, mathematical; hardware and other analogue models may be of value in some circumstances). To be of value, this representation should conform to 'reality', and so should be tested in experimental conditions; if the model is a valid representation, then it should either reproduce an aspect of the environment as it is/has been, or it should be able to predict accurately a future state. (A weather system model, for example, should be able to take the conditions yesterday and simulate today accurately, and should be able to take today's situation along with yesterday's and predict tomorrow accurately.)

There has been much debate among scientists and philosophers of science about the validity of the two approaches. The inductive is frequently criticised for its lack of critical experiments; it amasses information, but the validity of its findings is difficult to sustain because there is no unambiguous way of assessing whether they are right or not: the classic example is the 'all swans are white' scientific description which was then faced by the discovery of what were apparently 'black swans' in Australia; were they really swans, and if so, what now were the defining characteristics of swans? (For a full development of the 'poverty of induction' case with regard to physical geography, see Haines-Young and Petch, 1985.) This suggests that the deductive approach is the best. One starts with known information, deduces some consequence from that, and then designs a critical experiment to see if the deduction is correct. This ideal situation is less easy to apply than might at first sound, because it depends on the quality of the known information. In the study of some environmental systems, such as the atmospheric, it can be argued that all you need to know are certain basic physical laws, then you apply the relevant mathematics, and produce the needed deductions. Those physical laws are well established, and provide an apparently unambiguous input to the calculations, but what physical laws can be used to model the flow of energy in the Isle Royale ecosystem (Figure 2.1)? There are none available to represent, for example, the efficiency of moose in grazing the available biomass, or the efficiency of the wolves in hunting the moose (at different densities); these aspects of the environment can only be portrayed through empirical enquiry and represented as probabilities. The same is true of most aspects of environmental systems; while the ultimate goal may be to develop a viable mathematical model, this can only be done by obtaining empirical field data (perhaps accompanied by laboratory data from experiments simulating environmental conditions) that can be used to calibrate the models.

The collection of field data is rarely straightforward, particularly as for much work long series of data are required in order to describe changing conditions; environmental scientists have displayed a great deal of ingenuity in designing equipment with which to capture the data they need. But apart from the actual data collection problems, there are other difficulties inherent in the empirical approach. The first is that, even if the whole system is appreciated and general models of it exist, it is very difficult to collect data for all of the links/flows in a single experiment. Thus any one piece of research will probably focus on a particular part of the system only. For example, Thornes provides a general model of a fluvial system (Figure 2.11; see also Lane, 1995). One study of that system may focus on the link in the bottom left-hand corner only, between discharge and channel slope, and attempt to describe the relationship between the two. This will probably involve measuring the two variables at a range of sites, and regressing the one against the other to identify the relationship; the hope is that the relationship will be a strong one (i.e. a high correlation between the two variables, indicating that the channel slope value can be accurately estimated from the discharge variable). But channel slope is also affected directly by two other variables, according to the model. So where the value of the slope is not accurately estimated by the discharge variable, it could be concluded that this is because of the unmeasured impact of the other variables. Thus the next stage of the work might be to measure those two, and produce a multiple regression equation which estimated channel slope as a function of the three variables. (Alternatively, an experiment might be designed in which the effects of two of the variables were 'held constant' by studying only streams with identical valley slope and channel morphology characteristics,

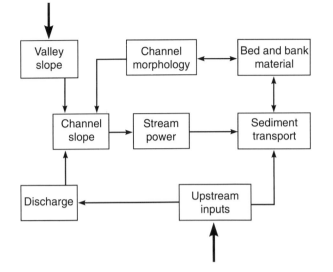

**Figure 2.11**   A model of the components and links in a fluvial system (redrawn from Thornes, 1987)

for example; such an experiment is almost impossible in field conditions, though it may be possible in laboratories.)

Much scientific work is incremental, adding together the results of earlier findings to provide an overall description; thus workers may seek a synthesis of understanding of the fluvial system by taking the results of one study on one of the links and those of another on a second link, and so on, to produce a general model. But this piecemeal approach overlooks that basic characteristic of a system, that 'the whole is greater than the sum of the parts', in at least two ways. First, since it is virtually impossible to 'hold all other influences constant' in field situations, the results of a partial study are difficult to evaluate, since it is not known what the values of the other critical variables (some of which may be only indirectly linked to those being measured) are. This makes the calibrated parameter values in any model of dubious value. Secondly, the variables interact, and when they do so can operate differently than when they are acting in isolation. (This is why some chemical processes require the presence of a catalyst; two chemicals interact differently in the presence of the third than when it is not present.) Thus if all of the relevant variables are not studied together the outcome may be a very incomplete, if not misleading, representation of the system.

The need for holistic studies is advanced further by arguing that the result of the interactions may well be a change in the 'dependent variable' which is not readily predicted by partial studies. A great deal of environmental science involves the application of relatively simple statistical procedures which assume a linear relationship between two variables; as one variable changes so does the other, in a constant ratio, so that if we are predicting channel slope from discharge, then a given increase in the discharge will produce the same change in the slope, whatever the initial discharge value. (This is the simplest linear regression model.) This does not mean that nonlinear relationships are necessarily ignored, but they are almost invariably treated as linear, through some transformation of one if not both of the variables; thus, for example, it might be found that the change in slope is greater when discharge increases by $x$ units from a low level than when it increases by $x$ from a higher level, which can be handled by, for example, a logarithmic transformation of discharge.

Transformation of nonlinear relationships to a linear form is an over-simplification of many relationships, especially in the holistic situation of systems, as Thornes (1987) has made clear in his argument for 'dynamic systems theory'. The mathematics is more complicated, as Wilson (1981b) has shown. In mathematics dealing with differential equations, the dependent variable is the change in one variable expressed as a ratio of the change in another; a simple example is population change over time.

$$x = d_p/d_t$$

where $d_p$ is the change in population, $d_t$ is the change in time, and $x$ is the differential ratio.

Such equations can be characterised by *bifurcation*, in which one of three things may happen at certain points in the trend (Figure 2.12). The first is

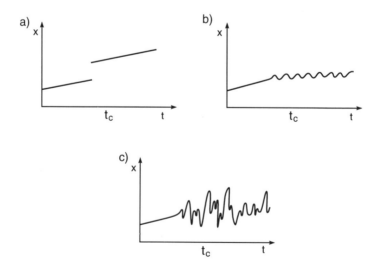

**Figure 2.12**   Three types of bifurcation (redrawn from Wilson, 1981b)

simply a 'jump'; the slope of the trend remains the same (Figure 2.12a), but there is a discontinuity in it, as some threshold is crossed. The second is a switch from a steady trend to some periodicity (Figure 2.12b), whereas the third is a switch to what appear to be random oscillations, or chaos (Figure 2.12c).

The relevance of the first two of these shifts to the study of environmental systems has increasingly been appreciated in recent years. The existence of thresholds, as examples of 'jumps', has already been noted in the example of the switch of a river from a meandering to a braided state (p.30); what is of interest to the scientist in such circumstances, and perhaps even more to the engineer, is being able to predict when the 'jump' will occur, what combination of values of the relevant system variables produce this quantum shift. With regard to periodicities, the earlier discussion of predator–prey relationships in the context of Huggett's (1980) diagrams (Figure 2.8) has shown that what was formerly an equilibrium could be transformed into a periodic relationship, as first the predators increase in numbers and the prey decline, followed by a decline in the predator population and a subsequent increase in the prey. Environmental scientists have also increasingly become interested in what are known mathematically as catastrophes, in which the relationship between two variables shows a complex form when a third is taken into account, because of the existence of bifurcations. Thornes gives an example of such catastrophe (Figure 2.13) in which the basic relationship being studied is that between sediment load in a stream ($Y$) and the ratio of

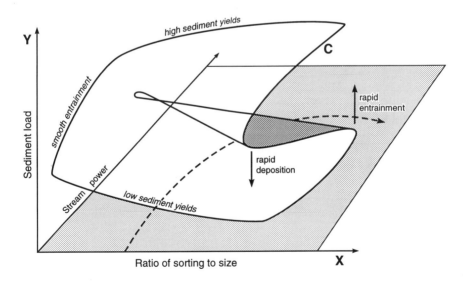

**Figure 2.13**   An example of a cusp catastrophe in three dimensions (redrawn from Thornes, 1987)

sorting to size of the sediment carried ($X$). When stream power is introduced as a third variable a cusp in the relationship between the other two is created, shown by the heavy shading, such that at certain values of $X$ there is more than one possible value of $Y$ – so no one answer is right. Outside the cusp there is only one value of $Y$ corresponding to each value of $X$, but in that critical area $Y$ cannot be predicted, which makes for difficulties both in modelling the rest of the system and in suggesting engineering solutions to environmental problems.

The relevance of the third type of bifurcation, apparently random oscillation (Figure 2.12C), to environmental systems is illustrated by May's (1976) ecological experiments which provided early evidence of the existence of such oscillations (or chaos). He took a very simple equation in which the size of a population, a herbivore say, is expressed as a function of its previous size: in brief, the size this year is a function of the size last year, which does not seem to be an unreasonable assumption to make. The equation is

$$x_n = ax(1 - x)$$

where $x$ is as the population at a given time, $x_n$ is the next value of $x$, and $a$ is the parameter of the equation which represents the rate of reproduction of the species concerned.

In May's mathematical experiment, $x$ took on values between 0.0 and 1.0, on the argument that all environments have a certain carrying capacity only. (The equation is thus that widely known as the logistic.) If we take the value of $a$ as 1.0, then the equation says that the next value of $x$ is determined by the present value (which is the proportion of the carrying capacity) multiplied by 1 minus the present value, or the unused capacity. Thus if $x$ is 0.4 (only 40 per cent of the carrying capacity has been attained) the next value will be 0.4 (0.6), or 0.24. The following year it will be 0.24 (0.76), or 0.18, and it will be 0.15, 0.13, and 0.11 in subsequent years. The species is slowly becoming extinct because it is not reproducing fast enough. If $a$ is increased to 2.0, however, then if we start with $x$ at 0.6, the next value is 2.0 multiplied by 0.6 multiplied by 0.4, or 0.48, followed by 0.4992, 0.50, and 0.50 thereafter. With a reproduction parameter of 2.0, the population stabilises at half of the carrying capacity; some shock to the system may take it up to 0.6 (a good summer with lots of grass perhaps) but it soon stabilises again at 0.5.

What May found, however, was that this stability only occurred with certain values of the parameter $a$. As it increased towards a value of 3.0, so the population remained stable; if $a$ is 2.7, for example, the value of $x$ stabilises at 0.6292. But with a value of 3.0 it alternates between 0.65 and 0.6825, and with $a$ at 3.5 the value of $x$ settles down to a four-year periodicity with values 0.3828, 0.8269, 0.5009 and 0.8750, which indicates very substantial annual variability from the same relationship which with lower $a$ values produced stability. What May had shown was that at low reproduction rates a species would become extinct; at medium rates it remained stable relative to the carrying capacity of the land it occupied; and at higher rates its numbers varied substantially, because as it approached carrying capacity so its numbers were cut, and it then grew again. In some ways this is not unexpected, but what May found is that with even higher $a$ values periodicity in the values of $x$ disappeared, and the result was a chaos of values, with no apparent pattern to them (except that there might be brief periods of periodicity before chaos set in again).

Two conclusions can be drawn from this finding (of which Thornes, 1987, pp.40–3, gives a further example). The first is that the fragility of the environment already referred to is perhaps even greater than initially expected, because in certain situations rapid changes in variables can occur; in the predator–prey example the two populations could both fluctuate wildly, and in the stream discharge/channel slope relationship the result could be rapid and frequent alterations in channel slope if there were periodicity, if not chaos, in the change in discharge over time. (Clearly there are issues of scale here; local differences may occur within an overall pattern of stability–changes in channel form in various stretches of a river need not lead to changes in characteristics of the river basin itself.) The second conclusion is that, if chaos is general in the environment, and Gleick (1988) argues that the accumulation of evidence suggests that it is, then not only do we have a fragile environment but we also have a very unpredictable one. Such a conclusion has clear implications for human interrelationships with the environment.

One final aspect of environmental systems related to the basic concepts already introduced is that of evolution, which is applied to geomorphological systems and to ecosystems, if not to atmospheric systems. Within geomorphology, for example, the concept of the 'normal cycle of erosion' associated with the work of William Morris Davis (see Chorley et al, 1973) is well known for its central argument that landscapes evolve from a youthful to an old-age stage, with characteristic forms at each, whereas in the study of ecology the concept of a climax vegetation, that most suited to a particular set of other environmental conditions, is also well known. Many people now consider such concepts untenable and inconsistent with the empirical evidence. They do not deny that landscapes and ecosystems change, however. In the latter, for example, the floral and faunal compositions of areas change as some species become more prolific and others move towards extinction, while species change in their characteristics as they adapt successfully to changed situations. But those changes may not be a part of teleological sequence towards a predetermined end, but rather consequences of the need to respond to new stimuli in the environment, which call for new structures. Thus the jump bifurcations in particular, which may be brought about by random events, such as volcanic eruptions or three good summers in a row, are the equivalent of evolution and suggest how aspects of the environment may change.

# HUMAN 'INTERFERENCE' IN THE ENVIRONMENT

Chorley and Kennedy (1971) and Bennett and Chorley (1978) argue that human societies, represented as systems, should be considered separately from systems in the physical environment because of two distinct characteristics: the ability of humans to remember; and the positive feedback that is common in human systems compared to the negative feedback they see as typical of environmental systems. Because of the former characteristic, humans are able collectively to learn much more about their physical environment than are other forms of animal life, and the advances in intellect that have been built on that characteristic have enabled humans to alter the environment, both intentionally and unintentionally, to a much greater extent than any other species. (It is for this reason that human activity is often considered 'interference' with the environment, rather than just activity within it; it is sometimes considered outside the 'natural' aspect of an environment, with the implication that human 'interference' is 'unnatural'. The distinction is really one of scale; all human activities are natural, but have far greater potential impact – *vide* the nuclear weapon – than those of any other species.) The second characteristic suggests that human societies have a tendency to grow *ad infinitum*, which is not a characteristic of other species. In strict biological terms this is probably not so, and there is no reason to believe that humans *per se* have a higher *a* value in May's equation (p.38) than other species. But what is undoubtedly the case is that combining the natural growth tendencies with the first characteristic – mental power – means that human growth has more impact on the environment than that of other species; the way in which that growth is organised is the particular concern of the next two chapters. The growth can be sustained to a greater extent because humans have developed an ability (limited, but we do not know how or to what extent) to extend the earth's carrying capacity, which other species do not have.

Human societies have 'interfered' with 'natural' systems in a great variety of ways, and are apparently increasing their 'interference' very substantially at the present time. The extent of the human impact on the environment has been fully documented by Goudie, who argues that 'the complexity, frequency and magnitude of impacts is increasing, partly because of steeply rising population levels and partly because of a general increase in *per capita* consumption [of food and energy]' (1986a, p.285).

It is not the purpose of this book to provide detailed illustrations of that interference (see Turner et al, 1990): nevertheless, a brief outline of its nature in a range of environmental systems indicates the salient features of human activity within the environment that are central to the arguments in the rest of this book.

Goudie's (1986a) material is organised to show the nature of human impact in six different types of system. The first two relate directly to ecosystems. A great deal of the earth's natural *vegetation* cover has been removed, particularly to extend agriculture, as with the massive deforestation that continues to occur (Williams, 1989). One of the most contentious current issues regarding vegetation change is that of the spread of desert conditions, especially in the Sahel area of Africa, a consequence according to Goudie of 'a combination of human activities...with occasional series of dry years' (1986a, p.49). Important outcomes of these human-induced vegetation changes have included the 'opening up' of soils to weathering and erosive forces, and a reduction in the diversity of plant species; new species have been developed, but many of these prove only weakly resistant to plant pests. By changing the floral environments, human activity is also imperilling the survival of many fauna, and Goudie identifies five major impacts on *animal* populations: domestication, dispersal, extinction, expansion and contraction (p.70). Some of these changes, especially extinction and contraction, are due to deliberate policies of reducing numbers, if not eliminating certain species, but many more are the indirect impacts of, for example, changing habitats through the extension of agriculture, pollution of habitats (as with water bodies), and the methods of clearing land (such as the impact of fire); there has also been the deliberate attack on micro-organisms in attempts to control disease of humans and other species, but these fall outside Goudie's coverage.

From ecosystems within the biosphere, Goudie turns to human impacts on the *soil*, which is 'one of the thinnest and most vulnerable human resources and is one upon which, both deliberately and inadvertently, humans have had a very major impact' (p.109). The nature of the soil in any place is a function of the interaction of five factors – parent material, topography, climate, organisms within the soil, and time. Human activity can affect each of the first four directly and indirectly, and thereby influence the time in which a soil has to develop. The chemistry of many soils has been affected by such activity, and the amount of anthropogenetically-induced soil erosion has increased very substantially in recent centuries, with clear consequences for the ability of the soil to sustain plant, and thus human, life.

Fresh and salt *waters* are also affected directly and indirectly by a range of human activities. They have been major receptacles of waste materials, for example, both as deliberate policies (as with the continued dumping of human sewage into rivers, lakes and seas and the current policies of depositing nuclear waste in certain ocean deeps), and as the reservoirs into which polluted rivers flow and polluted air is deposited through precipitation. They have also been modified in many ways, as is clear in the management of river channels (to control flooding and to extract water for other uses). In urban areas especially, the extraction of water from rivers and ground-water sources has major direct and indirect impacts, and the alterations in the nature of the ground cover have significant consequences in the movement of water through the hydrological system from atmosphere

42

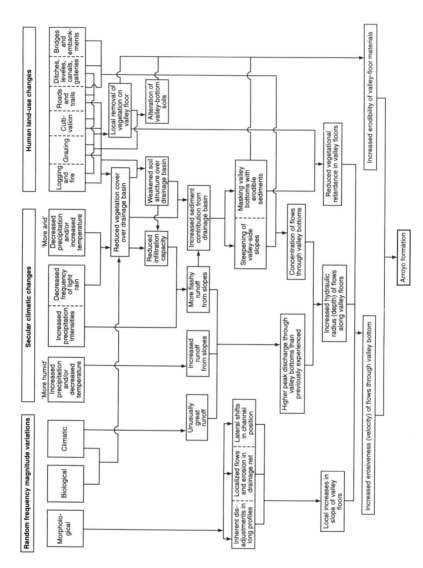

**Figure 2.14** A model of arroyo creation (redrawn from Cooke and Reeves, 1976)

to oceans; flood peaks increase, for example, with less infiltration and more rapid run off.

Human activity is a major *geomorphological* agent, stimulating the various processes of weathering, erosion and deposition involved in the creation of land-forms, at all scales. This is illustrated by Cooke and Reeves's model of the development of arroyos – deep gullies incised within broad valley bottoms and plains – in the south-western United States (Figure 2.14). Six types of land-use change, reflecting increased intensity of human occupance of the area, have led to alterations to both vegetation cover and soil structure, which have both exacerbated the erodibility of valley-bottom soils. Together with other factors related to both the nature of the local climate and short-term climatic change (themselves also possibly linked to human activity in the area and neighbouring districts) human activity has also increased the erosive force of the water flowing through the valleys.

Arroyo formation is an example of largely unintended interference with geomorphological processes, but, as with other aspects of environmental systems, there has also been much intentional interference too. This is because many aspects of geomorphological systems, especially those involving flows, are considered as 'hazardous' for human occupance of areas. Coasts provide excellent examples of this, where the rapid changes in, for example, beach form as a result of short-term changes in erosive and depositional forces threaten human investments and lives. They have been countered by a great range of coastal protection works, which themselves have had secondary impacts on other aspects of coastal erosion and deposition.

Finally, Goudie looks at impacts on *atmosphere and climate*, emphasising the impact of human activity in three ways–through the production of heat, alterations in atmospheric quality, and changes in the albedo of land masses and oceans (Figure 2.15). The role of the first two is relatively well known, even if not fully understood. The production of heat is well documented with regard to the creation of 'urban climates', in the areas where production is concentrated, and the nature of atmospheric pollution, with its consequences for the ratio of incoming to outgoing radiation, the creation of clouds, and the transfer of pollutants through precipitation (as with acid rain) is also widely discussed. With regard to the third impact, the albedo of a surface is its ability to reflect radiation; in general, the denser the vegetation cover, the lower the albedo, and the greater the proportion of the incoming radiation that is retained at the earth's surface. The higher the albedo, the greater the surface cooling, and the lower the convective activity in the lower atmosphere; with the removal of tropical forest, therefore, it is argued that climatic change (lower rainfall there, compensated by higher rainfall in the temperate zones but less in the Arctic latitudes) is a major consequence. Interestingly, this surface cooling in the tropics as a result of forest clearance is occurring at the same time as warming of the atmosphere there, as some argue, because of the greater concentration of $CO_2$ – the so-called

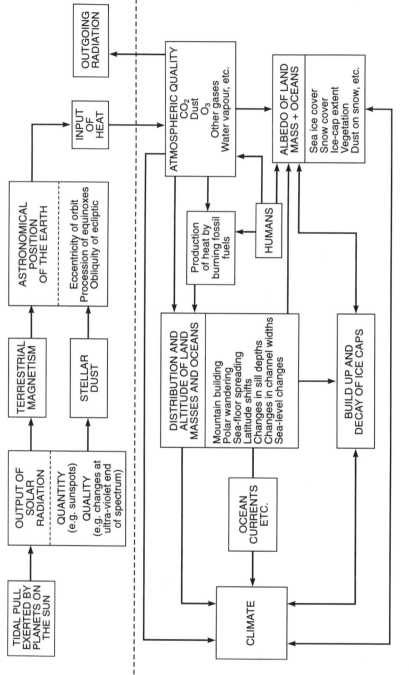

**Figure 2.15** A model showing human contributions to climatic change (redrawn from Goudie, 1986a)

greenhouse effect. Furthermore, a decrease in convective activity over the former area of tropical forest should lead to less cloud and less rainfall; there will then be more direct heating and less evapotranspiration so the area could become warmer. It is such complexity in the feedback mechanisms of environmental systems that makes the prediction of the consequences of action so difficult, and underpins the lively debates among environmental scientists.

Goudie's classification, supported by a very large number of examples and assessments of the extent of the impacts, shows not only that human 'interference' affects all components of the environmental system and is increasing in its quantity, but also that the consequences are widespread in both space and time. An activity in one place does not simply have direct impacts on the environment there; it has knock-on effects for other aspects of the local environment as energy and mass are moved through systems and call forth responses in the morphological structures. Further, those knock-on effects are not limited to the local environment but are transmitted, rapidly in some cases, slowly in others, to other places, because of the interlinking of systems. The movement of air through the atmosphere and of water through the hydrological cycle are the main transport agents, and since no part of the earth is isolated from all others none is immune from the potential consequences of human 'interference' elsewhere; even the remotest island can receive pollutants carried in the wind and/or rain and deposited there, and can receive others carried on and in the sea waters or by plants and/or animals which serendipitously arrive there.

All of these changes can be classified into those which are reversible and those which are not; the latter are clearly the most worrying, especially if they are increasing in magnitude, since they involve alterations to environmental systems that cannot be recovered. In one sense no impact, however slight, is reversible because once it has happened it has triggered other responses that may not be reversible; once a small piece of land has been destroyed, it can never be replaced in exactly the same condition. But there are cases of reversibility, especially with regard to flow resources which are naturally renewed; if certain types of air pollution cease then the air will be cleaner, increasingly so as the remnants of earlier pollution are deposited – though it may be more difficult to reverse the impacts of earlier deposition. There are other impacts which could be reversed, though the process may be very slow; soil deterioration could be countered by returning the ecosystem to its 'original' state (whatever that might be?) and allowing the slow process of soil creation to operate, which is the way in which some argue desertisation should be countered. Those which are not reversible include the extinction of plant and animal species, and also those which produce weathering and erosion; once a slope has been eroded it cannot be returned to its original condition.

Certain changes in environmental systems may be reversible, as the work of conservationists has increasingly shown over the last century, though the costs of many of the reversals are great and it would be much preferable if the need for reversal did not arise. Goudie lists nine arguments for restricting impacts. The *ethical* argument is that all species have rights and that nature is there for humans to share, not to dominate and alter for utilitarian ends. The *scientific* case is that we understand so little about environmental systems that we should preserve them for future study, while the *aesthetic* case is that ecosystems and landscapes should be retained to enrich human life and values (in part for their *recreational* value). These four are linked in a *future generations* case that we only have a 'leasehold' on the earth, and should sustain it for those who will follow. Linked to the future is the *genetic diversity* case, that once species are extinct they cannot be recreated; similarly, once landscapes are destroyed they cannot be replaced – which is associated with the *environmental stability* argument that the more diversity there is, especially in ecosystems, the 'more checks and balances there are to maintain stability' (Goudie, 1986a, p.291). *Economic* arguments suggest that because of our scientific ignorance we are as yet unaware of much of the wealth of the earth that could be exploited to sustain human societies. Finally, the *unintended impacts* case is, as argued here, that the nature of environmental systems is such that a change in one component of one can have substantial, unexpected, effects on another, somewhere else in time and/or space.

We are concerned here neither with detailing the amount of human interference nor with the arguments for its limitation, though both are central to much of the rest of the book (Turner et al, 1990, provide a major compilation of these changes). The sole purpose of this brief section is to highlight that human societies are able, wittingly or unwittingly, to affect environmental systems in myriad ways, with consequences that can be very large. If, as the evidence accumulated by Goudie (1986a) and others suggests, those consequences generally are deleterious to the contemporary environment, and they are increasing, then the conclusion must be that action should be taken to limit them. We need to understand what type of action, and we need to understand why those consequences are being produced in any case. That is the purpose of the rest of this book.

We must appreciate, however, that the scientific evidence is rarely conclusive, especially when it refers to processes and patterns of environmental change, as illustrated by the issues of global warming and desertification (Binns, 1990). To a considerable extent this is because of the complexity and interlinked nature of environmental processes stressed here, and the unpredictability which is a consequence of those characteristics. Thus at the time of the 1995 Berlin Conference on Climate Change the UK's Global Environmental Research Office (GER, 1995) published a list of 'Ten Interesting Facts about Climate Change':

(1) The Rio Convention on Climate Change was seeking to restrict its magnitude, not halt it.

(2) The scope and impact of human influence on climate change has increased greatly in recent decades.
(3) Climate change involves more than temperature increases: it also involves greater frequencies of extreme events, such as drought, floods, winds and sea levels.
(4) The impacts of climate change will vary regionally – some places will be wetter and windier, and others hotter and drier.
(5) As a consequence, some localities will benefit, but others will not.
(6) Global warming does not automatically lead to melting of the polar ice caps and sea-level rise, because it may generate greater snowfall.
(7) Although human-generated carbon emissions may contribute only 10 per cent of the 'natural' total, this is sufficient to perturb the carbon cycle.
(8) If $CO_2$ emissions were held at the present levels, atmospheric concentrations would continue to increase for 200 years.
(9) The greenhouse effect results from concentrations in a narrow wavelength band.
(10) Some pollutants produce net cooling effects, so reduction in their emissions may have positive effects.

The complexity of the chemistry makes prediction extremely difficult, therefore, and politicians have to decide whether the available evidence is sufficient for them to agree to precautionary measures being taken, even if the evidence for a forthcoming ecological disaster is far from conclusive (see p.4).

## IN SUMMARY

This chapter has illustrated the nature of environmental systems and their interrelationships with human societies, thereby raising two questions that are central to the rest of the book. With regard to the systems themselves, the chapter has illustrated the complex holism of the earth's environment, which can be disaggregated into separate parts for analysis and illustration but which in effect comprises one single interacting whole, with all parts affected, ultimately, but what happens in all others. To the extent that there are environmental issues and problems, therefore, they are global in scope, though they vary locally in their impact and extent.

Despite a great deal of scientific effort, much about these systems remains unknown, in large part because of their immense complexity and interactions. Study has suggested that many environmental systems are characterised by negative feedback, and so tend to maintain themselves in a steady state, although that may be interrupted by events in other parts of the system, or in what (for analytical ease at least) are other systems. But this steady state, or equilibrium, is in general very fragile, and can easily be disturbed, with potentially major consequences not only locally and regionally but also globally. Human activity can be a major interruption to the equilibria and there is a growing body of evidence to show not only how that activity has had substantial impacts but also that the quantity and quality of the impacts is increasing. Because of the complexity of the interactions within environmental systems, assessing the full nature of those impacts, and the likely consequences of further impacts, is extremely difficult; the weight of evidence, however, is that it is likely to be deleterious (though not all agree with this conclusion: see the alternative views of Council on Environmental Quality, 1982; and Simon and Kahn, 1984).

All human activity affects the operation of environmental systems to some extent. So what is important in evaluating the nature of the impact is the degree to which it is either reversible or limitable, since it cannot be avoided. This issue raises many unknowns because of imperfect appreciation of how environmental systems work (indeed, if the arguments regarding chaos are valid, it may be that we can never fully appreciate this); it means that we cannot be sure what we should not do, what we may do, at least to some extent, and what is relatively safe to do.

Hence we come to the main questions that are the focus of the rest of the book. The first concerns the production of these impacts: why do we need to make increasing demands on the environment? What is it in our societies that has impelled that development in recent centuries? Unless we can answer that question we cannot tackle environmental problems fully, since we will not know why we are producing them in the first place. The second question is how we tackle them. If it is accepted that human activity is having an increasing, and largely deleterious, impact on the earth's environmental systems, how can societies be mobilised to modify their activity in order to reduce, if not end, that impact? Since the environment is a whole, this implies that society must respond as a whole too, so how can collective action against environmental despoliation be undertaken?

# 3 Modes of Production

> In the social production which men carry on they enter into definite
> relations that are indispensable and independent of their will .... The sum
> total of these relations of production constitutes the economic structure
> of society – the real foundation on which rise legal and political
> superstructures and to which correspond definite forms of social
> consciousness. The mode of production in material life determines the
> general character of the social, political and spiritual processes of life.
> (Karl Marx, Preface to *A Contribution to the Critique of Political
> Economy*)

The previous chapter has introduced the importance of appreciating that the
earth is a complex of interdependent systems, the operation of which can be
substantially affected by human activities; they are complex, interlinked and
fragile. In order to appreciate why it is that the systems' operation is so
frequently and substantially influenced by human activity, we need to
understand the features of human societies that lead them to interfere with
natural environmental systems to such an extent that they threaten their
continued existence, if not indeed the existence of the earth itself. Only when
that appreciation is available can we turn to an analysis of how the
environment might be protected from the undesirable consequences of
human use. Thus this chapter looks briefly at the basic nature of human
societies, to assist in understanding their interrelationships with their
environments.

## THE BASES OF SOCIAL ORGANISATION

The fundamental goal of all individuals is survival. In certain circumstances
individuals can survive entirely independent of any others, can care for
themselves without even any contact with others. But they cannot survive
biologically for ever, and when they die there is no inter-generational
reproduction. Survival of the species involves collective action. It is possible
for two individuals to ensure this, with little or no contact with others, and for
their successors to do likewise, but the nature of human genetics makes this
unlikely as a continuing process over several generations, for two reasons:
first, it is possible that a couple either are unable to produce children, or can
only produce them of a certain gender, thus halting the reproduction process;
or, secondly, continual inbreeding tends to weaken the genetic stock, with
possible extinction as a consequence. So wider interaction is necessary to

ensure continued inter-generational reproduction. Species survival requires a social organisation.

If survival is a social issue, then societies must be organised towards that end. (See, for example, Dalton's introduction to Polanyi, 1971.) Survival need not be the only reason for social organisation, and much of what is undertaken collectively is not necessary to that end. But survival is fundamental – if a society cannot ensure its reproduction, both day-to-day and inter-generational, then all else will ultimately fail. The crucial element of a society's rationale cannot be left to either chance or pragmatic decision-making; the fundamental organising principles of a society must address the issue of survival, which means a focus on obtaining and then allocating sufficient food and water and, where relevant, raw materials for creating shelters from environmental resources.

Means of organising societies to ensure their survival have evolved over many millennia, in many different places and myriad ways. Differences between them reflect the environmental conditions in which the societies are located, but also the responses of individuals and groups to those societies and how they have learned to respond to the stimuli set. There is no implied environmental determinism, requiring a particular response to a certain type of environment. Some environments may be so hostile to human occupance that no societies have found a way of surviving in them over a long period, and others may be very constraining so that societies of similar types have evolved in them independently. But most environments offer a range of opportunities. These may not all be perceived by their inhabitants, who have to choose which opportunity to take up from those they have identified. But for a variety of reasons, of which chance may be one of the most important, different people in similar but isolated situations may identify different opportunities in their environments, and build societies accordingly. Those societies are cultural organisations, and the result is a complex cultural mosaic.

In detail, as much anthropological research has shown, that cultural mosaic comprises a very wide range of types of social organisation. But it is possible to simplify them to only three, using a typology introduced by Karl Polanyi (1971, p. 149) to represent the main forms of economic integration. These were seen by Polanyi as 'ideal types' (as Dalton stresses: Polanyi, 1971, p. 153), and many economic systems contain elements of two, if not all three.

## RECIPROCITY

The characteristic feature of a society based on reciprocity as its fundamental organising principle is collective rather than private ownership of property, especially the means of reproduction – notably land. The society's resources are held communally, and they are organised collectively – usually by groups tied together in kinship obligations – to ensure that sufficient food and other materials are obtained for all. There will be some division of labour, notably according to age and gender, and some individuals may have more influence than others on decision-making within the society, either because they impose themselves or because the society recognises their wisdom and is prepared to defer to them. Within the society, no group or individual will receive a disproportionate share of the products, the allocation of which is decided collectively and is thus considered equitable. It need not be equal, for the society may decide that certain individuals or groups should get more than their proportionate share; perhaps because of the nature of the work that they do, which is more physically demanding; perhaps as a small reward for some above-average contribution; or perhaps because of agreed rules drawn up to ensure survival. It may be, for example, that children are fed more than adults at certain times, such as those of relative food scarcity, as a recognition of their importance to the society's future. On the other hand, too many children may be seen as a threat to the future, because they consume much more than they contribute, leading to policies for sacrifice of some to promote the general good.

Over the full span of human history, societies based on reciprocity have almost all existed at relatively low levels of subsistence, and can best be described as *primitive communist* in their structure (although, as Polanyi stressed, reciprocity is not necessarily confined to small, primitive communities and can be a characteristic of a large and wealthy empire too). Nevertheless, reciprocity was probably the only mode of production for many millennia, pre-dating any more complicated organisational structures. The great majority of such societies almost certainly had precarious existences, subject to the vicissitudes of the environment. In resource-poor milieux, the chance of societies being decimated as a consequence of inability to support themselves, and even of being eliminated, was undoubtedly large; the quality of life was almost certainly low for most of the time, with very low life expectancy. Many such societies became extinct, and have left few if any signs of their presence. Richer environments have the potential for a better quality of life, but societies frequently bred to the limits of their environment so that in years when the environment was inclement, and especially in sequences of such years, there was societal hardship. Responses to this may have varied, including the voluntary or forced decision of some members to move away and find a new unoccupied environment where they could found a new society.

Such primitive communist societies lived in relative equilibrium with their environments, since they lacked the appreciation, and even more so the technology, with which to tackle the environmental vicissitudes. The degree to which they could control the environment and make it do what they wanted was extremely limited. In most cases that equilibrium would not have been a particularly pleasant one. Means of surviving in and with the environment permanently were evolved, as with slash-and-burn agriculture, but they allowed relatively little comfort or leisure, and life expectancy was short. It is not possible from the outside to evaluate the degree of contentment felt, of course, for there was little if any opportunity for developing feelings of relative deprivation. What is crucial here is to note that the relationship between a society and its environment was one in which the latter dominated, in the long term if not the short.

Primitive communism is not the only form of society based on reciprocity, and for much of the twentieth century up to one-third of the world's population lived in societies based, in stated principle if not in practice, on the tenet 'to each according to his needs, from each according to his abilities'. Those societies – termed *advanced communism/socialism* here – differed from the primitive communist in two main ways. The first was scale: whereas virtually all primitive communist societies have been very small, with populations of at most a few thousands only, their advanced counterparts have included the world's largest (the People's Republic of China, with more than 1 billion members). This scale difference is very much associated with and made possible by the second: level of technological ability. Advanced communist/socialist societies have thus had much more impact on their natural environments than is the case with the primitive communist, hence they are given considerably more attention here.

## RANK REDISTRIBUTION

Rank redistribution societies differ from those based on reciprocity because some of their members hold more power than others; these individuals and groups impose themselves upon the others, although they may use ideological and other means to try to legitimate that usurpation of power and their own positions as either natural or necessary or both. Quoting Aristotle, Polanyi (1971, p.93) notes that the 'three prizes of fortune' are: honour and prestige; security of life and limb; and wealth. Those with power in a redistribution-based society dictate to those without it, not necessarily with regard to all aspects of their lives but sufficiently so that the powerful, who are a minority, and probably a small one, are able to enjoy the three prizes of fortune based on work done by others at their command. In most rank redistribution societies the power of the elite group does not extend far into the lives of the others, but it penetrates those important areas concerned with meeting the elite's needs, well beyond what is necessary for subsistence and reproduction.

The origins of power in such societies are obscure. Archaeological evidence suggests that in most it was linked to either religious or military characteristics (and probably both: see, for example, Wheatley, 1971, on the origins of urbanisation). Individuals and groups claimed power over others by recourse to some magical or metaphysical source. Their power base was ideological, in that it was created by them and supported by the myth that they created and sustained inter-generationally. In brief, they claimed some kind of divine right to rule, a right sustained by a priestly cohort linked to those with power (if the priesthood were not the power-holders themselves) and with occasional recourse to claimed divine intervention – notably in the environment – to illustrate that power.

Although the ideology may have been necessary to secure the power of the elite, it was rarely sufficient to sustain control over the majority of the population, who may have been both resentful of the exercise of the power and sceptical of its claimed origin. So the ideology had to be supported by some form of coercive force involving a military presence. The military was used to ensure that the directives of the power elite were followed, and its demands met. Thus the military had to be sustained alongside the elite (and the priesthood), so that the powerless had to deliver sufficient resources (food, raw materials for shelter, clothes, weapons, means of movement and so forth) not only for the elite but also for the groups employed to support the elite and who were unable (rather than unwilling, as in the case of the elite) to provide for themselves. So there was a marked division of labour in the society at two levels: between the producers and non-producers; and, within the latter, between the elite and its functionaries.

Fundamental to rank redistribution societies is the unequal distribution of power, with a hierarchical social structure. The basis of that unequal distribution varied extremely widely between societies, as did the means of expressing and implementing the claimed superiority. The goal was the same: to enable the reproduction of the elite through the work of others. Slavery exemplifies this, where the individuals concerned – the slaves – were commodities owned by others, subject to their power and lacking control over their personal labour and reproduction; imperial Rome is an excellent example of such a society, in which the affluence of the elite was founded on their ownership of large amounts of slave labour. But, as Finley has argued, although slaves have been ubiquitous throughout human history in all modes of production, slavery has been the 'dominant labour force only in the west in a few periods and regions' (1983, p.441).

Of the many different types of rank redistribution society, that most relevant to the European experience is *feudalism*, in which the twin bases of elite power were land ownership and the institution of serfdom. Land, or at least some of it, and probably the most fertile, was not held in common by the society as a whole, but was owned by individuals, who determined how it would be worked. The work was done by a class of serfs, peasants who were obliged to work for part of their time for the landlord, to provide the means of self-reproduction for the elite, and worked for the remainder on land which they had been allocated; they obtained the means of their own reproduction from land which they did not own but merely held as part of their relationship with the landlord. The situation of these 'unfree' peasants was defined in law, and they were entirely subject to the lord's jurisdiction on all matters, being bound to the lord and unable to move to another estate.

In relatively primitive feudal societies there was a simple division between landowner and others, but in the more developed, larger in scale and spatial extent (reflecting the ability of military technology to control larger areas effectively), there was a hierarchy of landownership. In a threefold division of society, for example, there may be an overall landowner, a monarch perhaps, who allocated much of the land under her or his control to a class of lords, who could use the land as they wished in return for loyalty to the monarch, the payment of dues (to sustain the monarch's standard of living), and the provision of certain services, such as an army when required. Those subsidiary lords would then use their land either by requiring the resident population to work on it, providing them with food and shelter in return, or by allocating land to them and requiring certain payments (in kind or in money) in return for the land, from which the population could also obtain an existence. Most feudal lords combined the two, keeping some land to themselves on which their tenants were required to work but also allocating land among their tenants and making demands on them as well.

Although the 'unfree' peasants were a mainstay of the feudal mode of production they were rarely in a majority, for alongside them were the 'free' peasants, who were tenants of the landlords but owed them no labour. Their contribution to the elite's existence was not through the provision of feudal labour – working on the landlord's demesne – but through the payment of taxes of various forms which the landlord was empowered to exact from all tenants, and also through the ability of the landlord to require them to work (in mills and craft industries, for example), at a rate of recompense determined by the employer. In addition, the 'free' peasants were subject to a range of fines and rents, which required them to sell part of their produce in order to raise the needed money.

Feudalism did not comprise self-contained, self-sufficient societies, therefore, and although most of what was produced was not traded on open markets (either being consumed in the peasant households or being transferred from the peasants – in kind or in labour – to the elite) there was some buying and selling. According to Hilton, the pressures to market farm produce were twofold. First, there was what he termed the 'social division of labour between cultivation, manufacture, ruling and waging war' (1983, p.168) which required the labour of the cultivators to support the full-time or part-time activities of the others. Although some of that support could be demanded from the peasants, the latter became aware that if they produced a surplus to their own and their landlord's requirements it could probably be sold on the market, to their own benefit, thereby providing a motivation to greater production. Secondly, there were what Hilton termed 'the special needs of the ruling class' (p.169), whose consumption habits reflected much more than needs in a subsistence sense:

What was consumed was only partly a matter of enjoyment: it was also a matter of display and reward – in other words it had a political function. The consumption goods … were relatively small in bulk and high in price, and … they were produced a long way from the place of consumption – the Middle and Far East in particular. These goods were the commodities of international trade which in a stable feudal society could not be obtained, or at any rate only sporadically, by means of warfare and plunder. The feudal ruling class needed money to buy them, money which was obtained through rent and jurisdictional profits, and which peasants obtained by selling their surplus product on the local markets. (p.169)

Thus there were powerful growth impulses within feudalism, by which the landlords demanded increased production from their serfs and greater rents and other payments from their peasantry, in order to promote their own consumption habits and status. At the same time the peasantry was strongly pressured to increase its production in order to obtain the money needed to pay rents and fines, and also to purchase items of consumption for themselves. So feudalism was strongly tied to a system of markets and trade and to the growth of a network of market centres.

The details of the feudal mode of production vary widely, as historical evidence indicates. Bloch, for example, argues that feudalism developed in much of Europe as a response to the inadequacies of ties of kinship as a source of security in troubled times. In all places, it had two features that 'appear to have been indispensable' (1961, p.187) – the monopoly over the raising of armies held by the vassal lords, and the tie of vassalage (the obligations of the serf, who was 'the man of another man') as the predominant form of government. But given those two characteristics, different detailed forms of feudalism evolved: as Bloch remarks of England, it was 'a society of Germanic structure which … pursued an almost completely spontaneous course of evolution' (p.181).

Whereas most primitive communist societies were in relative equilibrium with their physical environment, albeit a dynamic and brittle one, most rank redistribution societies have not been, because of the tendency of the elite to increase the pressure on the powerless to produce more, either directly (by making greater demands on the labour of serfs) or indirectly (through market mechanisms, as described earlier). This pressure may have resulted simply from increased human requirements, as a consequence of population growth, or from acquisitiveness and greed. In the former case, for example, if a society is well organised and substantial supplies are provided for the elite, this could well lead to a high survival rate for its children, and hence a geometric growth rate in the elite population. The demands for resources will increase, and the powerless will be expected to produce more, with consequences for the environment. In order to ensure that more is produced and delivered, a larger military and/or priestly group may be needed, which in itself means an even greater increase in the demands on the powerless and the land that they occupy.

If the powerless are unable to respond by producing the needed extra resources, the elite class must reduce its demands. Over time, it may learn the limits that the local environment poses to its expansion – either in numbers or in its demand for goods – and may limit its size in some way. The result will be an equilibrium relationship with the environment. But such an equilibrium is less likely in feudal societies than in those based on primitive communism. Those with power will probably want to improve their lot, either in terms of the necessities of existence – a better diet, for example, or better housing – or in terms of 'luxuries', which would include ways of displaying their power through conspicuous consumption and permanent status symbols. These desires will be transmitted to those who provide for them; if they are unable to respond, then the elite may try to extend their control, occupying more land and bringing more people into a subservient relationship to them, perhaps through military conquest: Hilton suggests that warfare was 'the favourite occupation of the [feudal] ruling class' (1983, p.170). Whatever they do, in the long term the demands on the environment increase, to meet the direct and indirect demands of the elite. In part those demands were imposed as demands on the peasantry, and were the cause of conflict within feudal societies as the peasants tried to resist the increased requirements they were forced to meet.

## MARKETS

The fundamental principle in this third method of organising society is the market, in which goods and services are traded between buyers and sellers – *capitalist* societies are integrated through the market-place, rather than through the obligations of kinship and other social relations that characterise the other two, though not all interactions in capitalist societies are market transactions (as with social relationships within households, for example: see also Pahl, 1985). Within the general principle there are many variants, depending on the way in which markets are operated, the relative power of the buyers and sellers, and so forth. One of those variants, capitalism, has attained a dominant position in the contemporary world, having grown out of the previous modes, notably feudalism, and developed in a way in which the fundamental resource traded is labour power. Since an appreciation of capitalism is central to the arguments developed in this book, it will be given a more extended treatment than that allocated to modes of production based on rank redistribution and reciprocity.

## THE CAPITALIST MODE OF PRODUCTION

The capitalist mode of production involves the use of two naturally given resources, land and labour, along with a third, capital (which is a human creation), to produce the goods and services that people consume in order to ensure their self-reproduction and desired quality of life, and also to ensure inter-generational reproduction. Its dynamo is the accumulation of wealth, which is derived from the profits of production. It is a mode of production which cannot be static, and as a consequence cannot sustain an equilibrium with its environment. Appreciation of that point is fundamental to much of the remainder of this book.

Capitalism is sometimes equated with industrialisation, and sometimes with the operation of markets for goods and services, but while both are significant features of capitalism, they are not defining characteristics of the mode of production. According to Desai (1983, pp.65–6), capitalism has six major characterising features:

(1) Production takes place for sale rather than for consumption by the producer.
(2) Labour power is bought and sold in markets, with the buyers agreeing contracts with the sellers over rates of payment (either for items of work or for periods of work) and the conditions of work, including the length of the period of employment.
(3) Exchange is almost universally through the medium of money, which is the most flexible way of redeploying the rewards of production. The importance of money gives financial intermediaries a particularly significant role in the operation of capitalism.
(4) The capitalist (or a managerial agent acting on behalf of a capitalist or a consortium of them – e.g. the shareholders in a company) who purchases the labour power of others also controls the process of production, determining how products are made and sold, and in what quantities.
(5) The capitalists and their agents also control financial decisions, which include those to borrow in order to invest, what to invest in, and where, and so forth. The sellers of labour power (the proletariat) have no control over those decisions, which determine their livelihoods.
(6) There is competition between segments of capital, for labour, materials on which labour works, and markets. This competition is subject to laws of value which force the capitalist to adopt new techniques and practices which will cut costs, and to accumulate to ensure the provision of improved machinery. This constant revolution in value is an important feature of the dynamics of capitalism.

Capitalism originated in a transition from feudalism in the parts of Europe where accumulated wealth was available to be invested in new ways, and where the nature of social relationships enabled this to be successful (Hechter and Brustein, 1980). Substantial new wealth was accumulated through, for example, the investment of capital in trade involving slaves, agricultural production, precious metals and simple manufactured commodities. It then evolved into its industrial phase, with substantial investment in routine production of commodities in factories through the employment of large, disciplined labour forces, and then into its later stages (variously termed 'finance capitalism', 'monopoly capitalism', 'post-industrial capitalism', 'disorganised capitalism' and so forth) in which relatively small numbers were involved in the actual processes of production and many more in both its facilitation and the organisation of distribution and exchange.


## MEANS OF PRODUCTION

Capitalism operates through the mobilisation of the three means of production – land, labour and capital. To some there is a fourth means, enterprise, but in the argument developed here enterprise refers to the way in which capitalism is operated and is not a separate resource on which the mode of production draws. Each of the means of production is privately owned, and this is fundamental both to the operation of capitalism and to its ideology.

*Labour* is the power to work, and is a personal attribute, even though much work involves collaboration with others. In some types of society, such as those based on slavery, the individual's labour power is owned by another. This is not the case in capitalism; the individual is free to sell his or her labour power to anybody who wants to buy it – or not to sell it at all, in which case the individual must have an alternative means of support. Labour power has two components: the physical power to work, and the mental ability to undertake tasks. The former is genetically derived, though it can be either enhanced or reduced; the latter is a genetic endowment that can be enhanced through training and experience. The genetic endowments and the degree to which they have been enhanced comprise the commodity which individuals take to the labour market. They sell that commodity in order to be able to obtain their needs and demands, in order to live; because they lack the ability to meet those themselves, they must obtain the means to purchase them – i.e. to buy the products of other people's labour.

*Land* provides the resources on which people work, and is fundamental to all production, even though not all people deal either directly with the land or work on its products; the majority of people who work in most capitalist societies are involved in neither primary (production from the land) nor secondary (manufacture of products from the raw materials yielded by the land) occupations, but rather in the tertiary and quaternary occupations involved in the organisation of production and the distribution of the outcomes. Land also comprises two main components: the raw materials which can either be consumed or transformed; and the environment within which other raw materials (such as foodstuffs) can be developed. It too is privately owned, and just as the owners of labour can determine how they will use that resource, so the owners of land are free to determine how they will use that means of production.

*Capital* differs from the other two means of production in that it is not a naturally occurring phenomenon but a human creation. Yet it plays a central role in the mode of production: without capital, land and labour cannot be employed. It is in effect a collective term for a variety of phenomena used in production, distribution and exchange; it includes the buildings within which work takes place, the machinery therein, and the money invested in those fixed assets, and is also used as a term to define the stock of wealth held by an individual or group. Capital is fundamental because unless money is invested in the work process, for example in building factories, installing machinery and fuelling it, purchasing raw materials, employing labour, and selling the resulting products, no goods are created, nothing is available for people to buy and survive on, no jobs are available for people to earn money with which to obtain the means of reproduction, and so forth. So how does it come about, and why is it invested?

Capital is the result of labour, specifically the surplus derived from employing labour. That surplus is created because the income from the sale of the products of the purchased labour is more than the costs of employing it, and the land resources on which it worked. The surplus value of any product is the difference between the cost of making it and the price received when it is sold (the production costs include the selling expenses, such as marketing and advertising). It accrues to the person or group who invested in the production process, and is generally known as the profit. (The technical definition of profit in this labour theory of value is given in Harvey, 1982, Chapter 2.) That profit is added to the person's or group's stock of wealth, and can be used either to purchase goods and services or to invest in further production, and hence further profit-making. If profits are not made, the investors have no returns on which to sustain themselves. More importantly for the mode of production as a whole, they have no available money that can be used as capital to invest in further rounds of production, and hence in providing employment for labour. The dynamic of capitalism requires both that profits be made and that capital be invested in making more profits.

The difference between capital and land and labour, therefore, is that the one is the product of the other two. This raises important questions about the origins of the initial capital. Answering them lies outside the main arguments of this book. All that is important here is to note that capitalism developed as a mode of production in areas of feudal societies, where the wealth of the elite was directed, through a sequence of stages and much trial and error, into the creation of the capitalist mode of production. It emerged in societies where most individuals possessed only their labour power and were dependent on the owners of land for their livelihoods. Those powerful owners of land used some of their amassed wealth either directly in the employment of labour or indirectly by investing in those who themselves intended to employ labour. Capitalism grew out of societies based on inequality, and extended that inequality.

## EMPLOYING LABOUR AND MAKING PROFITS

The motive force of capitalism is the accumulation of wealth derived from profits. If people do not want to amass wealth, then they do not want to make profits, and if they do not invest in making profits, nothing is made, people do not have work, and reproduction becomes impossible. Thus the desire to accumulate wealth from profits had to be accepted as the 'natural' way of organising society, and that ideology had to be promoted by those who already believed in such a method of organising society. The success of that ideological experiment can be assessed by the contemporary role of capitalism.

How did the mode of production develop? Early capitalism involved both direct and indirect purchase of labour power by those with available capital. The direct route involved employing people either in agriculture or, increasingly, in manufacture. Investment in manufacturing began in many places by people investing not in factories, in which they set employees to work, but in raw materials on which they employed people to work in their own homes; profits were made by paying those people less than what the goods they produced could be sold for. The indirect methods involved not employing people directly, but rather buying goods from them, which were then sold elsewhere, at a profit; again the investor had to have available money to bridge the gap between the purchase from the producer and the sale to the consumer, and any costs involved in getting from one to the other. In every case, the investors' decisions were determined by their interpretation of the market-place: they would not invest in a commodity if they thought they could not sell it, and they would not pay more for it than a percentage (less than 100) of the price they expected to obtain. Markets determined what was produced; if there was no likely sale there would be no investment, since if the product could not be sold profits would not be made, and the investors' stock of wealth would be reduced rather than enhanced. This principle remains central to the operation of capitalism.

At this early stage, then, we can identify three groups within the population. The largest by far was that comprising individuals whose only available resource was labour power; in order to survive they had to sell it. The others were those who, in addition to their labour power, possessed other means of production. There were those with land, who employed labour in order to produce saleable commodities from the land; in addition to the land, they needed some capital to cover the costs of employing the labour in the period before the products were sold. Finally, there were those with capital, obtained in a variety of ways (inheritance, borrowing, gifts and so on). They invested this either directly in production or indirectly in facilitating production through trade. Those with only labour power depended on the other groups for their existence, and thus were relatively powerless; those with land and/or capital were much more powerful and it was their investment decisions that formed the direction of the society's development. For a long period those investors with available capital operated as individuals, and so the major distinction within society was between those with capital – the capitalists – and those without – the labourers. Over time that distinction was replaced by another. As capitalism expanded, the capital investment requirements were increasingly greater than those that individuals could meet from their amassed wealth (or were prepared to 'gamble' on a single venture). It was necessary for them both to combine and to borrow from others to obtain the necessary sums. Thus the precise distinction between capitalists and labourers disappeared, and was replaced by that between the labourers and those who employed them, who benefited in part from the outcomes (their incomes were conditional on successful profit-making) but who were accountable to a wide range of other investors (i.e. the capitalists' agents, to use Desai's term; see p.57). Increasingly the difference within capitalism is between the managers of capital and the workers, which is not to deny the existence of many individuals and families with great wealth based on their investment in labour. The workers have been indirectly incorporated to the capitalist structure. Most contribute to pension funds, which involves their money being invested in capitalist operations with the sole objective of making profits so as to guarantee members a sufficient income on retirement. In the UK alone, pension funds' assets totalled over £700 billion in 1993, equivalent to more than 70 per cent of GDP. Somewhat paradoxically, the managers of those funds may indirectly influence their members' livelihoods in a negative direction by their choice of investments (Bluestone and Harrison, 1982); a UK court ruled in 1984 that the managers of the National Union of Mineworkers' pension fund were legally required to make the best investments in terms of potential returns, even if that meant directing the money overseas and into industries whose development might threaten miners' jobs.

A mode of production based on the trading of agricultural products and the outputs of relatively unsophisticated manufacturing processes requires an infrastructure, which has two components. The first is the built environment, comprising the transport networks and the vehicles that traverse them, the buildings in which trade is to be conducted, and so on. The second is a facilitating environment, providing in particular the services on which trade is based – the most important is an agreed currency. These too called for investment, by people who perceived that capital used in that way would produce a return – i.e. would be profitable. New sectors of the economy emerged to facilitate the basic processes of producing, distributing and exchanging: all were subject to the same basic principles – only invest if profit will ensue.

## COMPETING AND SELLING

In the 'ideal' capitalist economy there is a very large number of sellers and a probably much larger number of buyers. As a consequence, no one buyer or group of buyers and no one seller or group of sellers can determine the price of a commodity with little or no reference to the others; the price is a function of demand and supply. In such a market buyers are seeking the cheapest items, at a given quality, or at least within a certain quality range, and in order to sell to them the producers of the goods must meet the buyers' criteria. Success in the market therefore involves producing goods at a price and quality acceptable to the buyers. To a large extent price and quality are relative rather than absolute criteria. Clearly there are price limits beyond which consumers will not go – because they cannot afford to, given the many other demands on their available resources – and there are quality limits below which they will not buy. But in most situations the alternative goods on display offer an equivalent return, and customers are seeking the 'best buy'; this usually means they are looking for the most competitive price.

Producers are well aware of this, of course, and their decision whether to produce a certain commodity reflects their evaluation of the market. But having entered it, they face competition, which will change as others enter and some withdraw. To succeed they must compete successfully. In the market for any commodity the successful competitors are those whose production costs are lowest. If the price is fixed they make the largest profits; however, if they are prepared to lower their price they may reduce the profit on each individual item but, by increasing their sales volume, increase their profitability overall, and relative to their labour costs (even though they may employ more workers). How, then, do they ensure that they succeed in such ways?

If the largest profits accrue to those with the lowest production costs, there must be differences between producers in the costs that they incur. These can come about in a variety of ways; one producer may have access to a cheaper raw material source than another, for example. But raw materials are the product of labour power, indirectly if not directly, and ultimately virtually all variations between producers depend on the relative costs of their labour – relative, that is, to what they produce. The more productive a unit of labour, measured as the amount produced for every pound spent on that person (both directly, in wages, and indirectly, in the materials provided and the machinery used) the greater the profit from the expenditure. If a commodity can be sold for £20, the investor who produces it for a £10 investment will make more than the person who pays £12. Greater productivity means greater profits.

*Productivity* is of fundamental importance, then; the more workers produce, relative to what they are paid and is spent on them, the more profits they generate for their employers. Thus the differences between producers' relative success in the market-place reflect differentials in their workers' productivity. Those differentials may reflect different capacities of the workers – they are fitter, or more able – but are usually the product of investment (in training, for example). In other cases they may reflect the resources used – one farmer has more fertile soils than another, for example. But in the majority of cases they reflect the amount and efficiency of work; the more efficient the work process, the greater the return on the wages paid.

Greater work could simply involve greater expenditure of effort; one employer's staff works harder for the same amount of money than does another's. But differences in the effectiveness of work are most likely to produce the greater profits, because one group has better tools to work with than another. Increased productivity is usually achieved by replacing labour by machines. This is sometimes called replacing 'live labour' by 'dead labour', since machines are themselves the product of labour. The machines may be expensive to install, but are so much cheaper to run (fuel and maintenance are less expensive than labour) that the investment promises to repay the initial outlay with interest and so can be afforded; the cost of buying and running the machines is less than the cost of producing by using 'live labour'. Some operations are more readily performed by machines than others, and some production processes are entirely automated – but machines cannot invent and maintain machines, so labour is needed somewhere. Where labour can be replaced by more efficient machines – which frequently means that a skilled operative is replaced by a semi-skilled or unskilled machine-minder – the potential competitive advantage in the market-place from the investment in the replacement of labour will probably be realised.

The drive to increase productivity and thus profits is ever-present, because it means greater wealth acquisition. It is particularly pressing when competition is intense, perhaps because the market is more or less saturated, and even more so when it is in decline. In the latter situation, producers are competing for a declining market; in order to maintain their profitability they must increase their market share. To do this they must be competitive; the winners are the producers with the lowest costs and/or the best products, because they can outsell their competitors. In particular, those with the lowest production costs can undercut the prices of the less efficient, and force the latter out of the market. In periods of buoyant demand the relatively inefficient may be able to survive, but as competition becomes tougher it is the fittest who survive.

So far, the discussion of increasing productivity in order to compete successfully has been presented in terms of the production of goods. But it applies equally to service industries, which depend on labour for the distribution and exchange procedures, and for facilitating the operation of the whole system. The retailing industry has been subject to drives to increase productivity in a variety of ways in recent years; supermarkets replace labour by space in giving customers access to the goods, for example, and high technology at the checkouts increases the number of customers that an employee can handle in a given period, for a certain wage. (And this book has been written on a word-processor, which is quicker than longhand and removes the necessity for a secretary–typist.)

There are three probable consequences of increased productivity. The first is that the process of survival of the fittest means that the relatively inefficient producers are eliminated from the competition. Eventually, the number of producers still active is sufficiently small for them to collude if they wish to fix the price, and so to some extent protect themselves from possibly losing in the continued competition. The ultimate expression of this is the creation of a monopoly in which a single producer gains control of the market for a product – either by causing all other competitors to fail or by buying them out. A monopolist is less subject to the constraints of the market than is the case when there are many competitors, though the degree to which monopolists are released from the rigours of the market-place depends on the elasticity of demand for their products. Monopoly situations can lead to a range of consequences considered undesirable both for consumers and for the future of the capitalist system: monopolists are less likely to invest in further improvements if their profits are ensured, which could initiate a downward spiral of production and consumption.

The second consequence is also a result of success. The market for most products is not ever-expanding, particularly if the product cannot easily be transported several thousand miles. Thus as productivity increases, so the ability to produce more than the market can consume comes ever closer. The technological advances that allow productivity increases result in the production of more goods than can be sold (a condition known as either 'overproduction' or 'underconsumption'), and so in the end the drive to increase profits leads to the situation in which the making of profits becomes more difficult, even for the more successful, efficient producers. The only answer to this is for the producers either to seek new markets or to switch their investment into other product lines where the market is more buoyant and the promise of profitability brighter.

Linked to this problem in certain circumstances is the situation in which increased productivity itself reduces the demand for goods. Products are bought by people using their wages. But if they are made redundant by the productivity increases – fewer people are needed to produce the same volume of goods, and those who are still employed are paid less because they are less skilled – then fewer people have wages to spend and those who have, have less to spend. (The workforce becomes increasingly polarised between the well-paid, skilled workers who design and maintain the machinery that increases productivity, and the poorly paid, unskilled operatives.) Competition in the market leads to the market being destroyed. This tendency is countered if capital is invested in new lines of production, creating new jobs. This may involve bringing into the capitalist system the production of goods and especially services that was formerly outside it. The growth of leisure-based industries in recent years is an example; increasingly people purchase leisure (television programmes, for example) from producers, rather than creating their own entertainment. This is the process of commodification whereby, as a consequence of its very success, the capitalist system has to invade more aspects of life in order to survive.

The third consequence of increases in productivity is that they may lead to increased conflict between employers and their employees over two main issues: wages and the conditions of work, and job security. On the first, employers are concerned to hold wages as low as possible relative to prices, in order to sustain profitability levels. They may be prepared to make some additional payment as a reward for productivity increases, but not so great as to wipe out the benefits to their profits from the investment in greater productivity. Employees, on the other hand, are concerned to increase their wages in order at least to maintain if not to increase their spending power and level of living. Alongside these debates over wages (over the proportion of the selling price that should go in wages relative to the proportion that goes into surplus value) may be others over the conditions at work. Employees may claim that they are being asked to work harder, or in more dangerous conditions, and seek recompense accordingly, either directly – in higher wages – or indirectly – through a shorter working week, for example, or longer holidays, or other fringe benefits. These disputes become more contentious, and the power of the employees in them increased, if the employees act collectively through a trade union or similar body. By negotiating in strength, and with the ultimate sanction of withdrawing their labour, which will of course hurt them but will also have immediate impact on the profitability of the organisation, the workers are better placed to win concessions from their employers than are individual employees.

This conflict between employers and employees is fundamental to the operations of capitalism, since all changes introduced by employers to enhance their profitability have consequences for their employees. In the short term it is the employees who have most to lose, since they do not have the cushion of accumulated wealth to sustain them during a period when they are not earning. If they are prepared to hurt themselves, however, they may win concessions from their employers whose potential profits are rapidly being eroded by the loss of production and income. But this success merely writes the script for the next act of the conflict; having made concessions, the employer will then want further productivity increases in order to survive in the competitive market.

## LONGER-TERM COMPETITIVE CONSEQUENCES

In this brief description of how capitalism works, the earlier statement that it is necessarily a dynamic mode of production has been clearly illustrated.

People's survival is dependent on their being able to find work, so that they can buy the goods that they need for personal and societal reproduction. They can only find work if others with capital available are prepared to invest it in making things for sale, and they will only do that if they believe that there is a market for the products in which they can compete successfully and make profits. Having determined that they can, and so entered the market, they then find that to survive in it they must continually increase the productivity of their operations, without which they will fail, their workers will be wageless again and there will be no profits to invest in creating further jobs, products, and the means of survival. Capitalism is a competitive activity in which continued improved performance is a necessity, and if people do not succeed, many others lose.

One of the consequences of this system is that it contains within itself the seeds of its own destruction; success can be the cause of failure. Increasing productivity can mean that the ability to produce goods far outstrips the ability to consume. The result is a crisis, alternatively termed a crisis of overproduction or of underconsumption, depending on the point of view. Whichever term is used, the result is the same; too much is produced, and profitability suffers. Whenever profitability suffers, investment slows, jobs are at risk, and with them people's life chances.

The actors within the capitalist system are aware of these issues, and are continually seeking ways of countering them. In the short term their response is to try to increase profitability by the traditional routes: cheaper raw materials, perhaps from another supplier whose labour is cheaper; more efficient production using fewer (and preferably cheaper) workers and better machines; more effective advertising and marketing, expanding the demand for the product either by convincing those who formerly did not buy it to do so or by convincing those who did to replace their existing purchases more frequently. These may involve geographical strategies, searching the world for cheaper materials, cheaper labour and more markets.

But there are limits to these strategies. Sooner or later the market will become saturated and sales cannot be increased, and the limits to increased productivity will be approached. Profitability will be eroded, and only the fittest will survive. The only solution then for most competitors in that sector of the system will be to withdraw, and to find alternative uses for their capital: fixed capital (buildings, machines, raw materials, even land itself) may be put to alternative uses that can yield profits, as also may labour. This may be painful; many people may find themselves unemployed, temporarily at least, as the transition occurs, and they may need to be retrained to participate in the new activities. But if those activities can be identified, and then developed, the problems should be short-lived.

What happens, however, when such a need to restructure occurs not just in one sector of the economy, or even in a few firms, but in very large segments of it, affecting the jobs of very many people and the capital investments of large numbers too? And are such major events likely? The evidence of the history of capitalism, and certainly of the last 200 years or so, is that there is a major slump, affecting many parts of the economy at the same time, about once every 50 years. Profitability declines in a number of important sectors concurrently, with the result that the possibilities for alternative uses of capital are limited: buildings cannot be transferred to other uses, there are no new tasks for which labour can be retrained, and so on. Eventually each of these slumps has been followed by a new period of prosperity, built on a new generation of industries – the outcome of investment in research and development – creating and then meeting a new set of demands and, it seems, drawing more of the world into their sphere of influence. But the restructuring is often painful, as capital is withdrawn very substantially from certain activities, which almost certainly means certain places, and is eventually placed elsewhere. In the interim, the capital-holders may perceive no worthwhile investments and prefer not to commit themselves to ventures unlikely to increase their stock of wealth, and which may even erode it. In such situations they may prefer to use their money in ways that are much less likely to create jobs for others, for example by investing it in commodities like land, precious metals, jewellery and works of art, whose exchange value they believe will increase in the long term.

Such 'unproductive' use of capital cannot go on for long, since it will lead to a decline in the store of wealth and also to a crisis in the system as a whole, as insufficient investment in production means not only fewer goods and services produced for consumption but also fewer workers with incomes to spend on those goods and services. The dynamo will wind down, unless capital is directed towards potentially profitable investments. Harvey (1982) has illustrated this with his representation of three circuits of capital (Figure 3.1). The primary circuit involves investment in the production of goods and services, from which surplus value will be extracted and profits made, with consequent wealth accumulation. But during periods of underconsumption capital is moved into the secondary and tertiary circuits. The former involves investments in fixed capital, such as the built environment, in the expectation of profits from this investment, either in rents from the use value or in enhanced exchange value. The tertiary circuit involves investment in science and technology, in the expectation of advances in production methods that will enhance future wealth accumulation strategies, or in improving human labour, as with education. In both cases much of this investment is made collectively, through the institutions of the state, because individual capitalists are unlikely to make investments in the potential long-term advantages. This provides part of the argument for the necessity of the state in capitalist societies, as developed further in later chapters; at this stage we note that the long-term survival of capitalism requires institutions which ensure investment in the infrastructure (both physical and mental) necessary to the continued operation of the dynamo of wealth accumulation.

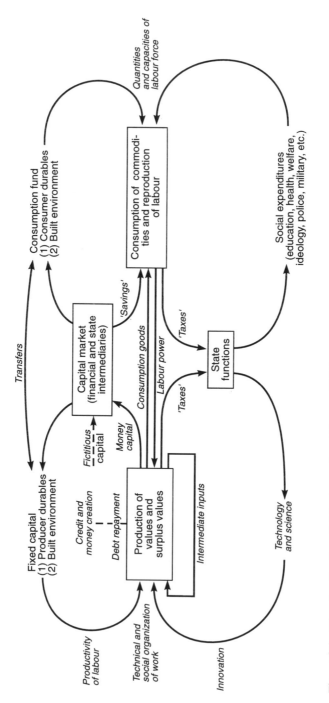

**Figure 3.1** The circuits of capital (redrawn from Harvey, 1982)

CAPITALISM AND PLACE

This brief description of some of the elements of the capitalist mode of production carries with it a number of major geographical implications, since the prosperity of people is intimately tied up with the prosperity of the places in which they live. But the geography of capitalism is not simply an outcome of the operation of non-geographical processes; the continual restructuring of geography is an integral part of the continual restructuring of capitalism. Capitalism makes, destroys, and remakes places.

The basic process of creating and changing geographies (or places) is well portrayed in a model developed by Ann Markusen (1985). This represents the life of an industry as a profit cycle, comprising four stages. In the first stage, a new product is being developed and profitability has yet to begin: investment in research has been forthcoming because potential profitability has been perceived, a market is thought either to exist or to be creatable. At the second stage, the market is being opened up, returns on the initial investment in research and development are being obtained, and profitability begins. The initial developers who invested in the product may reap a rich reward at this time if the market does develop as predicted, because of their near-monopolistic position. Eventually, however, their success attracts competitors, who can enter the market without the expensive research and development investment. Competition increases and profit levels decline overall, but vary between competitors depending on the degree to which they increase productivity-enhancing investment – which will depend on their perception of the future market trends. By the fourth stage market saturation has been reached, and the crisis of overproduction (or underconsumption) of the product has set in. As the level of profitability declines, many of the competitors will choose to disinvest from the sector, seeking alternative outlets for their money and expertise, and those remaining will be less inclined to invest in further profitability increases. The market for the product may entirely disappear. More likely, however, is the continued existence of a relatively static level of demand, and some producers remaining to serve this, probably those able to survive because of relatively low costs.

The geography of this profit cycle reflects the differences between the stages; increasingly that geography is being written and rewritten globally rather than nationally, let alone regionally or locally. At the first and second stages the development is contingent on the availability of both capital and skilled labour; it is most likely to be found in places where those are relatively abundant (on the geography of venture capital see Thompson, 1989). With the move into the second stage factories are established which need skilled labour, because of the newness of the product and the processes involved; their workers may be relatively highly paid, not only because of their skills but also because their relative monopoly allows the employers to meet the wage and other demands (which they are immediately able to add to the price of the good or service), in order to ensure continued production and high profits. This may be to those workers' disadvantage at the third stage, when the production process becomes much more routinised, because they will probably be highly paid relative to those of firms who have entered the industry at the routine stage and established their factories in places where labour is relatively cheap. The initial manufacturers may find it necessary to shift to such locations as well, which means that the original incubation areas for the industry lose out in the mature stages of its development. At the final stage, it will be the factories with the most productive workers who remain in production, which could well be in regions where skills are few; their prosperity is based on providing cheap, relatively amenable workers for routine production – profits are not great but are relatively assured by employing them.

To some commentators, the spatial dispersion of production activities envisaged in the profit cycle model is a characteristic of a form of capitalism that is increasingly becoming obsolete. In the era of 'Fordism' the mass production of commodities took place in large factories with production line organisation and mainly semi-skilled labour. But 'Fordism' is now being replaced, it seems, by what is variously termed 'post-Fordism', a 'regime of flexible accumulation', and 'disorganised capitalism' (Lash and Urry, 1987), characterised by much smaller production units and a greater integration of factories and workshops into production complexes comprising interdependent units most of which survive on subcontracted work (Thrift, 1989). Thus while 'Fordism' allowed great spatial flexibility to producers, and apparently led to a decline in large cities as investors sought cheap production locations (a process widely known as 'counterurbanisation'), 'flexible accumulation' requires spatial proximity of linked production units, and is restimulating the growth of major cities and regions (Scott, 1988).

A major feature of this profit cycle is that the pace of operations has increased substantially in recent decades; the length of the period of 'excess profits' in the second stage is now much shorter than it was only a few years ago, and the competitive years of the third stage are both fewer and fiercer. Restructuring takes place more frequently, so geographies change more often.

This process of restructuring involves a geographical process of 'uneven development', whereby the fortunes of places change rapidly, but within a well-recognised overall structure. Basic to the geographical structuring is a division of the capitalist world into two main zones – a core and a periphery. Within the core are concentrations of two main types of activity – the financial institutions which facilitate the operation of the global capitalist system, and the research and development clusters. The core is where the innovations develop, and where the factories of the 'excess profits' second stage are located. It is where the investors live. The periphery lacks skilled labour and capital in large quantities, but has resources and cheap labour to offer. It is where factories are opened in the third stage, and where those that survive in the fourth are likely to be found. But many of them are owned by organisations located in the core, and the profits from peripheral activities are thus likely to be destined for the core (where the financial institutions will reallocate them, perhaps to other areas of the periphery).

Places in the periphery therefore have a fragile economy relative to those of the core. A few may be able to rise up into the core, via a semi-peripheral stage, as the result of exploiting local advantages – as with Japan in the present century – but for most peripheral areas escaping that status seems a remote possibility. Within the core, different areas compete for power. In each of the major boom periods of the world economy in the last three centuries, one core area has dominated, but the strains of success usually lead to its replacement in the next. These strains are related to the politics of core status also, which sees the state in which the core area is located becoming overstretched geopolitically and therefore unable to assist the core in the restructuring process of the switch from one period of the cycle to the next. Thus the major concentration of political power has migrated around the core, but the relative position of core and periphery has remained substantially unchanged for long periods.

It is common to associate the core–periphery division of the capitalist world economy with the geography of the nation-states of the contemporary world political map. This is a substantial generalisation, because the processes creating cores and peripheries are really class processes. Thus while it is proper to see the division of that map into cores and peripheries, as a consequence of colonial and imperial processes, it must also be recognised that individual countries (in both the core and the periphery on a global scale) contain their own cores and peripheries, as indeed do individual cities (see, for example, Hechter, 1975). Thus the processes of uneven development operate at a variety of spatial scales, producing complex maps of economic power and complex movements of investments and profits.

## CAPITALISM IN SUMMARY

Capitalism is an extremely complex mode of production, and this introduction has only sketched some of its features which are fundamental to understanding the genesis of and possible approaches to solving environmental problems. In brief, the survival of capitalism depends on the continued circulation of capital, invested in the production of commodities (goods and services) in order to create surplus value and thus increase the stock of capital. It is difficult to improve upon David Harvey's (1985b) summary of the basic features that underpin the circulation of capital, in the following ten points.

(1) The production of an ever-increasing stock of capital depends on continual expansion of the value of commodities produced. Growth is necessary to capitalism, so that it must be sustained and legitimated through a pro-growth ideology.

(2) Growth can only be achieved through the profitable sale of the products of human labour.

(3) Profits are obtained through the exploitation of labour, from the surplus value which is the difference between the costs of production and the selling price of commodities.

(4) Since the success of capitalism depends on the buying and selling of labour power, there is a class separation between those who sell labour power and those who buy it; without that separation, and the social relations that it implies, capitalism could not operate.

(5) The relationship between the classes implies antagonism and conflict, over wages and working conditions.

(6) The competition that underlies capitalism requires continued technological and organisational advances, so that some investors can increase their competitive advantage over others.

(7) Technological and organisational development require investment, in advance of profit-making; the survival of capitalism requires ensuring that continued investment.

(8) Capitalism is crisis-prone, because growth and technological progress are antagonistic; this will occasionally result in major crises of capitalism with disruption of the circulation process.

(9) The usual manifestation of crisis is that of overproduction, in which the surplus capital yielded by profits cannot be absorbed by further rounds of investment.

(10) In order to surmount the crisis of overproduction, it is necessary to devalue the surpluses by writing off capital investments.

Harvey's analysis thus focuses on the importance of crises in the operation of capitalism. As will be argued in the next chapter, those crises, and the growth dynamics from which they emerge, including the increased value of commodities in circulation and the need for continued investment in technological and organisational improvements, produce responses that are likely to have particularly severe consequences for the physical environment. Their resolution also requires the institution of the state, as discussed in Chapter 5.

## ADVANCED COMMUNISM/SOCIALISM

These two linked modes of social organisation differ from capitalism in the relative importance of the basic components of an economic system –

production, distribution and exchange. Under capitalism, it is production and exchange which are dominant, and together they provide the dynamo which keeps a system in operation. Furthermore, growth in the volume of production, and hence also of exchange, is a necessary element of capitalism's health; continued accumulation drives the capitalist mode of production, and if it fails to occur, decay is the consequence – stagnation, over more than a short period, is inconsistent with the capitalist mode. Under advanced communism/socialism, on the other hand, the major focus is on distribution, on the allocation of the fruits of production among the members of society, through mechanisms which may not involve exchange as it is understood in the capitalist system. Thus the two types have very different ideologies promoting their acceptance: the capitalist ideology focuses on the creation of wealth within society, and argues that the operation of markets is the best means of assuring that this privately produced wealth is widely distributed through society; whereas the communist/socialist ideology focuses on the collective production of wealth and its equitable allocation by mechanisms other than markets which, it is argued, are rarely equitable in the distribution of power between buyers and sellers.

Therefore capitalism and advanced communism/socialism differ in their apparent need for central co-ordination and control. Capitalism is dominated by independently operating markets; the decisions on what to produce and what to purchase are made by individuals according to perceptions of markets and needs. On the other hand, if decisions on production and distribution are to be made collectively, as is the case with communism and socialism, it is necessary to have an institution within which those collective decisions can be made; such an institution would need the acceptance of the population it serves. This is clearly a case for a state, or some institution similar to that which we term the state, that can draw individuals together in a collectivity, determine their goals, and develop means of attaining them.

Although the origins of advanced communism/socialism can be found in many sources, the ideology gathered momentum during the nineteenth century, particularly under the stimulus of the work of Karl Marx. As he and his followers developed it, the ideology saw the communist mode of production as a successor to capitalism, with socialism as an intermediate stage. Indeed, communism was seen as the logical outcome of capitalism which contains within itself the seeds of its own destruction; the in-built antagonisms between capitalists and workers would eventually lead to the latter overthrowing the former and taking over the economic and political organisation to promote their own collective ends.

Communism is a mode of production and social organisation in which the means of production, distribution and exchange are collectively rather than individually owned and in which there are no class distinctions based on the buying and selling of labour power. It is created out of the successes of capitalism, but because of its failures. The successes of capitalism are its ability to solve the problems of production; the inventiveness of individuals in the creation of ways of making products that contribute to a high material quality of life. The failures include its inability to ensure that the high material quality of life is available to all; under capitalism, according to marxian arguments, there must always be major disparities in levels of living, because the success of the mode of economic organisation depends on class inequalities. This failure will increasingly become apparent to those who suffer from the inequalities, who can be politically mobilised to create a new form of social organisation, a new mode of production, in which such disparities disappear. Under capitalism, goods and services are produced if they can be sold; under the new mode of production they would be produced if the population wanted them, and would be equally available to all.

This new mode of production – which is termed advanced communism here to distinguish it from the primitive communism described earlier – would be achieved by the appropriation of the privately owned means of production by the state, on behalf of the population at large. This could occur in one step, through a revolution, or it could be a steady process of the continued advance of public ownership and the decline of private property. State ownership of the means of production, distribution and exchange would ensure that decisions about what should be produced, for whom, and how it should be allocated would be made by the population at large (through a representative body which had their popular support) rather than by a small number of owners of large wealth whose decisions were determined by profit-making potential rather than 'real needs'. It should be noted, however, that not all those who accepted the analysis of the successes and failures of capitalism subscribed also to the prescriptions of communism. For example in *The Future of Socialism* (1956), an important book that influenced Labour Party thinking in Britain for a generation, Crosland argued that equality could be achieved through planning involving co-operation between the state and the capitalist organisations, without major nationalisation and public ownership; he promoted instead a system of 'competitive public enterprise' in which

> ownership is thoroughly mixed up – a society with a diverse, diffused, pluralist, and heterogeneous pattern of ownership, with the State, the nationalised industries, the Cooperatives, the Unions, Government financial institutions, pension funds, foundations, and millions of private families all participating

and concluded that

> State ownership of all industrial capital is not now a condition of creating a socialist society, establishing social equality, increasing social welfare, or eliminating class distinctions. What is unjust in our present arrangements is the distribution of private wealth; and that can be cured

in a pluralist as in a wholly State-owned economy, with much better
results for social contentment and the fragmentation of power. (1956,
p.340)

According to those who accepted the communist prescription, as socialism
spread through a society so private ownership would be diminished and
collective control over the economy would replace it. Once this was achieved
the transition to communism would be complete and, according to some, the
need for a central state would disappear. *Anarchism* would replace it, using
that term in its original sense and not as a synonym for chaos; society would
be organised through myriad small communities, in each of which all were
equal and had equal negotiating rights in determining the priorities and
programmes of larger collectivities. Central direction through a state would
be unnecessary, and individual freedom would be maximised (thus removing
one of the fears of Crosland and some other interpreters of communist
societies, that economic equality could only be achieved at the expense of
individual liberty).

According to this set of views, communism builds on the prosperity created
by the successes of capitalism, and transforms the way in which that
prosperity is enjoyed; it is fundamentally a global mode of production,
promoting the interests of all. Thus socialism should develop, as the
precursor of communism, in areas of greatest capitalist success. In general
terms, this has not been the case. Whereas some countries in which
capitalism has been successful have seen social democratic experiments
(notably in Sweden and New Zealand) these have not moved far towards the
goals of collective ownership promoting equality. In several of these
experiments, the collectively owned enterprises have been very similar to
privately owned capitalist enterprises in their modes of operation – expected
to make profits, for example, and to react to market signals. In recent years
there have been major shifts away from the socialist experiments, as the
capitalist ideology has gained renewed support among the population at
large, as reflected in the politics of the parties elected to run their societies.
(Some parties with socialist roots, and still to some extent promoting socialist
ideas, are clearly now not socialist in what they do when in power; New
Zealand's Labour Party in the mid-1980s provides a clear example of this:
Johnston, 1993.)

Where it has been introduced, notably in the countries of eastern Europe
and east Asia, communism took over from modes of social organisation
where capitalist success had not been achieved; the societies were either in an
early stage of capitalist penetration, and with low material living standards
for the great majority of their populations, or had not yet attained even that
level. Thus there were few successful capitalist operations to be taken over in
a socialist revolution, which could make a wide range of goods and thereby
ensure high overall levels of material prosperity for all, if the products were

equitably distributed. Instead, the development of a very strong state has been necessary in those countries, a state which would plan the achievement of such high material levels of living by a programme of industrialisation which would achieve what had been attained in western Europe and North America by the very largely unplanned operation of capitalism. The level of direction necessary and the control imposed on the population is seen by many as totally contradictory to the ideology of communism, with its emphasis on freeing the individual from the control of others. Apologists for totalitarian regimes argue that they represent a necessary transitional period because the communist revolutions occurred away from the areas of capitalist success (and have not been assisted by the capitalists); only when high material levels have been achieved could the promised liberation be allowed. Thus instead of being achieved out of capitalist success, communism was being attempted without it.

The goal within communist societies is to attain levels of material welfare equivalent to those of capitalist societies, without the excesses 'enjoyed' by small proportions of the population in capitalist societies, where consumption levels (in, for example, house size) far exceed what can really be described as 'needs'. In large part, this is because residents of the communist societies are aware of those levels, and wish to emulate them; in the long term, if the communist society fails to deliver such standards, it will be deemed to have failed. Only in a few cases, as in Tanzania, has there been much explicit promotion of levels of consumption well below those attained elsewhere, on the grounds that such standards are neither necessary nor sustainable. In general, the communist ideology is that the material standards achieved in the capitalist world can similarly be achieved in the communist, through a different mechanism. Thus the production goals in the two are very similar in terms of what is wanted, and this is important to later discussions of relationship with the environment.

Most of the advanced communist/socialist states failed in the late 1980s and early 1990s. Their single-party-dominated political machines were dismantled, and replaced by multi-party democracy on the liberal model; this collapse was heralded by Fukuyama (1992) as 'the end of history', his term for liberal democracy's global triumph. (One-quarter of the world's population remained in a single-party communist state, however – the People's Republic of China. It made a number of concessions to capitalism at the same time but was much more restrictive of individual freedoms than was the case in eastern Europe and the former USSR.) The collapse resulted from a number of related internal and external causes. In a society without market signals it became difficult to motivate workers to increase productivity; the rewards for doing so were uncertain and, it seemed, insufficient. The state ideology was questioned by some and ignored by many more, whose material living standards were relatively low, although subsistence was maintained and life expectancies were much higher than in the Third World (Johnston, 1989).

More importantly, the leading bureaucrats in the party and state apparatus hierarchies were concerned about external and internal threats. They perceived a strong desire in the 'West' (especially the USA, by then the predominant world economic power) not only to contain communism within its current borders but also to replace it by democratic structures and a market economy. Thus the Soviet Union maintained a large military presence, participated in the nuclear arms race, and became involved in a number of geopolitical wars beyond its borders (Agnew and Corbridge, 1989; O'Loughlin, 1989). This was extremely expensive. So too were the costs of internal surveillance; the state bureaucrats felt a strong need to ensure that no threats to their power base could develop, and so implemented a complex system of controls involving secret police and other agencies.

The costs of containing the perceived external and internal threats eventually became too much for the advanced communist/socialist states to bear – especially the USSR, which dominated the remainder (with the exception of China). Agricultural and industrial production could not be increased sufficiently to meet the material demands of the population and too large a proportion of the state budget was committed to surveillance. The structure crumbled, the Soviet yoke over its eastern European satellite states was removed, democratic electoral systems were introduced, and the transition to a market economy prepared for (see Taylor and Johnston, 1993). That transition is proving extremely difficult, with negative consequences on material standards, life chances and life expectancies (Johnston et al, 1995).

The collapse of advanced communism/socialism over a very short period is a special example of Kennedy's 'overstretch' thesis, which applies to capitalist states as well. Each of the long cycles of the capitalist world economy has been characterised by a dominant geopolitical force which is also the pre-eminent economic power; the two go together, with military support being used to sustain the successful economy (especially in its external relations). As the cycle (often termed a Kondratieff wave; Taylor, 1989a) enters its downturn and the economy goes into decline, so the relative costs of geopolitical activities threaten the dominant state's position. Its weakness may be challenged by other states, where thriving new industries signify the upturn associated with the next cycle, and a major war may be fought between the two protagonists – with other countries implicated. Wars are major drains on an economy and can hasten the economic decline of a once-dominant power, even if it wins – as the British case in the twentieth century makes clear.

The USSR was suffering substantially from a condition very much akin to overstretch by the mid-1980s; it could not sustain its armed forces, participation in the arms race, and very extensive surveillance operations. It needed _détente_ with the USA – which also required cuts in its military and related budgets because of overstretch at a time of substantial economic challenge (albeit not supported by military force) from both the European Union (especially the Federal Republic of Germany) and Japan. *Détente* was achieved in negotiations between Gorbachev and Reagan, but was insufficient to save the faltering Soviet economy and regime; the collapse came a few years later and the major cold war antagonisms were removed.

The transition to liberal democracy in the former communist countries has been far from straightforward, however, and the democratic structures have been significantly overturned in a number of countries since. Of the 12 republics created out of the former Soviet Union (excluding the three Baltic states of Estonia, Latvia, and Lithuania), by 1995 only two (Moldova and the Ukraine) were not characterised by strong presidential rule. Opposition parties have been banned in a number (Armenia, Azerbaijan, Tajikistan, Uzbekistan), parliament has been dissolved in others (Belarus, Kazakhstan, Kirgizia), and rule by presidential decree is common elsewhere (Georgia, Russia, Turkmenistan). To some commentators, this confirms the model described above that democracy follows economic development, rather than preceding it; all 12 have experienced massive declines in real GDP per capita during the 1990s.

## SPHERE OF PRODUCTION, CIVIL SOCIETY AND THE STATE

The discussion so far in this chapter has focused exclusively on the economic base of a mode of social organisation, hence the term 'mode of production'. That economic base is fundamental; if a society cannot organise its survival then other aspects of its members' lives are irrelevant. The foundation of any mode of social organisation, therefore, must be the way in which production is organised to ensure societal reproduction.

But although the economic base of a society is fundamental to its existence, the organisation of production is not the only distinguishing feature. Indeed, even casual observation of contemporary capitalist societies will show that although they share that economic base they differ in many other ways. Profit-making and wealth accumulation are central features of all of those societies, and they all experience the crises associated with overproduction. But they differ in many other aspects of their social and political organisation, differences that are often summarised as cultural.

The origins of these cultural differences often lie in the pre-capitalist societies, which in turn reflected local responses to their physical environments. Those cultural practices became part of the capitalist heritage, and were allowed to remain in place so long as they did not impede the operation of the capitalist system. And as capitalism developed, so new cultural practices emerged that were unique to particular societies. Thus, for example, the political development in many capitalist countries of western

Europe saw the emergence of an electoral cleavage between the employer and employee occupational classes. But such a cleavage was not necessary; capitalism did not require it, and it failed to appear in some countries, such as the Republic of Ireland (as well as the United States). The politics of capitalism does not necessarily involve the two economic classes in opposition in the electoral arena. (On electoral cleavages, see Taylor and Johnston, 1979; Harrop and Miller, 1987.)

One model of the entire structure of capitalist societies divides them into three major sectors; the sphere of production, the sphere of reproduction, and the state (Urry, 1981). Discussion in the present chapter has focused on the sphere of production, on the organisation of the means of survival. With this, although the fundamental organising principles are common – the making of profits through the surplus value accruing from the employment of labour within capitalism, for example – there are many variations from place to place in how that is done, both on an international scale (as documented in detail in Lash and Urry, 1987) and locally within individual countries (as exemplified for the British coal-mining industry in Griffiths and Johnston, 1990). Thus one can have a geography of the operations of capitalism in its mode of regulation.

The sphere of reproduction, also referred to as the sphere of consumption and as civil society, refers to the organisation of social life outside the workplace. Social life must be organised in ways that are not contrary to the economic goals of a society, but the limits are very broad. Modern capitalist societies, for example, differ very widely in the nature of the relationships between the sexes, in the nature of education and religion, in the dominant sports and recreation activities, and so forth. All these are part of the local culture, and add to the richness of the geography.

An illustration of this cultural richness, and of its links to the geography of modes of production in the contemporary world, is Todd's work on family structures. He identifies seven different types of structure, each of which is characteristic of certain areas of the world, producing a set of anthropological regions. The value systems inherent in those different family types provide what he terms the infrastructure of society: 'it determines the temperament and ideological system of the statistical masses which make up sedentary human societies' (1985, p.196).

Importantly, according to Todd, the geography of that infrastructure is not in itself determined, but rather is 'incoherent':

> it is completely independent of its economic and ecological environments. Most family systems exist simultaneously in areas whose climate, relief, geology and economy are completely different. It is impossible to perceive any global coincidence at all between ecological or economic factors and family types. (pp. 196–7)

Nevertheless, different family types do promote different types of social development, which are linked to economic structures, as he argues in a later book which links his anthropological model to the processes of 'development' (Todd, 1987).

Variations in cultural values are also relevant to an understanding of environmental use, since environmental attitudes also vary between societies. Blaikie (1985) illustrates this with examples of societies where cattle are kept not just as food sources but also as status symbols; cattle are 'a store of wealth' as well as a 'source of income', and status is positively related to the number of cattle owned. The acquisition of greater status can have deleterious effects on the environment, through overgrazing, and agricultural advisers believed that they could reduce that problem if higher-yielding cattle were made available; stocking densities could be reduced but the same level of output achieved. This failed to take account of the status symbol importance of cattle; the result of the activity was that cattle densities increased, not decreased.

This brief example is just one illustration of the importance of appreciating cultural values in developing a full understanding of societies and their relationships with their environments; as many attempts to alter agricultural practices have shown, people are influenced by a wide range of factors other than those involved with the economics of survival. So in attempting to alter land-use practices it is necessary to appreciate that economic arguments may be insufficient to promote change. In this book, however, the main concern is with the economics and politics, and the cultural variations receive little attention; the aim is not to provide a complete guide to the understanding of the origins and solution of environmental problems, but simply to stress the need to appreciate both their economic origins and the political limits to action.

Those political limits are defined in the third sphere of society, the state. As will be argued in more detail in Chapter 5, modern analysis suggests that the state is necessary to the capitalist mode of production, in ways that are not relevant to pre-capitalist modes (see Johnston, 1982a). The state must be there to do certain things, otherwise capitalism will fail. But there are many ways in which those roles can be performed, many ways in which the script can be interpreted by the actors. And the state is not constrained only to actions linked to its necessary roles. The state is the focus of non-economic power in society, and can be used by those who win control of it to promote goals other than those related to the accumulation of wealth. Again, we can see that those goals vary considerably between states, and over time within the same state; certain states, such as the Irish, are much more influenced by religious goals than are others, such as the Swedish, for example.

There are, then, three main sectors in modern societies, but the sphere of production is the foundation for the other two. Each requires the other; the sphere of production requires a state and a civil society, and neither of the latter pair could exist without a successful method of organising production. But the mode of production does not require a particular form of its civil society or of its state; these vary considerably from place to place, and can have significant impacts on the relationships between society and environment. Here and in the next chapter the focus is on the sphere of production, and in the following two it is on the state.

# 4 Resources, Land and Environmental Use

> Capitalist production . . . develops technology and the combining together of various processes into a social whole, only by sapping the original sources of all wealth – the soil and the labourer. (Karl Marx, 1977, p. 475)

All life on earth depends on that earth for its existence; for most forms of life that dependence includes a reliance on other forms of life. Thus sustaining life is only possible if other life forms are present – which for humans means many different plant species and a smaller number of animal species. (Some people survive, to a greater or lesser extent, without dependence on animal species; none do so without dependence on plant species.) Most humans differ from other forms of animal life in that their continued existence has been organised so that it depends on other materials from the earth as well. This is not because of 'natural', or genetic, differences between human and other species, but rather because of the way the human species has evolved to its present condition of ecological dominance, if not predominance. That evolution began with the use of inanimate materials as tools, and has been extended to the contemporary situation in which an extremely large range of products is created by transforming animate and inanimate materials obtained from the earth into commodities that are defined by human societies as 'useful'.

The earth is thus the resource base on which human societies rely. The nature and content of that resource base are fixed by the processes through which the earth has evolved, but the identification of aspects of the environment as resources is not 'natural' in most cases (Spoehr, 1956). Resources are defined by humans themselves, and the process of resource definition is one of continual change, as new uses for earth materials are identified, and previously unused materials are translated into resources by the discovery of ways in which they can be made useful. (The exceptions to this general case are air and water; humans are genetically created to identify these as necessary resources, on which their individual reproduction depends.) Thus even with foodstuffs, whether or not a given plant or animal provides desirable food is a human determination, and groups differ in what they identify as desirable; what is acceptable to some, according to their cultural norms, is not acceptable to others. Part of the cultural geography of the world comprises different interpretations of the natural environment and whether its various components are usable resources for sustaining life.

The previous chapter showed that the most dynamic of modes of production, capitalism, is based on forever extending the range of goods and services offered to people for sale. It depends on a parallel extension of human appreciation of what can be done with the raw materials of the earth (not just its surface and the other inhabitants of that surface, but also its core and its atmosphere). Thus capitalism requires an ever-expanding resource base – and, according to the argument of the preceding chapter, so has advanced communism/socialism, because one of its major goals appears to be mimicking capitalism in the range of material goods produced and distributed. Resources are 'created' by humans, through their relationships with the earth. But there are limits to that 'manufacturing' process provided by the nature of the earth itself, and so this chapter begins by identifying the interrelationships between humans and their environment which define the spatially varying nature of the resource base.

## THE NATURE OF RESOURCES

A number of classifications of resources has been proposed, many based on the distinction between renewable and non-renewable, or stock and flow, resources (see, for example, Rees, 1985).

### STOCK RESOURCES

Stock resources are inanimate components of the earth, and are fixed in quantity. Thus human use is limited; once the stock has been exhausted, it is no longer available. Reliance on stock resources for the production of goods and services therefore means that societies must be prepared to change their demands when the stock runs out – or when it is no longer possible to make use of the remaining stock (as in capitalist societies where the costs of obtaining the resource are greater than the return that can be obtained from the products made with it). Stock resources are a stimulus to human inventiveness, therefore, in that at some stage they will have to be replaced; either an alternative material for the same product must be identified or a new product to replace it must be invented.

A basic distinction within stock resources is between those which can be consumed only once and those which can, theoretically at least, be consumed many times. Fossil fuels exemplify the former category; once they have been burned they have been destroyed. Most minerals are examples of the second category. They can be transformed into a great variety of commodities, but the technology is available – in most cases at a substantial price – to regain the original mineral resource from the discarded product: the extent to which this is done depends upon the 'need' for the mineral, relative to the costs of winning more supplies from the ground and of developing alternatives. With some, it is possible, again theoretically at least, to recycle them, so that there is no loss of stock at all.

A crucial feature of stock resources, especially those that are used only once, is that once consumed they do not simply disappear but rather are transformed into other states. The output from burning fossil fuels, for example, involves the creation of 'waste products' or 'pollutants', many of which are emitted into the atmosphere and, through the operation of the hydrological cycle, distributed through most ecosystems. Some, such as coal, also produce a residual mineral, and such 'wastes' may be redefined as resources if uses can be found for them, in which case they become another stock resource. Further uses have not as yet been found for most wastes, however, and their disposition (as with the wastes from the generation of nuclear power) may cause considerable problems to the producers.

The degree to which the earth's stock resources, especially minerals and fuels, have been depleted already is the cause of much debate and concern. Simmons (1991, p. 127), for example, quotes estimates that reserves of lead and zinc had lifetimes, at expected consumption levels, of only 14 and 25 years respectively in the late 1980s, and very few reserves of other minerals (iron and chromium are the main exceptions) are expected to last for more than another century. This is despite increased efficiency in their use, including recycling: in the USA in 1990, for example, 73 per cent of the lead consumed, 50 per cent of the aluminium and 56 per cent of the iron and steel came from recycled material (Emel and Bridge, 1995). But globally, as the developing world economies become more industrialised, so demands for those metals increases; between 1977 and 1987 the Third World's use of copper and zinc as a percentage of the global totals rose from 10 to 18 and 16 to 24 per cent, respectively. In order to sustain supplies of the needed raw materials, exploration and exploitation are increasingly focusing on less tractable (i.e. less rich) sources, harder to extract (within the Arctic Circle, for example), which increases both the fixed and the variable costs. With copper, for example, the average grade mined was 8 per cent some centuries ago (and up to 30 per cent in some of the richest sources, such as Montana) but it is now only 1 per cent (and 0.6 per cent only in the USA); environmental disturbance is thus increased, as more ore must be extracted for the same use volume, more overburden has to be removed, and more tailings and other wastes from the purification process are produced.

## FLOW RESOURCES

Flow resources comprise the great majority of those used by human societies; they differ from stock resources in that they are constantly renewed by processes external to their use by humans. Most stock resources are renewed too – the processes by which oil is created continue alongside the consumption of oil – so the real difference between flow and stock resources is the time involved in their replacement. The production of new stock resources is a very slow process, taking millennia in some cases and so much slower than the rate of human use. Flow resources are constantly reproduced, at rates which may equal those of their use.

The critical feature in the use of flow resources is thus the rate at which they are replenished relative to the rate at which they are used. At the extreme, the resource can be exhausted in one of two ways. First, exhaustion can result because no more of the resource is available. It is not destroyed, but it is limited in quantity, as with the amount of solar energy entering the earth's atmosphere each day. (Human activity can alter that amount somewhat, as recent debates concerning the greenhouse effect suggest.) Similarly, the amount of water passing a point on a river in any one time period is ultimately fixed (river control measures can regulate the flow but not increase its amount, except where water from other sources is introduced, with consequential losses there), so that the amount of power that can be generated from its passage is limited, and once that amount has been achieved the resource is exhausted.

According to this first definition of an exhaustible resource, the amount available is fixed, but is always there to be used. According to the second definition, the resource can be destroyed and so no longer available. The latter are what Rees terms 'critical zone' resources, to distinguish them from the 'non-critical zone' resources described in the previous paragraph. In the critical category, the rate of resource use is crucial. If it exceeds the rate at which the resource is reproduced naturally, then the resource will be depleted, eventually reaching a stage at which reproduction ceases and the resource is exhausted. All plant and animal species fall into this category, and many have become extinct because of human exploitation – either directly, because the species has been used by humans, or indirectly, because the species consumed by humans is no longer available to the others dependent on it in the ecological web of life. Barbier et al (1994, pp.10–11) report estimates that some 484 recorded animal species have become extinct since 1600, the great majority of them since 1850; Myers (1979) suggested that tropical deforestation would lead to the extinction of a million plant species between 1975 and 2000 – or 4 per cent of all species per annum. More locally, Peters and Lovejoy (1990, p.357) report that of the 82 known species of birds which have inhabited the islands of Hawaii, 53 per cent were extinct by the time of Captain Cook's arrival in 1778, and a further 23 native species have been lost since then, along with 177 native plant species; 30 bird and 680 plant species are currently listed as endangered there.

Soil is a resource that falls somewhere between the stock and flow categories, but is probably best identified with the latter. It renews itself naturally, more slowly than most plant and animal species but much more rapidly than the minerals identified as typical of the stock resource category. If used in certain ways, its fertility and ability to support plant life can be sustained and its natural processes of regeneration supported. But if the fertility is removed rapidly, in a variety of ways, then in effect it is being 'mined' in the same way as a mineral; its ability to support plant life is diminished, and eventually it can no longer do so. (As an intermediate stage, it may be able to support some plant life, but not the sorts of plants that are perceived as a resource by the human occupants.) Recent estimates suggest that the rate of soil loss through wind and water erosion is up to 17 times that of soil formation; even if the soil is not eroded, its fertility can be depleted by about one-third (Pimental et al, 1995). Current estimates of the volume of soil erosion in the USA are 17 tonnes per hectare per year on cropland alone. The total annual cost of that erosion is estimated at $44 billion (of which $20 billion is the estimated value of nutrient losses), and to reduce it to 1 tonne per hectare per year would cost $8.4 billion per annum: current expenditure is only $1.7 billion. These figures are extrapolated to a global cost of $400 billion per annum. Not surprisingly, perhaps, such estimates are contested, but the existence of a potentially serious problem is widely recognised (Glantz, 1995).

Some, though not all, flow resources can be enhanced by human activity – either intentional or otherwise. For example, pastoral practices may increase the number of animals in certain species, but such an increase has a cost, in the long term if not in the short term. If we accept that the total resource base of the earth is fixed by the amount of solar energy entering the atmosphere each day, then there are limits to the earth's carrying capacity. Those limits may be nowhere near being reached at present, as human ingenuity discovers yet more ways of increasing the flow resources (through multiple cropping, for example) without destroying the base of stock resources. Yet ultimately use of the earth will be exhausted, using the term in the first of the two meanings introduced here, so that increasing the volume of some flow resources can only be achieved by decreasing the volume of others. The management of the earth's resources involves determining the most effective way of approaching that level of exhaustion.

## RESOURCE LIMITS

This categorisation of resources indicates clear environmental limits to human activity. Just what those limits are, and how soon they will be reached, is the cause of much debate. Optimists argue that we are at present so far from them that to all intents and purposes we can assume that they do not exist. The carrying capacity of the earth may not be infinite, but it is so much greater than it is currently being called upon to sustain that there is no need for concern. The pessimists, on the other hand, argue that the limits are near, and that the problems induced by approaching them are being exacerbated by the nature of human use (misuse/abuse?) of the environment.

An example of the debate between the optimists and the pessimists concerns the availability of oil as a major fossil fuel. According to the pessimists, the likelihood of discovering further major and as yet untapped reserves, and particularly reserves that can be recovered at acceptable financial costs, is remote. According to the optimists, there are many areas where the search has so far been very limited and the experience of earlier decades of prospecting suggests that the chances of major finds are high. With regard to exploiting difficult reserves, the optimists argue that only a few decades ago it would have been impossible to exploit the oilfields beneath the North Sea. That is now being done on a large scale, and if that problem can be solved so too, it is argued, could the problem of exploiting reserves found, say, under the Antarctic ice cap. (On this general issue, see Odell, 1989.) In other words, the optimists believe both that the earth's resources available for human use are very much greater than currently appreciated and that technological developments will ensure that society can always respond to new challenges regarding their exploitation.

Also relevant to a discussion of resource limits is the issue of food supply and hunger. Is the earth reaching its carrying capacity in terms of human numbers, particularly given the rapid growth of population in recent decades? There are two aspects to this. The first concerns population growth: pessimists argue that it is out of control and that a catastrophe will soon occur because the earth cannot feed the extra millions (World Commission on Environment and Development, 1987); optimists claim that the recent rate of growth is but a small blip in a long-term trend of much less rapid expansion of numbers (Woods, 1989). The second aspect concerns not so much the ability of the earth to produce the needed food but rather the ability of human societies to organise food production and distribution to ensure that all are adequately fed. In this part of the debate, the optimists point to the current overproduction of food in much of the core of the world economy, which is leading governments to pay farmers not to produce, or at least to reduce the intensity of production. If that is possible, then surely a different way of organising the means of production, distribution and exchange would ensure adequate food for the many  millions who are now starving, or virtually so, and on whom the pessimists focus their attention.

Much of the debate about the carrying capacity of the earth focuses on the physical constraints, whereas others direct their attention to the social, economic and political limits. Those favouring the latter recognise both that there are ultimate limits and that these may be either reached more quickly or reduced by environmental practices; those favouring the former accept that social, economic and political change is important in ensuring effective winning of resources from the earth. (Beckerman, 1992, quotes Sen, 1981, who says that 'Famines in recent years . . . seem to have been more the result of appalling policies, civil strife, and discrimination, than of acute physical food shortages in any given area'; much the same is said about the Irish famine of the 1840s.) What is crucial for both to appreciate is the extent to which environmental practices, and hence the approach to the limits, are largely determined by economic forces – by the mode of production – and also that the extent to which those practices can be altered requires an appreciation of the nature of the political forces that operate. Advancing such appreciation is a major goal here, since without it the creation of a self-sustaining interrelationship between society and the environment will not be possible. The remainder of this chapter thus looks at the relationship between mode of production and environment, and the next chapters turn to the state and political forces.

## PRIMITIVE COMMUNISM, FEUDALISM AND ENVIRONMENTAL USE

In looking at the relationships between various modes of production and the environment, most attention will be paid to capitalism. This brief section looks at primitive communism, as an example of a mode of production based on reciprocity, and on feudalism in Britain as an example of one based on rank redistribution.

*Primitive communist societies* have had the most intimate relationships with their environments, because in many senses they have been most dominated by nature. Their level of technological development has been such that they have 'controlled' their environments to a limited extent only, having (of necessity because of their levels of technological and societal sophistication) developed a pragmatic alliance with the environment, living in a fragile ecological balance with it. The nature of that alliance has varied very substantially from society to society, partially reflecting the variability of the environment; different physical circumstances call forth different responses. But it also reflects different sequences of human learning in different places. Most environments offer a range of possibilities to humans seeking means of survival within them – which fruits to gather, which animals to capture, how to prepare foods, and so forth. For a variety of reasons, many of them closely linked to chance, those possibilities have been appreciated and acted upon differentially. The nature of the relationship with the environment created then becomes part of the society's culture, of the inter-generational inheritance of practices which allow survival within the environment. Those practices will change over time; change may be 'forced' by an environmental event – a drought, for example, may stimulate a search for an alternative source for part of the diet – or it may come about pragmatically as the result of a 'chance' discovery (eating a previously ignored fruit, perhaps). The result is a complex mosaic of people–environment relationships, which is the foundation of the current cultural geography of the earth.

Although the environment offers many possibilities in most situations, it is likely that similar practices will have evolved in most where the range of possibilities is virtually the same, for one or both of two reasons. The first is that some of the possibilities offer better life chances than others, and it is likely either that eventually separate societies will discover these and adopt them (albeit perhaps with some differences of detail) or that those which do not will eventually perish while only those that find the most appropriate survive. Secondly, similar environments are usually adjacent, and there is likely to be contact between their separate societies and a sharing of expertise; again, the outcome will probably be similarity in the general nature of the practices adopted, even if there are differences in detail.

An example of this similarity in general but differences in detail is provided by the patterns of land tenure within the Pacific prior to the penetration of its island chains by capitalist agriculture and land-holding conventions. Crocombe (1972, p. 219) illustrates this:

> Within the Pacific area people often emphasize the great diversity of tenure systems . . . But in world perspective, all the tenure systems in the Pacific had much in common, both in the environment and in the cultures of the peoples, and these factors set the boundaries within which each tenure system evolved and operated.

Thus inheritance was the standard way of obtaining land, for example, and there was no market for its sale. In New Guinea and Polynesia, however, inheritance was mainly patrilineal; in Micronesia it was matrilineal; and in Melanesia (apart from New Guinea) 'there are both patrilineal and matrilineal systems, as well as ambilineal and bilineal' (p. 227).

The Malthusian spectre is always present in primitive communist societies: either they will breed beyond the carrying capacity of their environment, or a change in their environment (even a relatively minor one, such as a drought for two years) means that they can no longer sustain their numbers. Over time, they may learn ways of changing the balance, either by improving the carrying capacity in some way or by developing means of surviving periods of relative famine. Their general situation is a dynamic equilibrium with the environment, of the type described in the discussions of predator–prey models in Chapter 2. Their level of technological development is such that they cannot deliberately alter that equilibrium substantially, at least in the short term. Over long periods of time, they may (intentionally or, more likely, inadvertently) destroy the environment by their overconsumption of the flow resources in a small area; their only hope for survival then is to find another environment nearby that will support them, while perhaps that which they have deserted is rehabilitated because they have not completely destroyed the major flow resource – the soil – and this can be regenerated naturally, as fauna and flora recolonise the areas abandoned by humans. (For detailed data on the practice of swidden and other types of agriculture in such societies, see Bayliss-Smith and Feachem, 1977.)

Most primitive communist societies do degrade their environments, however, as Allen and Crittenden (1987) illustrate with the Kakoli people of the New Guinea Highlands. They had three types of land-use practice. On the valley floors and floodplains there were permanent open fields where sweet potatoes (introduced about 400 years ago) were cultivated; and on gully-sides there were swiddens, where crops were grown for a few years, followed by a fallow period of 10–15 years while the land recovered: in both cases, equilibrium was maintained. But on the upper slopes, at the forest–grassland boundary, they employed a 'crop and abandon' practice. Gardens were cleared and cultivated for two years, and then left fallow, when they were colonised by weeds and woody plants. The land was then cleared again and turned into a permanent sweet potato garden, in which cultivation continued until yields fell to such a level that replanting was not worthwhile. The land was then abandoned; it was colonised by cane grass, which could be used for pigs, but it never regained its original vegetative cover. Cultivation moved further uphill, so that over time there was a belt of abandoned, degraded land separating the villages from their current hillside gardens. The Kakoli sustained an ecological balance with parts of their environment, but not all of it.

*Feudal societies* differ from primitive communist in many ways. For the present discussion, however, the most important is that they may have within them a growth process that puts increasing pressure on the environment. As in societies based on reciprocity, that process may be produced simply by population growth and the tendency to breed up to the limits which the environment can support. But in a rank redistribution society, the problems set are greater because a proportion of the population, however small, comprises non-producers. If that proportion grows, then the entire burden of supporting it has to fall on the remainder of the population (the peasants). And if (as is almost certainly the case) the landlords and their retinues have the highest material standards of living, then their offspring are more likely to survive and to have greater life expectancy than those of the peasants, with obvious consequences for the demands for food and other 'needs' to be won from the land.

Increased demand for agricultural production from this source leads to an alteration in the ratio between producers and non-producers in the agricultural economy, and can only be sustained in the long term by increasing the productivity of the former group. The same is true whatever the source of the increased demand; the monarch may call for a greater contribution to the country's military, for example, either to provide a more secure defence or to wage an aggressive campaign against others. Or the feudal establishment may wish to increase its material standards in some way – greater investment in the built environment, for example, requiring more craftsmen who must be supported by others.

In feudal England all of these sources of demand were present, and stimulated a range of agricultural innovations. For a substantial period, from the Norman conquest on, the environment apparently coped, for the population tripled between 1066 and 1348. Part of this increase was catered for by extensions to the settled area, and in part it was sustained by improvements in agricultural practice, such as the development of the three-field system and crop rotation. But according to one agricultural historian (Postan, 1973), by about 1300 the limits of this expansion had been reached and England, with about 6 million inhabitants, was overpopulated. Subdivision of land had proceeded to such an extent to cater for the increased population that holdings were in many cases too small to sustain their occupants; at the same time, some of the more affluent landholders had increased the size of their holdings and so expanded their relative wealth, and in some areas industrialisation proceeded apace based on local wool production. Further, much of the marginal land brought into use was unsuited to grain crops, and there was a shortage of animal manure as fertiliser. Others accept Postan's case that England's population was reaching its Malthusian limits at the time, but argue that the real cause of the problems was the unwillingness of the parasitic aristocracy to invest in improvements to agricultural technology. The pressure was ended by the arrival of bubonic plague in 1348, which presaged the major fall in population over the next three decades known as the Black Death; growth only recommenced in the sixteenth century, when the incipient capitalist system stimulated increased investment in improvements to agricultural productivity.

Many scholars looking for evidence that land degradation occurs under most types of mode of production and not just capitalism focus their attention on contemporary peripheral areas of the world economy. Blaikie and Brookfield (1987b) have pointed to the important evidence provided by the histories of the Mediterranean region and of western Europe in the last two millennia, however, though in such exercises it is often very difficult to evaluate the relative impact of land-use practices and other variables, such as climatic change (such as the so-called Little Ice Age of Europe in the late medieval period: Grove, 1988). With regard to the circum-Mediterranean area, however, they argue (with Shaw, 1981) that human intensive occupation of the area may have retarded rather than accelerated rates of erosion, and that it was only when and where management standards were poor – with terraces poorly maintained, for example, so that heavy storms could stimulate active degradation – that environmental deterioration occurred. Such deterioration has certainly occurred, because land that once supported forests now clearly cannot (the cedars of Lebanon, for example; Mikesell, 1969), and what was the 'breadbasket' of the Roman Empire (the Carthage region) no longer sustains intensive agriculture. Thus it may not be human 'interference' with the environment *per se* that promotes its degradation, but only badly managed 'interference'; the fertility of land with its 'natural' vegetation removed may be maintained if it is 'well' farmed, but not if it is opened up to erosive forces.

Similarly in northern Europe, Blaikie and Brookfield (1987b) suggest that accelerated erosion in parts of France and Germany was a consequence of the interaction of human and climatic causes, rather than either one or the other. In the *département* of Haute-Marne, for example, there was substantial damage to the land in the 1780s as the result, it seems, of human response to a series of bad harvests and a drought in 1784–85. Many cattle died because of the drought, farmers were unable to replace them because of high prices, and the decrease in livestock numbers led to a substantial decline in soil fertility (because of the lack of manure). Better management of the land was required to ensure that the pressures of increased demands could be met without land degradation, and it was the improved management practices of the agricultural revolution in the period from the sixteenth century on (as, for example, with the enclosure movement in England) that allowed societies to increase the pressure on their environmental resources and to some extent escape the constraints that these resources posed to the existing level of environmental understanding.

Another environment in which the case that bad management practices (themselves perhaps a response to environmental stress), rather than 'interference' with the environment *per se*, probably led to degradation occurred among the so-called 'hydraulic civilisations'. Wittfogel (1956, 1957) characterises these by their large-scale water works built both to promote production (i.e. via irrigation) and to provide protection and flood control. There have been many such civilisations in arid and semi-arid areas, with social and political structures distinguished from those of other feudal societies by the extent of state power which was needed because of the demands not just for large amounts of labour but also for it to be integrated in major public works programmes – the irrigation and flood control systems:

> In hydraulic economy man extended his power over the arid, the semiarid and certain humid parts of the globe through a government-directed division of labor and a mode of co-operation not practiced in agrarian civilizations of the non-hydraulic type. . . . The development of such a work pattern meant more than the agglomeration of large numbers of men. To have many persons co-operate periodically and effectively, there had to be planning, record-keeping, communication and supervision. There had to be organization in depth. And above the tribal level this involved permanent offices and officials to man them – bureaucrats. (1956, p. 156)

This centralised control meant that 'the hydraulic farmer maintained a man–nature relation that involved unending drudgery on a socially and culturally depressing level' (p. 161) – a way of life described by Wittfogel (1957, p. 136) as 'benevolent in form and oppressive in content'. So where the control could not be sustained, and the management practices declined in efficacy, the hydraulic civilisations collapsed. (Wittfogel, 1957, implies that the failures often resulted from autocratic despots losing the support of the bureaucracy necessary to run the hydraulic culture.) It was not that an equilibrium with the environment was unsustainable but rather that the organisation of the society prevented it, in the long run – though some hydraulic civilisations lasted several millennia.

Blaikie and Brookfield (1987a) come to a similar conclusion with regard to the current situation in Nepal where, according to some observers, the farming practices and destruction of forests undertaken to cope with population pressure are causing accelerated erosion and increased flooding of the Brahmaputra and other rivers in India and Bangladesh. They point out that some commentators suggest that farmers, because of the pressures on them, choose management options which lead to accelerated land degradation. But some farmers, especially the richest, may be able to take other options which protect their land, so that 'poverty is the basic cause of poor management, and the consequence of poor management is deepening poverty' (p. 48). According to this argument, the problem of land degradation under feudal and other rank redistribution societies is not simply that human 'interference' with the environment necessarily leads to such degradation; rather it is the nature of the social and economic system that encourages bad land management practices. This leads to a deterioration, rapidly and apparently continuously in a high-energy environment such as Nepal but only rarely, and usually at times of environmental as well as economic stress, in temperate environments such as those of north-western Europe. Thus understanding the origins of environmental problems requires appreciating the nature of the social, economic and political organization which leads to their generation; the problems are not inherent to human 'interference' with the environment, but are the consequence of how that 'interference' is managed.

## GAMES AGAINST NATURE

The environment provides all societies, and not just those based on either reciprocity or rank redistribution, with limits to growth linked to the available agricultural technology and land-management practices; it both constrains what they do and provides them with wide opportunities. The stability of such societies depends on their learning the nature of those constraints and developing an appropriate set of agricultural practices within the opportunity set. This is illustrated in a classic paper by Gould (1963), which is relevant to the study of all decision-making in the context of an uncertain environment whatever the mode of production but is especially important to societies which have little ability to 'control' or modify the environment and so must learn to live with it.

Gould uses as his example a village in Ghana where, for illustrative purposes, years are either wet or dry. The village farmers know about five different crops, and experience tells them what yields they can expect in a wet and in a dry year. Those yields (in arbitrary units) are:

| Crop | Wet year | Dry year |
| --- | --- | --- |
| Yams | 82 | 11 |
| Maize | 61 | 49 |
| Cassava | 12 | 38 |
| Millet | 43 | 32 |
| Hill rice | 30 | 71 |

Yams offer the best return in a wet year, but their yield in a dry year is very low. So should they plant yams, and gamble on it being a wet year; should they plant maize, which has by far the highest average yield over the two types of year; should they plant yams in some years, maize in others, and so on; or should they divide their land among the crops, to minimise the risks of a food shortage in any given year?

To answer these questions, Gould uses the concept of a 'saddle-point' from the mathematical theory of games; the saddle-point in a table is the minimum row value that is also its column maximum – it is simultaneously the lowest high point and the highest low point (as illustrated in Abler et al, 1971, p. 480). He drew up a diagram comprising two scaled columns (Figure 4.1), with the wet and dry years forming the columns and the rows scaled by the yields for each crop. The saddle-point is the lowest point on the polygon (shown by a solid line) which forms the uppermost boundary to the diagram; it occurs at the intersection of maize and hill rice, with a yield of 54. This can be attained either by planting 77.4 per cent of the land with maize and 22.6 per cent with hill rice in every year (so that in a wet year the high maize yield compensates for the low hill rice yield, and vice versa in a dry year), or by planting all of the land with maize in 77.4 per cent of years and with hill rice in the other 22.6 per cent. In the long run it does not matter for the average annual production will be 54 units, but, as Gould (1963, p. 293) puts it:

> when men have experienced famine and have looked into the glazed eyes of their swollen-bellied children, the long run view becomes somewhat meaningless. Thus, we may conclude that the farmers will hold strongly to the short-term view and will plant the proportions each year since the truly catastrophic case of hill rice and wet year could not then occur.

This planting pattern is the 'rational' response to an uncertain environment which the farmers cannot alter and in which there is no ability to store food

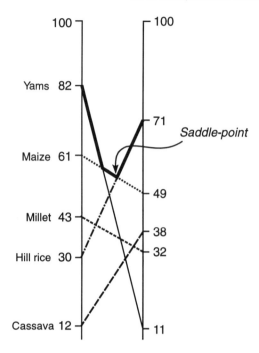

**Figure 4.1**   Graphical representation of the yields from five crops in Gould's example of the game against nature (redrawn from Gould, 1963, p. 292)

(the 'surplus' of a good year in which production exceeded 54 units) for the bad years that are bound to come.

Development of the abilities to store food and to transport it from areas of 'surplus' to those of 'deficit' has enabled societies to break out of the game against nature portrayed by Gould. They now play other games in which they can change the yields, and the probability of getting them whatever the climatic conditions, through environmental control.

## INTO CAPITALISM

The replacement of feudalism by capitalism as the dominant mode of production in western Europe was intimately associated with increased agricultural productivity, since the ability to produce food and industrial raw materials more efficiently was necessary to sustain the growing concentration of people in non-agricultural occupations. The ability to transport and to store materials was equally important, since capitalist expansion was built on both urbanisation and the growth of long-distance trade. Thus it was the willingness of those with power in society to invest in increasing agricultural productivity and the necessary restructuring of society which enabled the transition to capitalism, a process which markedly altered the relationships between societies and their environments; the agricultural and industrial revolutions of the sixteenth century onwards, which are generally associated with the transition to capitalism in north-west Europe, saw the technocratic interpretation of the environment come into its own.

Those changes in agriculture are clearly illustrated in England during that period, and also in the expansion of English influence over much of the rest of the world (see, for example, Butlin and Dodgshon, 1989). There were many institutional and technological changes in English agriculture from the sixteenth century on, and especially in the century after 1750, as the result of much trial and error and of the willingness of individuals to invest in such experiments in the expectation of substantial gain. Their experiments involved not only the relatively small, affluent elite but also a wide range of the farming population, as in the enclosure movement. In terms of agricultural practices, new crops were introduced and productive strains were developed. The new ones were mainly root crops, which were used as winter feed for livestock. This enabled much larger numbers to be retained through the winter rather than slaughtered in the autumn, and the greater volumes of manure thus produced could be used to fertilise the arable fields, increasing the productivity of grain farming (the staple for human food) as well as of the root crops and hay that sustained the wintered-over animals. Other new crops, such as clover, were widely planted, to benefit from their efficiency in fixing nitrogen from the atmosphere in the soil and thereby increasing its productivity during the fallow period. There were technological improvements, too, as in the development of more efficient ploughs to work the land.

There were also institutional changes, introduced to improve the management of the land. Most important of these in much of England was undoubtedly the process of enclosure, whereby the former open fields, in which each tenant had a number of small strips of land, were replaced by consolidated tenant holdings. Those holdings, with their fields enclosed (usually by hedgerows), allowed major developments in livestock farming in particular, with which came the creation of new ecosystems, such as those associated with the ubiquitous hedgerows of the English Midlands. Selective breeding was possible, and the productivity of the land was increased enormously by the development of high-yielding breeds.

The major difference between these agricultural developments and those preceding them was that they were not basically a response to the Malthusian spectre resulting from the society having reached the limits to growth. Rather they were the outcome of investments because people wanted the benefits that increased productivity brought in terms of what they could do with the yields from their land – using the additional money earned. This was especially the case with the large landowners, who sought increased rents to spend on more conspicuous consumption (bigger homes surrounded by landscaped parks, for example) and to invest in increasingly profitable trade and industrial ventures. Accumulation of wealth was their goal, which they promoted by encouraging their tenants to want improved material standards too, and which were accessible to them through purchase if they invested in increased productivity. (Thus in many villages, the tenants as well as the landowners favoured enclosure.) For the major landowners, therefore, increased agricultural productivity on their own lands provided wealth that could be invested elsewhere. (Indeed, according to some analysts, the particular landowning system of several parts of north-western Europe and the possibility of accumulating large wealth from it facilitated the emergence of capitalism and the industrial revolution there; Hechter and Brustein, 1980.) Increased rents from tenants aided that accumulation of wealth. The demands for greater rents stimulated the tenant farmers to increase their productivity, a stimulus much assisted by the fact that they were not just handing over tribute as in the feudal system but were also able to earn additional income that they could either spend on or invest in themselves.

## PRODUCTIVITY OF LAND AND LABOUR

Progress is achieved under capitalism by increasing labour productivity, thereby creating greater surpluses per unit of input (usually measured as labour time). In part, pressure to increase labour productivity can be assisted by increasing the productivity of the materials on which it works – the smaller the proportion that is wasted, the greater the returns from the investment. This is perhaps more clearly seen in agriculture than in other activities, because the productivity of the material – land – can be increased very substantially (as exemplified by the removal of hedgerows in parts of eastern England to enlarge fields).

As already outlined with regard to the agricultural revolution in England from 1750 on, increases in land productivity have been very substantial in recent centuries, when measured in terms of output per unit area. These have been achieved through the selective breeding of plants and livestock to obtain higher-yielding strains, and by changing the basic land use in many cases. The enclosure movement was associated with a substantial switch away from grain farming, largely for subsistence purposes, into livestock rearing (with the associated cultivation of root crops as winter fodder), because the returns from livestock (£ per acre from the wool, for example) were greater than those from grains and other products, reflecting the demand for industrial raw materials. Forest land was eaten into also, replacing its relatively low yields by either crops or livestock – a process that continues to the present day with the clearance of very large areas of tropical forest, albeit with potentially very deleterious long-term ecological consequences.

The changes which brought about increases in the productivity of land were largely associated with the plants and animals that it supported, with few direct links to the parallel industrial revolution. But industrial technology was increasingly applied to the task. A large chemical industry has developed in the twentieth century to produce fertilisers that will increase soil fertility more efficiently than animal manures do, thereby releasing farmers from the need to keep stock in order to produce their own fertilisers and, where it is economically sensible, turning the majority of their land over to arable farming. The fertilisers also allow this to be a permanent switch, removing the need for a fallow period (one year in three, five or seven). And technological solutions have been found to other problems; the introduction of relatively efficient movement of water up from the water table, for example, has allowed large-scale irrigation developments, as on the High Plains of the United States.

Alongside the investments aimed at increasing the productivity of the land (and thus indirectly of labour) have been those undertaken to increase labour productivity directly. Much agricultural machinery has been introduced for this purpose, although some activities – such as sheep-shearing – remain labour-intensive. The milking of cows is now done by machines, for example, allowing one person to milk very many more animals in an hour, and advances in the design of not only the machinery but also the milking-sheds (such as the herring-bone cowshed of New Zealand) have been promoted for the same reason. In arable farming, the development of machinery for planting, tending and harvesting crops has similarly increased labour productivity greatly; no longer are very large gangs required to pick the hops in Kent or raise the potatoes each October in Scotland (the reason for a mid-term break in universities as well as schools), and combine harvesters do the work that formerly involved not only several tractor drivers with harvesters, but also those who threshed the grain and baled the straw. (According to Roberts et al, 1989, the pressures on American farmers to invest continually in new machinery to increase productivity mean that they are on a 'technological treadmill', although increasingly farmers do not invest in the machinery themselves but contract with specialists to provide the services on demand.) To accommodate the new machines, such as combine harvesters (which also improve land productivity to some extent since they are more effective), fields have had to be enlarged, destroying many miles of hedgerows in parts of England where they formed the field boundaries and bringing not insubstantial additional areas under production (see Goudie, 1986a, pp. 84–6).

The extremes of these developments are what is known as factory farming, which involves an increasing divorce of animals from the land in livestock rearing. Instead of allowing the animals relatively free range in the fields, they are confined to buildings and are fed the products of those fields. Since arable farming is generally much more efficient than pastoral farming in transforming the products of the land into food (i.e. the energy equivalent of the production of animal-based foods from a hectare of land is much less than that from arable use of the same area), this means that productivity can be increased very substantially indeed, since the animals' land requirements (area occupied in the 'factories') are small and the same area of land is supporting a much higher stock density than if the animals freely roamed the fields. The pressure is then to increase the productivity of the arable land as much as possible, through mechanisation, the use of fertilisers, and field enlargement, to provide more food for the captive animals. There are negative environmental consequences, however, such as the increased volumes of animal wastes (slurry) to be disposed of; this is proving increasingly difficult because of the volume produced in very small areas, and some material is entering natural stream courses with consequences for water quality and use.

More so than in many other sectors of capitalism, therefore, it is possible in agricultural and pastoral activities to increase the productivity of both land and labour. As in all sectors, of course, the increased productivity of land results from the application of human labour, either directly – and thereby increasing its productivity as well – or indirectly, through the use of 'dead labour' (i.e. machines). But it is probably the case that the productivity of the land resource can be increased more in this sector than in any other, which is crucial in understanding the demands that are made on the land in the dynamic of capitalist society. If, as argued in the previous chapter (p. 69), the continued health of capitalism depends on technological and organisational changes designed to ensure a continued flow of surplus value, then the ability to increase productivity via two routes in agriculture should be particularly attractive to investors; the result would presumably be that the crises of overproduction and underconsumption would be especially apparent in that sector – could the increased volume of food produced be successfully marketed at acceptable prices?

## INCREASING LAND PRODUCTIVITY

The capitalist dynamic requires increased productivity in order to survive. The move to greater productivity may occur at different rates at different times and places, and may be greater in some sectors than others.

### ORGANISATIONAL CHANGE IN ENGLISH AGRICULTURE

English agriculture developed out of a feudal system in which the land held by the feudal lords was divided into separate farms, the majority of which were allocated to tenants who paid an annual rental for the use of the land. Over time, some of those tenants purchased their land and became freehold occupiers, as the landlords decided to sell for a variety of reasons. Thus an increasing proportion of the farmed land became a marketable commodity, and the organisational structure of landownership became more variable, allowing changes in order to promote increased productivity. Nevertheless, for long periods relatively little altered.

Much has changed in recent years, however, as a major British study has shown (Whatmore et al, 1987a). Although British farms are predominantly owned and managed by individual families, the traditional concept of the 'family farm' (see, for example, Williams, 1963), only partly incorporated within the capitalist system, is no longer appropriate. Instead the situation is of 'a wide range of productive, labour and business relations representing neither an empirically nor a theoretically discrete category' (Whatmore et al, 1987a, p. 27).

Whatmore et al suggest a typology based on the extent of what they call 'subsumption' in both the internal and the external relations of the farm unit. Subsumption involves the capitalist transformation of agriculture through one or both of: direct methods, involving the 'full commoditisation' (1987a, p. 27) of labour relations and the influence over technical procedures by external capital; and indirect methods, involving the appropriation of some of the surplus produced on the farm by external investors. The typology comprises four ideal types defined according to the degrees of direct subsumption of internal relations and of indirect subsumption of external relations:

(1) The *marginal closed units*, comprising farms low on both. Families own and manage the land and the business, provide most if not all of the labour, and have few debts. They are usually small-scale units, 'surviving on the margins of commercial agriculture' (p. 32), and contain family members living partly on other sources of income (such as state benefits).
(2) The *transitional, dependent units*, which employ some hired labour and carry some debt; many are on the edge of viability and need more capital, and perhaps more land, in order to avoid being marginalised.
(3) The *integrated units*, in which capitalist relations dominate, with high levels of capital input and credit, and with contract marketing quite common: 'Such businesses are firmly set upon the technological treadmill and must continue to be dynamic and expansionist in order to remain viable' (p. 33).
(4) *Subsumed enterprises*, which occupy the highest positions on both scales. The family farm has been taken over by corporate capital, is run by a manager and has strong links with external capital, for both technological inputs and marketing.

They apply this typology, which in its ideal form implies farms moving from the first stage, through the next two, to the fourth, in three case-study areas in southern Britain, showing that movement along it had been greater in some areas (those close to London) than others (west Dorset; Whatmore et al, 1987b). As they move through the stages, so farmers become increasingly tied in to the growth dynamic of capitalism, reflected not only by their mortgage and capital indebtedness but also by their links to chemical and pharmaceutical companies which are playing an increasing role in the food chain via developments in biotechnology (Barlow, 1988a). As Barlow (1988b, p. 117) sees it:

> The processes of technological change will be selective, hence the pattern of uneven development will be maintained and the trend towards regional monocultures based on the requirements of the food processing industry reinforced.

Capitalism is 'invading' agricultural practices at different rates in different times and places, with consequent variations in both the geography of agriculture and the geography of land despoliation.


ECOLOGICAL IMPERIALISM

It is not always easy to achieve substantial increases in the productivity of either land or labour in areas where the land has long been occupied and farmed within the capitalist mode of production. Thus in order to obtain the profits from the sale of agricultural products in markets that are expanding because of population growth, it may be sensible for those with capital to invest to put it into lands currently outside the capitalist mode, which offer great potential for both initial profits and rapidly increasing productivity. This is what occurred in medieval England with the destruction of the forests and the draining of the wetlands. From the sixteenth century on, it happened at a much wider spatial scale, as an increasing proportion of the earth's surface was drawn in to the capitalist system. As Peet (1969; see also Chisholm, 1962) has shown, a global system of agricultural zones focused on the North Atlantic core of the capitalist system emerged during the nineteenth century, as advances in transportation technology (such as refrigeration) enabled long-distance movements to markets: in the early 1830s, the average distance that butter imports travelled to London was only 262 miles, whereas by c.1910 it was 3120 miles; the comparable figures for wool and hides were 2330 and 10 900 miles, respectively. The result was very substantial changes in the earth's land cover: Richards (1990, p. 164) estimates that between 1700 and 1980 the global area of forest and woodland declined by 18 per cent, whereas that of cropland increased by 466 per cent: in North America the respective figures were 7.3 and 6667 per cent; in south Asia, 46 and 296 per cent; and in Europe, 8 and 105 per cent.

    Expansion took place in two basic ways. In the first, ecological imperialism, people from the capitalist countries occupied 'new' lands where they imposed

their own organisation. Most of those lands were already occupied by either
rank redistribution or reciprocity societies, which were in some way or
another dispossessed of their ownership (in some cases, such as the
Aborigines of Tasmania, they were virtually eliminated). Such processes
characterise much of what is known in Britain as the 'New World', including
almost all of the North American continent as well as Australia, New
Zealand and parts of southern Africa.

The important feature of these 'white settlement' areas for the present
analysis is that the nature of the land-use pattern imposed was almost entirely
geared to production for markets elsewhere. This was particularly the case with
Australia and New Zealand; the former was initially settled as a prison camp
and the latter was reluctantly colonised by Britain when it was used as little
more than a refreshment stop for whaling and other expeditions, but within a
few decades each country had been transformed into a great food-producing
appendix to the British Isles. This involved, as Powell (1977) persuasively
argues, the development of images of those lands as 'attractive and bountiful
rural landscapes', and the purpose of settlement was to obtain that bounty for
the British Empire. Not all settlers had the same image, and there were
conflicts in some places about the best way to organise the occupation of the
land and reap its harvests, as Powell (1970) illustrates in his detailed study of
the conflicts between the official vision of the settlement of western Victoria, as
a landscape of small farms in the image of rural England, and the perspective
of the initial European colonists, who wanted the land organised in large sheep
stations; the latter won. Similarly, in South Australia, as illustrated in the
classic work of Meinig (1962), the pattern of settlement and land use resulted
from a pragmatic learning process as people with a particular image of the
rural scene came to terms with what, for them, was a new and fickle
environment: he termed it 'a quick mass-testing of the land and the revelation
of its qualitative patterns at an incalculable social and economic cost' (p. 207).

The settlers not only organised land tenure and practised agriculture
according to perceptions which had been learned in very different
environments many thousands of miles away, with production geared to the
markets there; they also wrought major changes to the local ecosystems. One
of the first detailed studies of that process was called *The Invasion of New
Zealand by People, Plants and Animals* (Clark, 1949). Its relatively neutral
description was shunned by Crosby four decades later; his book is called
*Ecological Imperialism: The Biological Expansion of Europe, 900–1900*
(Crosby, 1986). When the pakeha occupied New Zealand, they found no
mammals and relatively few species of flora and fauna, consequences of the
islands' long isolation. The settlers introduced not only animal and plant
species necessary to their agriculture, while destroying much of the native
population, but also installed many other European flora and fauna, to create
an environment as similar as possible to that left behind. For at least a
century, each New Zealand province had an Acclimatisation Society, whose

purpose was to introduce and propagate 'innoxious' flora and fauna, both useful and ornamental: the first report of the Otago Acclimatisation Society summarised its goal as to ensure that

> the sportsman and lover of nature might then enjoy the same sports and studies that make the remembrance of their former homes so dear, the country rendered more enjoyable, our tables better supplied, and new industries fostered. (Swann, 1966, p. 3)

The outcome was the introduction of 130 species of birds, 40 of fish and 50 of mammals, of which 30, 10 and 30 respectively became established in the wild. One of the mammals introduced (to Australia as well) was the rabbit. It bred extremely rapidly, and was the cause of much soil erosion, especially in the South Island high country (see Cumberland, 1947; McCaskill, 1969, 1973); the problems caused were such that both eating rabbit and owning rabbits as pets were legally proscribed.

The impact of the rabbit on New Zealand and Australian environments is just one example of the consequences of ecological imperialism. As Crosby puts it, the Americas and Australasia have provided European-based societies with a major windfall during the last four centuries in terms of an environment that could be exploited for great gain. But the costs of the pursuit of that exploitation have been great. The 'Dust Bowl' created in the Great Plains area of the United States during the droughts of the 1930s provides clear testimony to this (Worster, 1979); there were fears in the summer of 1988 that it would be repeated (see Ungar, 1992), despite the many lessons regarding land-use practices apparently learned from the first episode. The Dust Bowl in the 1930s further illustrates Blaikie and Brookfield's contention (see p. 94) regarding the importance of management practices in the impact of human 'interference' on physical systems. According to Worster (1979, p. 5):

> there was . . . a close link between the Dust Bowl and the Depression . . . the same society produced them both, and for similar reasons. Both events revealed fundamental weaknesses in the traditional culture of America, the one in ecological terms, the other in economic.

He argues that no other word than 'capitalism' sums up the reasons for the Dust Bowl; the pressures on individual farmers to increase their personal wealth through exploiting nature led them to ignore all environmental limits, with the ultimate disastrous consequences, just as 'Wall Street ignored sharp practices and a top-heavy economy' (p. 7) which together contributed to create the Depression:

> In a more stable region, this sort of farming could have gone on exploiting the land much longer with impunity. But on the plains the elements of risk were higher than they were anywhere else in the country,

and the destructive effects of capitalism far more sudden and dramatic. There was nothing in the plains society to check the progress of commercial farming, nothing to prevent it from taking the risks it was willing to take for profit. That is how and why the Dust Bowl came about.

Settler colonies such as Australia, New Zealand and the United States are not the only milieux in which ecological imperialism has been practised. Indeed, it has probably produced greater degradation of the environment in other parts of the world invaded by capitalists who either did not intend to settle there permanently or later decided to leave. Some areas of plantation economies in the humid tropics illustrate this; as Blaikie (1985, p.144) argues, the environmental attitudes implemented there led to rapid exhaustion of the natural resource base before the 'imperialists' moved on, in a process somewhat akin to slash-and-burn agriculture, except that the capitalists were probably less concerned that the soil's natural fertility should be replenished by a period of fallow. Cheap land was often available, and governments were prepared to subsidise the provision of an infrastructure, thereby making the investment even more attractive. Alternative investment opportunities elsewhere suggested that rather than seek to maintain the soil's productivity, it was better to 'mine' them and move on, an attitude encouraged by potential political instability which threatened the security of long-term investments. The commitment of the capitalist to the environment being exploited may be very low, therefore, with the obvious consequences. And yet, as Blaikie (1989) argues with regard to removal of forests from many parts of the Third World today, local interests in the conservation of environmental resources are difficult to defend against such ecological imperialism; the short-term gains of the economic activity generated are accepted at the sacrifice of the environment's long-term health.

## CAPITALIST PENETRATION

In this second, and more widespread, method by which capitalist agriculture expanded, lands formerly occupied by non-capitalist modes of production are slowly penetrated, not by their forcible removal, as with ecological imperialism, but rather by their incorporation within the capitalist world economy. This is how the peasant economies of many parts of Europe were replaced by capitalism, and contemporary developments are but a continuation of that process, on a very large scale. However, much of what is happening now is in tropical and sub-tropical, arid as well as humid, environments less able to withstand the increased pressures than the European temperate humid regimes.

This process of penetration comes about through contact between peasant and capitalist societies, in which each seeks to benefit from the other. The capitalist societies want to obtain the products of the peasants' land; the peasants are persuaded to 'want' the material benefits of capitalist consumption. To achieve them, the peasants must sell products to obtain the income that they need to finance material purchases; if they do that, then the capitalist societies obtain the increased volume of foodstuffs and other raw materials that they require.

At face value, this appears to be a symbiosis that brings mutual benefits (and it is sometimes presented as such in political programmes; Brandt, 1980; 1983), but it is usually the case, in the long term if not in the short, that the peasant societies are weaker and gain least. As stressed in the previous chapter, competition in the capitalist world calls for continued increases in productivity, in agriculture as much as in other sectors of the economy. Thus in order to increase their money incomes, and sell in the capitalist markets, peasants must increase their productivity; they must put greater pressure on their land. This need is accentuated by the nature of the markets in which they are competing. The peasants have little if any influence on the demand there, but must react to it. The crops and animal products that they offer for sale must be those that the outsiders want; they are competing to sell to them in buyers' markets – if the outsiders do not buy, then there is no sale. And so they are at the mercy of the market, and must respond to its signals. Their usual response, whatever the signal, is to try and produce more to sell, thus putting more pressure on their land.

Why is this so? Assume that a peasant family has decided that it needs a certain money income in order to live at the desired material standards. It thus produces enough to sell on the markets in order to yield at least that level of income. Neighbouring peasant families are doing the same, with the result that they sell and earn the income they need. Others perceive their success, and decide to enter the market too. The result is that the supply–demand ratio is altered as the price falls, in the buyers' favour. The only sensible way for each individual peasant farmer to react to this fall in income appears to be to produce more, to increase land and labour productivity. The result is even more products on the market, a further change in the supply–demand relationship, and a falling price. There is continuing pressure to produce more, with clear consequences for the environment.

Sooner or later the market will become saturated, and not all that is produced will be sold. The individual peasant family will probably then respond by seeking to increase market share, by undercutting competitors (in exactly the same way as described in the previous chapter), which can only be achieved – if a constant income is to be sustained – by increasing productivity. Alternatives, such as either collective action to keep prices high and production down or a move into other products, are less likely to be undertaken; the first because of the difficulties of achieving it, the second because it involves substantial investment in some cases and a loss of income for a period in most – investment in buildings, equipment, livestock and even plants (such as orchards) may have to be written off before the 'natural' productive life is completed, and new investments may take time to yield returns (with forests, for example, this could be several decades).

Exactly the same will probably happen if the market is not saturated and prices are high. For some peasant households, the ability to earn sufficient income for their needs may be the only driving force and the potential for more will be irrelevant; they will not respond to the market by sending more products to it. Others will, however, because their contact with the capitalist system, its growth ideology, and the promotion of consumption via advertising (Sack, 1988) will convince them that extra income is desirable, a conviction probably strengthened by the pressures outlined in the next paragraphs. Thus whatever the short-term situation, as peasants are incorporated into capitalism so they will continually seek production and income increases. After a good season, for example, yields will have been high but prices consequentially depressed; to recover, more must be sold next year. After a bad season, with yields low, prices are relatively high, and there is pressure to produce more next year to benefit from the greater income potential.

As peasants are drawn in to the capitalist system, therefore, so they increasingly adopt its dynamic, and in particular the need to increase the productivity of both land and labour (see Bradley and Carter, 1989). This will probably further their incorporation into the capitalist system (their 'subsumption' according to Whatmore et al: see p. 101), because they will realise (or are 'convinced' by outside agents) that the increased productivity that they require can only be achieved by capital investment in agricultural practices. This means either investing part of their income in the purchase of machinery and other capital goods, rather than using it for immediate consumption, or, more importantly, borrowing money to facilitate the investments. Paying off the debts so incurred becomes a further pressure to increase productivity. And this will probably mean that they switch an increasing proportion of their land and labour resources into production for the capitalist markets and away from their own subsistence, which means a shift towards monocultural practices; more and more of their effort involves producing for exchange rather than for use values (Watts, 1983). Increasingly, they come to rely on the markets for their day-to-day requirements, which only increases the pressure further, especially when the markets for their own products become saturated and competition to sell becomes fiercer.

In general, the terms of trade move against peasant producers operating in the market system, especially over the long term. The *terms of trade* is the technical term for the ratio between the costs of imports and exports, which for an individual household is the difference between the costs of purchases (and, by implication at least, their labour) and the income received from sales. Within capitalism, this changed ratio often comes about because of the effects of inflation: goods cost more and so it is necessary to work harder to

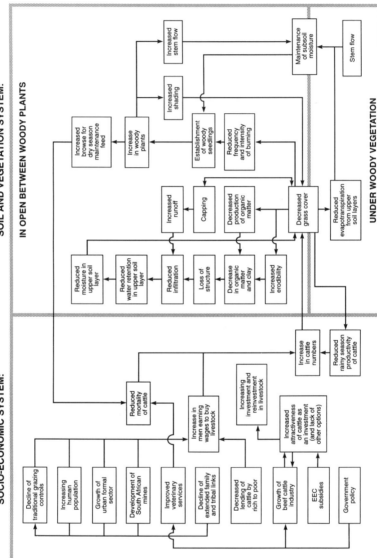

Model of ecological change on a sandy loam in intially carrying bushed and wooded grassland

**Figure 4.2** The origins of land degradation in Botswana (redrawn from Blaikie, 1985)

keep up one's level of consumption. Peasants on the edge of capitalism suffer from this; the manufactured goods that they have been convinced they need are increasing in price, and the only way they can cope is to increase their production. They are further disadvantaged because the trend in prices for foodstuffs and other raw materials is frequently downwards, as more and more production is encouraged to reduce the costs to importers. The pattern of uneven development described in the previous chapter is based on inequality in the market-place, whereby the producers in the periphery are at the mercy of the purchasers in the core. As a consequence, the terms of trade often move against them: the costs of imports rise and the values of exports fall, and the peasant producers can individually have little impact on either.

The overall consequence of these pressures is an increase in demands made on the physical environment, and its eventual degradation, as argued in Blaikie's (1985) analysis of the political economy of soil erosion. For example, the pressure to grow peanuts for the capitalist economy in parts of Niger led to accelerated soil erosion, because of the displacement of pastoralists and the disruption of the ecological balance they had achieved with the environment and because the techniques used to produce the peanuts removed nutrients from the soil at much greater rates than they were restored by natural processes and by fertilisers. In Botswana, a doubling of the cattle herd in the Ngwaketse district between 1963 and 1982 was the result of increased commercialisation of agriculture which, along with other extensions of the capitalist system and the incorporation of local labour into other activities, promoted major changes in the socio-economic system (Figure 4.2). Grazing was no longer communally controlled, and pressures on the environment increased in order to earn incomes from beef cattle, but

> the increased cattle population reduces grass cover and encourages soil erosion, which in turn reduces the productivity of the grass. Fewer and cooler fires result which enables more seedlings of woody plants to survive. Reduced competition with grasses also aids the survival of seedlings. Once established, woody plants shade out grasses and intercept rainfall, so that grass cover is further reduced. The decline in grass cover reduces the productivity of cattle in the rainy season, so that more are needed for the same output. The increase in shrubs helps survival in the dry season, so that fewer cattle die. The vicious circle is completed. (Blaikie and Brookfield, 1987c, p. 195)

This entire process of incorporation of the peasantry, accompanied by its impoverishment and marginalisation in many cases, plus the consequent degradation of the environment, has been termed 'silent violence' by Watts (1983) in his major study of northern Nigeria. It is silent because people suffer and die not because of intentional acts against them – called behavioural violence (see Johnston et al, 1987) – but rather because of the operation of the structure of the global economic system of which they are part. The argument regarding structural violence is closely linked to the concept of a core–periphery organisation of the capitalist world economy, in which the periphery is exploited for the benefit of the core. At a national scale, this is shown in, for example, relative rates of GNP increase, state indebtedness and wealth accumulation. At the individual scale it is shown by differences in the quality of life, as exemplified by people's life chances. Thus, if the capitalist world economy can sustain an average life expectancy for French children of over 78 years but only 40 years for the residents of Sierra Leone, then structural violence is being enacted on the latter in order to improve the life chances of the former. Johnston's (1989) analysis of these differences in life chances shows the amount of structural violence present in the contemporary world as a consequence of its core-periphery organisation. If the life expectancy of the French was enjoyed throughout the world, those born in 1985 could anticipate a total of 8 520 012 million more years of life than they will achieve because of the current differentials in life expectancy at birth; of those lost years, only 0.23 per cent will be in the 19 countries designated as 'industrial market economies' by the World Bank, which house some 8.7 per cent of the world's population.

Watts's (1983) work on the Hausa peasants shows how they had learned to survive in the fickle environments of northern Nigeria before British colonisation; they coped with climatic uncertainty and food shortages. But incorporation into capitalism eroded their coping mechanisms, so that they could not readily survive famines as they had in the past. Hence, according to Watts (1983, pp. xxiv–xxv):

> The contradiction of colonial rule in Nigeria was that while the success of metropolitan capital depended upon expanded commodity production by households who subsidized the reproduction of their own labor power, the demands of capital and the effects of commodity production simultaneously undermined (and occasionally threatened) the survival of those upon whom it ultimately depended. There is, then, a structural relationship between famine and the political economy of colonialism that legitimately warrants the use of the term 'violence'. This structural causality and the absences and neglect that mark the history of famine in northern Nigeria . . . is the 'silent violence' . . .

As Watts (1989) points out elsewhere, this does not mean that Africa is in a chronic state of crisis, but it does stress the point that it is the nature of the relationship between society and nature, and specifically the way in which human 'interference' with nature is managed under capitalism, that is the cause of much land degradation and the appalling human consequences that stem therefrom.

Perhaps the clearest example of this degradation is the process of desertisation that has taken place in the Sahel region of Africa in recent decades, and led to the major famines that gained international media coverage in the early 1980s. (*Desertisation* is the preferred term of some for the process by which an area becomes a desert; *desertification* is reserved by them for such processes that clearly are catalysed by human 'interference'.) The nature of the causes of that degradation is a topic of much debate (see, for example, Hulme, 1989, on whether overgrazing has stimulated the onset of drought conditions). Many observers believe that increased pressure on the land in the semi-arid areas has contributed substantially to the creation of desert conditions, however: Hare et al (1977, p. 336) refer to the process as

> the effects of interaction between mounting pressure on land and vegetation and the incidence of naturally occurring droughts, which are a normal part of desert margin climates. It is possible that desertification amplifies itself by means of the albedo feedback mechanism . . . [see p. 42 above], but the large-scale climate is, in the end, able to reassert more humid conditions. Damage to ecosystems during desertification may, however, make the recovery of surface productivity lag well behind the climate.

Goudie's (1986a, p. 48) model of how desertification has been stimulated in northern Kenya (Figure 4.3) has the sedentarisation of nomads and their increased numbers as the crucial human factors, and the increase in their cattle herds as the catalyst for land degradation. (See also Grainger, 1990.) Once again, however, the fundamental concern is not with human 'interference' with environmental systems *per se* but rather with the quality of the management of that 'interference'.

This argument has been developed by Thomas and Middleton (1994, p. 88), who suggest that:

> it is tempting to discern that the central theme is the conflict between a culture which demands a constant supply of a predictable commodity – meat – and an environment which is unable to support constancy simply due to its inherent natural variability. Approaches to resource use designed for a less variable environment [i.e. the temperate zones] inevitably lead to problems when applied to the more dynamic dryland scene.

They quote a Kenyan study (Millington et al, 1989) which suggested the following sequence leading to soil erosion: low incomes stimulate outmigration of males from the dryland area; because of low wages available in cities they stay there longer, which reduces the availability of labour on the farms; farm productivity declines; there is an increased burden placed on the women who remain; paid labour moves to the wealthier farms, leaving the poorer farms with labour shortage; this means that terraces and other soil management practices are neglected; and soil erosion is exacerbated. In other words, desertification is stimulated by 'Ignorance, poor planning based on inadequate understanding of the dryland environment, and the adoption of inappropriate techniques' (Thomas and Middleton, 1994, p. 97), a conclusion which applies to developed world drylands (such as the US Dust Bowl),

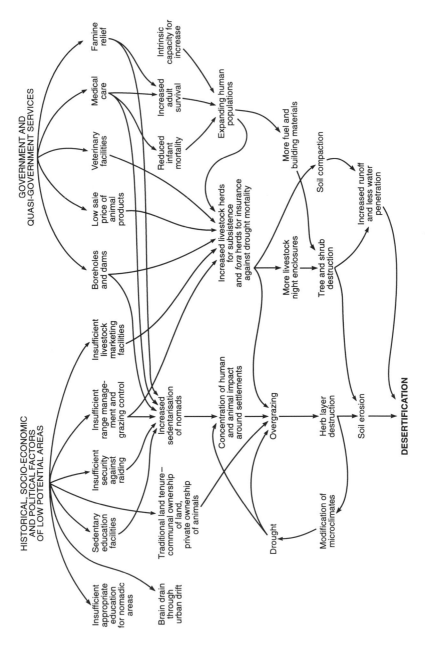

**Figure 4.3** Causal factors of desert encroachment in northern Kenya (redrawn from Goudie, 1986a, p. 48, after Lamprey, 1978)

especially in times of drought, just as much as to the developing world, although in the latter cases centuries of living in ecological equilibrium with the dryland environment are destroyed when the demands of external markets lead to lifestyle changes and demands for greatly increased productivity from monocultures.

Many communities incorporated into the periphery of the capitalist world economy are usually relatively powerless within that economy and its associated political structures, in many cases because of their dependence on providing a single commodity for which there is a buyers' rather than a sellers' market. They share these characteristics with 'one-industry town' communities located within the core regions of the world economy (Blowers and Leroy, 1994), except that it may be more feasible in the latter cases to mobilise political action against the environmental problems being stimulated by the particular land uses being practised there. Peripheral communities within the periphery of the world economy have least power, and they and their environments are most prone to exploitation for the benefit of others living elsewhere.

## OTHER RESOURCES

The discussion so far in this chapter has focused on flow resources, and especially those of the land system involved in agricultural production, which Rees classifies as in the 'critical zone' (i.e. they can be exploited to exhaustion: see p. 86 above). The arguments advanced apply equally as well to other critical zone flow resources, such as fish (over which there is increasing international concern) and forests. But what of the flow resources in the non-critical zone (which cannot be exhausted) and the stock resources?

### NON-CRITICAL ZONE FLOW RESOURCES

Resources in this category cannot be exhausted, as they are naturally self-regenerating – as with water moving through the hydrological cycle (though, of course, changes in the global environmental system can affect the amount of water available, through in particular the waxing and waning of the polar ice caps). They can be degraded, in ways to be discussed in a later section, and they are limited in the extent of their use. Thus the problems with such resources reflect the extent of use and of degradation.

With regard to use, relative to the limits available, there are pressures within the capitalist mode of production to increase exploitation and therefore reduce overall availability. The dynamo of capitalism, as previously described, depends for its continued operation on increased levels of consumption of goods and services. Thus it is necessary for people to be convinced of the need to consume more in general – hence the pro-growth ideology of capitalist societies – and for commodity producers to convince people of the need to consume more of what they have to offer. The latter is crucial because, as already argued, a static situation is rarely tenable for long under capitalism. In a competitive situation, if consumption of the good or service concerned is not increasing profits will probably fall; if consumption is not increased, the volume of investment in the production will fall, so everything must be done to ensure that more is consumed. (Investment may be transferred to the production of commodities for which demand can be increased, but this is easier with some resources than others – farmers only have their land.)

This growth syndrome has many consequences for the environment, as already described in the discussions of critical zone flow resources. It usually involves the promotion of goods and services which draw on the environment to a greater or lesser extent in either the creation or the operation of the product. In recent decades, for example, there has been increased use of electrical appliances, with consequences in the demand for the generation of power to be consumed in the home, and also of appliances driven by batteries, increasing the demand for the raw materials from which they are made and the production of toxic wastes that have to be disposed of.

In some circumstances non-critical zone flow resources themselves may be marketed. An excellent example of this is water, and its provision for consumption by capitalist companies whose goal is to make profits from the sale of that naturally occurring commodity. This is illustrated by Walker and Williams's (1982) study of Santa Clara County in California. There, as the land was settled and more intensively used, requiring irrigation for farming and urban growth, so the demand for water grew; increasingly it had to be imported from outside the county boundaries. Much of the water is supplied by private companies, with the remainder either provided by municipal agencies or self-supplied (e.g. from private wells). Walker and Williams suggest that the motives of both private and public sector suppliers are geared to promotion of increased water consumption, with little or no reflection on 'the economic value of water uses against costs of demand management' (1982, p. 107). Agency zeal (the promotion of growth) and inter-agency competition are both cited as reasons for these attitudes, which are sustained by local water law; any right to use water granted to a company or agency in California must be taken up within three years, or it is forfeit. Alongside these social and legal factors are those that are purely economic. 'The rule of profits' (1982. p. 111) means that short-term profits and long-term market growth are necessary to company success. Although American public agencies do not exist to make profits in the normal sense, because they are largely financed through the sale of bonds, they have to make the equivalent of profits in order to ensure returns to their investors: 'A good record of growth makes raising capital easier and cheaper' (p. 111). Thus continued expansion of water demand and delivery is typical, leading Walker and Williams (1982, p. 117) to conclude that:

*efficiency in water supply and water use is not a major policy concern* . . .
Inefficiency and overdevelopment will be tolerated or even encouraged if
growth is anticipated or is proceeding apace. This is not to condone such
inefficiency, only to see it in the harsh light of the real political-economic
purposes . . .

Privatisation of water companies in countries where they were previously
publicly owned, as in the UK, is stimulating similar trends, despite the efforts
of the government-appointed regulators to control profit levels and ensure
'environmentally friendly' usage.

The California example implies that many of the natural resources in the
non-critical zone may be treated as commodities in the same way as the
products of both stock and critical zone flow resources. The implications for
the environment can be profound, because the goal of the profit-makers is to
accelerate consumption of the resource. There are limits to that
consumption, because of the finite amount of the resource available.
Efficiencies can be gained, by ensuring as little waste as possible (perhaps
through pricing policies) and by recycling the resource – which with water
means using it as many times as possible during one sequence of the
hydrological cycle. Water is not only a scarce resource globally, and even
more scarce locally in many parts of the globe; it is also a necessity for human
reproduction. Thus the extent that water consumption – and by implication
that of other non-critical zone flow resources too – is promoted in order to
enhance profit-making and wealth accumulation is critical, since it means that
eventually choices will have to be made on how to use a limited amount of
water available in an area, which could well be through the price mechanism
of the capitalist market; the highest bidder would win, water would become
more expensive, and the costs of survival to the individual would increase.
Making those choices in any area could be delayed by importing water from
others, as increasingly has been done during the last two centuries of rapid
urbanisation, but paying for those investments and their upkeep means that
the water becomes more expensive. (Water consumption is not properly
valued in many places, however. In most parts of the UK, for example, there
is no metering and consumers pay a standing charge rather than a price for
the amount consumed. This, some argue, leads to waste; if people paid
according to the amount consumed, they would be more efficient in their
use.)

## STOCK RESOURCES

The critical issues for stock resources are their rates of consumption, and so
their potential denial to future users. Debates about those issues can be
clarified in terms of two polar positions. At the one extreme, there are those
who argue for great caution in resource use, and the need to avoid waste at

all costs, because of the problems that will be faced when exhaustion occurs. In moral terms, this is often expressed as protecting the resource base for future generations and only exploiting that part of it which can be justified; it is extremely difficult, of course, to develop normative standards of what is justifiable. (Sagoff, 1988, 224, presents the moral argument fully, claiming that environmental legislation is necessary in the United States to 'express Americans' perceptions of themselves as a nation, called upon, to an extent, to appreciate and preserve a fabulous natural heritage and to pass it on reasonably undisturbed to future generations'.) At the other extreme are those who argue that although the stock resources are finite in volume, that volume is so great, relative to past, present and anticipated future use, that there is no foreseeable problem of scarcity, especially since the lesson of the past is that we are likely, aided by increasing exploration and exploitation technologies, to discover more stocks than we are currently aware of. In any case, the optimistic argument often continues, human ingenuity is such that even if a stock does become either exhausted or too expensive for continued exploitation, alternatives will be readily found.

Whatever the merits of these two arguments and the long-term availability of certain stock resources, there remain issues of their exploitation and the impacts that this can have on other aspects of the environment. To the extent that the stock resources are viewed as commodities to be sold in competitive markets – as most of them are in capitalist societies – so there are pressures to exploit them as cheaply as possible in order to promote profitability. This can often have major environmental impacts, at least locally.

An example illustrates this. Banaba, or Ocean Island, is a small island in the Pacific, much of whose area has been covered over millennia with bird guano that has been transformed naturally into phosphate of lime (as was the case on the nearby, better-known island of Nauru). That lime was an attractive stock resource, for there was great demand for phosphate to be used as fertiliser in Australia and New Zealand. Companies were launched to exploit the resource, employing local labour. As the resource was worked, so the other resource of the island – the land on which the Banabans grew their food – was slowly reduced; as Binder (1977, p. 55) expressed it:

> their little island diminished. In fact it was worse than diminished; it was packed into sacks and disappeared altogether . . . Even where their precious food trees were spared, or replanting promised, the mining chasms made access impossible.

The Banabans were persuaded by the local colonial administration, first to give up their land, and then, if they were not to remain as indentured labourers working in the phosphate mines, to accept resettlement in the Fijian islands. The latter happened with a shift to Rambi in 1946, while Banaba itself became a 'moon-scape nightmare of mined-out stark coral pinnacles (Binder, 1977, p. 183). The initial agreement allowing mining of the phosphate signed with the British Phosphate Commission (BPC) required replacement of the earth and trees destroyed. BPC subsequently argued that this was impossible and it has not been done; Banaba is now uninhabitable.

This example illustrates two major issues concerning the winning of stock resources. The first is that removal of the resource has both direct and indirect environmental impacts. The direct impacts are just the removal, and the resulting 'hole'. The indirect impacts are not only the consequences of that 'hole', such as the subsidence in many areas of underground mining and the removal of artesian water, but also the disturbance to other environmental systems. That disturbance may be temporary, as it could be possible either to restore the systems to their original state or to create new, acceptable systems in their place, as with the rehabilitation of tip heaps alongside many coal mines to form grassy hills. But such rehabilitation costs money, which can only come – in the absence of collective action – from what would otherwise be profits. In a competitive situation, the organisation that threatens its profitability by returning some of the income into non-profit-making activities such as restoring the landscape threatens its own viability. This does not mean that it will not be done in some cases (even if not required by government regulation); for a variety of altruistic reasons, people will use part of their profit to enhance the landscape and so promote values other than those of the capitalist dynamo. But that can only be done if the profits continue to be forthcoming. The need to make a profit from the exploitation of stock resources, in a competitive situation, means that there are strong pressures to minimise expenditure on clearing up the mess created by mining the resource.

## INDUSTRIALISATION AND URBANISATION

A major feature of the expansion of the capitalist mode of production has been the immense growth in the range of commodities available for purchase and consumption. Much of this involves the transformation of raw materials obtained from the stock and flow resources in the environment through increasingly sophisticated and complex industrial processes. Those processes have considerable impacts on the environment.

### WASTES AND POLLUTION

Most transformation processes produce wastes, either parts of the raw materials that are not required or transformed aspects of the materials that similarly are not integral to the new product being created. Some of those wastes may be of use in other production processes, and are consumed accordingly. Others are not, and so remain as by-products of the process.

They can be classified into stock and flow wastes, in the same way as natural resources are classified. Each type provides a particular set of problems, in that they have to be assimilated by the environment, frequently to its detriment.

With *stock wastes*, the most straightforward of the problems is disposal; they take up space. Thus ways of disposing of the ash from coal-fired power stations have to be found, for example; in some cases it has been deposited in the 'holes' created by mining, but in others it has simply accumulated in piles. Such disposal is rarely insignificant in its local environmental effects. An ash-heap alters local geomorphological and ecological systems; the ash put in a pit does not replace the soil that may have been removed. Some of the wastes are naturally degradable through biological and mechanical processes, however, and are broken down into their constituent parts. This is problematic if those constituent parts then taint the environment – as, for example, with chemicals that enter water courses, either directly or through the soil. Particular problems are created by especially toxic wastes that are dangerous to other life forms; the wastes from nuclear power generation come into this category, and great problems regarding their disposal are being faced because of their toxicity and great longevity.

The problems with *flow wastes* are of a different order, since their entry to the environment is often more difficult to control than is that of stock wastes; control usually involves substantial costs through the even greater sophistication of the transformation processes. The emission of waste products from power generation through the burning of coal illustrates this. By-products are released into the atmosphere, and the chemicals are then carried through the hydrological cycle to other locations where they are deposited through precipitation (the 'acid rain' phenomenon) and enter local ecosystems, with consequent deleterious effects on plant and animal life. Controlling the emission of those wastes requires investment in 'cleaner' power stations, which reduces their potential profitability because higher prices must be charged; items produced with the power are thus more expensive, which threatens the profitability of industrial operations. New plant may be needed; it may be more energy-efficient, which, as the example of water resource development above showed (p. 114), is not necessarily in the interests of the power industry. Furthermore, changes in the generation of power may involve the creation of new (probably stock) wastes that need to be disposed of, and increase the demand for other resources to be used in the power station (such as lime as a bed for the burning – which has to be mined and transported to the power station, both of which activities generate environmental disturbance).

Stock and flow waste generation is not confined to the production processes in capitalist (or any other type of) industrialisation. These are also consequences of consumption, either because not all of the product is consumed or because there are by-products. An example of the latter is the production of CFC gases, through the operation of electric refrigerators and aerosol sprays; those gases are believed to be destroying part of the ozone layer that protects the earth from certain types of radiation, with consequences for human health (especially skin cancer). With regard to wastes from consumption itself, most consumption is only temporary and the products are eventually discarded, often in their original manufactured state, as with a car or an item of clothing. The waste materials may be reusable, either to make the same product again (perhaps of an inferior quality, as with paper), or in the production of another product, or as a fertiliser for the soil (the 'shoddy manure' produced in the Yorkshire 'heavy woollen district'), though elements harmful to the environment may have to be removed first.

Because capitalism requires continued growth in the value of production, and thus in the volume of commodities consumed, the problem of wastes increases. As production increases, so also will wastes generated as by-products of production and/or consumption. Furthermore, capitalism's growth dynamic requires waste production through consumption to be speeded up. To sustain profitability, people have to be convinced to cast off items long before they are redundant; much clothing is discarded before it is so worn that it fails to fulfil its function, for example, and many motor cars are scrapped which could continue to be used for thousands of miles. (Packard, 1961, graphically satirises this, with the forecast of factories on cliff-tops dumping their production directly in the sea below without it ever being 'consumed'.) The ever-increasing production of waste is part of the capitalist system, and calls for the application of human ingenuity to counter it if environmental degradation is not to proceed at least at the same pace.

## URBANISATION

Some of the by-products of industrial processes are one example of a larger category of products known to economists as externalities, which are the (usually unintended) effects of one person's actions on another, over which the latter has no control. Externalities may be positive, in which case the recipient gains something of benefit, free of charge. But many are negative; the recipient suffers the consequence of an action, which may involve a cost, and cannot prevent its occurrence. At the local scale, a negative environmental externality could be the ash from a fire falling on a neighbour's garden; at the international scale, the acid rain phenomenon exemplifies the same relationship, with Britain presumed to be the producer of an externality and Norway and other 'downwind countries' the unfortunate recipients.

Most externalities are limited in their spatial extent; the further you are from the source of a pollutant, the less you are affected by it. Some may have a very wide impact, as suggested by the simulations of nuclear explosions (whether disasters or the consequences of bombs; Openshaw et al, 1983); a few may be global in their direct effect, but many more are so indirectly, as the arguments summarised in Chapter 2 indicate. Because most are local, this means that there is a geography of externality production, and of receipt (in the case of airborne pollutants this means downwind of the source, which is why so many urban areas in Britain have their higher-status residential areas upwind of their industrial districts). There are two important spatial scales in these geographies.

The first of the scales is the global, and refers to the core–periphery division of the capitalist world into a pattern of uneven development. That pattern was initiated with the transition to capitalism in parts of north-western Europe, where the core was established, and the areas concerned have remained within the core to the present. The core has expanded, however, taking in most of western Europe and North America, plus Japan. The remainder is in the periphery, at varying levels of economic development, as defined in capitalist terms, although some countries – such as the so-called 'Asian tigers' (Hong Kong, Singapore, South Korea and Taiwan) – are now rapidly rising through the semi-periphery towards the core.

Industrialisation emerged within that core and the processes of transforming raw materials into commodities for consumption were launched there. In many ways, therefore, it is in the core – widely recognised as the most 'advanced' areas of the world economic system – that most negative environmental externalities have been created, through the production of pollutants as by-products of industrial processes, and where large areas of land have been made derelict. Similar dereliction characterises many places in the periphery, too, where the winning of resources has led to substantial modifications of the physical environment – as in the goldfields of Australia, for example, where the separation of the gold by chemical processes sterilised large areas of land. Thus the map of wealth in the world is correlated with the map of environmental degradation caused by industrial, rather than agricultural, processes. As industrialisation proceeds in the periphery, however, so similar pollution processes are introduced – as exemplified by the Bhopal chemical plant disaster in India. In many cases, the industrial technology introduced to the periphery is far from the most sophisticated, and claims are made that core country corporations are 'exporting' their pollution-creating processes to the Third World.

At more local spatial scales, the map of environmental degradation shows considerable geographical variability, within the periphery as well as the core. The major reason for this is the process of urbanisation, whereby the industries and the people who work in, and otherwise benefit from, them are massed in high-density concentrations to benefit from the internal and external economies of scale that characterised the growth of industrial complexes: the internal economies arise from the efficiencies associated with large size; the external economies arise from the efficiencies that result from proximity to suppliers, servicers and customers. Urban areas are thus major concentrations of both the production of wastes and the generation of negative externalities. Their greater density often exacerbates the concentration of pollutants, with major consequences for the local environment, as exemplified by the major smogs over cities such as Los Angeles and Lima, caused by the burning of fossil fuels, especially oil and its derivatives (and illustrated by the rapid increase in the proportion of British children living in urban areas who suffer from asthma). Similarly, rivers in the industrial cities have received some of the greatest volumes of pollutants as the by-products of production and consumption processes, with the consequence that many have 'died' and are no longer able to support fish and other life.

Urbanisation has other major impacts on the environment because of the indirect consequences of replacing the 'natural' environment by a built one; their full range is detailed by Douglas (1983). They are clearly seen, for example, in the difference between urban and rural areas in local climates, a consequence of differences between their two surfaces and the materials involved (see Chandler, 1965; Landsberg, 1981). Urban areas tend to be warmer than the surrounding countryside and the lower-density suburban areas, especially at night, because of the radiation of heat; this is exacerbated by the air pollution in towns, which helps to form a dome over them that traps the heat in. Cities also tend to be less humid because there is less evaporation, a consequence of the relative absence of vegetation; because of the greater number of nuclei in the air above them, resulting from the emission of pollutants, they tend to have slightly more precipitation, however.

The building of urban areas interferes with other environmental systems, such as those involved in the movement of water. In rural areas, some of the water received as precipitation goes straight into streams, but much more is either stored temporarily in vegetation and soil or moves only slowly through those media towards the open channels. In urban areas, the lack of vegetation removes that control (and also reduces the amount of moisture returned directly to the atmosphere via transpiration), while the covering of the land surface by buildings and various paving surfaces denies water access to the soil. It thus moves rapidly across those surfaces into the water channels, which have to cope with a much higher peak load during storms than is the case in the countryside; one result is greater erosion by urban streams and more expensive engineering works to compensate – with an increase in the 'natural hazards' of urban areas as the alternative (Perry, 1981, illustrates this for Britain, and both Jones, 1990, and Gardiner, 1990, outline human impacts on the environment of that small, densely occupied island).

Urbanisation has proceeded furthest in the core of the world economy, where a greater proportion of the population lives in cities rather than in the countryside; the periphery, on the other hand, now contains some of the world's largest cities and some of the worst examples of environmental degradation as a consequence. Douglas (1983, p.vii) notes their size, and records that:

> The people of those cities will live in an environment created by human endeavour, often made unpleasant by the side-effects of human activity, frequently full of risks derived from crowding, inadequate housing and poor sanitation, yet by no means immune from the extremes of natural processes, such as floods, tidal waves, landslides and earthquakes.

Until relatively recently, these major urban centres have been spatially contained as very high-density concentrations, clearly separated from the small settlements of the countryside. With the growing mobility facilitated by widespread car ownership and the investment in road systems, however, urban development has sprawled over very large areas. The densities are relatively low, and the impacts on the climate and hydrology less than in the older cities, because of a greater area of vegetation and untarmacked soil, but the general spread has had many consequences for the natural environmental systems. Furthermore, such cities, and their suburban areas especially, house the most affluent people in society who have the highest consumption levels and thus produce large volumes of waste which has to be disposed of; for many city governments, waste disposal is a major problem and some transport it many miles to acceptable receptacle sites.

This outward expansion of urban areas has been associated with greater overall prosperity, which has a number of characteristics. With the great increases in productivity many people are required to work fewer hours in the day, fewer days in the week, and fewer weeks in the year. This decline of demand for time at work has been compensated by the growth of leisure time and recreation activities. Much of this is reflected in the continued dynamic of the capitalist system, as the provision of leisure and recreation facilities becomes commoditised, at home and beyond. Part of it is reflected in increased pressure on the environment for recreational use.

Recreational use of the environment focuses on certain favoured landscape types, especially in areas of preferred climates (i.e. warm and sunny). Mountainous areas and, especially, coasts with beaches are particularly popular, and there has been increasing pressure to make these available to a growing number of people for short and long visits. Tourism is one of the most rapidly expanding service industries, stimulating a great deal of built environment creation, again with clear consequences, direct and indirect, for natural environmental systems. The rapid development of resorts throughout the Mediterranean countries illustrates this, with not only the provision of the accommodation and transport facilities that people are led to demand but also the transformation of large areas of the environment into 'pleasure parks' of some form or other and the disposal of wastes into the sea. Even in relatively remote landscapes, increased pressure has substantial environmental impacts, as in the erosion of the natural soil cover under footpaths in most of the favoured rambling areas of upland Britain.

The tourist industry is typical of recent trends in capitalism as it seeks to counter the problems of overproduction. People are being encouraged to take several holidays per year rather than just one, to travel further, and to demand a higher standard of facilities. Holiday resorts which previously operated for a few months only now cater for visitors all year round. As the demand continues to be stimulated, so the pressures on the environment that it creates are increased too (not least through the greater volumes of travel, by air and by car, which increase energy consumption and the production of pollutants – in some cases threatening the very sights that the tourists are visiting). To some, we are now in a post-industrial society and the evils of the polluted cities of the nineteenth and early twentieth centuries are behind us. The current growth industries produce their own environmental externalities, however, as the capitalist dynamo speeds up the processes of consumption to which the environment is for ever committed.

## ADVANCED COMMUNISM/SOCIALISM

According to Marx's interpretation, one of the major features of the capitalist mode of production is its basis in the alienation of the individual from other individuals and from nature. In pre-capitalist modes, survival depended upon community among individuals and community between individuals and nature; people were interdependent, and personal survival was conditional upon that interdependence. Similarly, people were dependent for their survival on personal interrelationships with nature, since they drew sustenance directly from it. Those two forms of interdependence form the essence of human existence. With the development of capitalism, however, people lost their essential humanness because both labour and nature were commodified. People no longer relied on each other in any sense of reciprocity; instead they interacted through the buying and selling of their labour power. Similarly, their alienation from nature came about when nature's products became marketable commodities to be bought and sold. Thus, as Kolakowski (1978, p. 222) expresses it:

> Marx's starting point . . . is . . . the fact that individuals are alienated from their own labour and its material, spiritual and social consequences in the form of goods, ideas, and political institutions, and not only from these but from their fellow beings and, ultimately, from themselves.

Marx's goal was to end that alienation and to restore humanity to people by abolishing the alienating mode of production – capitalism – and its base in the commodification of labour and nature. Thus communism, to be achieved through socialism, was to restore people to their pre-capitalist state, without denying them the opportunity to achieve high levels of material satisfaction. The implication is clearly that under that new mode of production people will once again live in relative harmony with nature, in a condition of relative ecological equilibrium from which all of the environmental problems of the modern capitalist world will be absent. As Blaikie (1989) and Carter and Turnock (1993a) argue, there was little evidence that such harmony was achieved in the twentieth-century communist/socialist countries, and plenty of evidence that environmental degradation there was as substantial as elsewhere. Komarov (1981) shows that although Article 18 of the USSR Constitution required that:

> In the interests of the present and future generations, the necessary steps are taken in the USSR to protect and make scientific, rational use of the land and its mineral and water resources, and the plant and animal kingdom, to preserve the purity of air and water, and ensure production of natural wealth, and improve the human environment

and although in addition Article 67 states that:

> Citizens of the USSR are obliged to protect nature and conserve its riches,

nevertheless there was a 'ravaging of nature', generating an 'ecological alarm . . . [that] cannot be too loud nor too premature' (1981, p. 19). Similarly, Smil (1987, p. 214) refers to land degradation in China as an 'ancient problem getting worse'.

The reasons for environmental problems in those countries lie in the nature and origins of their societies. As already stressed, in the ideal-typical sequences of societal development, socialism and advanced communism would come after capitalism and so benefit from the technological achievements therein. But that sequence has not been followed, and instead the 'overthrow' of capitalism in most of those areas preceded the true onset of capitalism itself. As a consequence, it was necessary to replicate the technological achievements of capitalism (or at least a large number of them), a necessity accentuated by the political isolation of the advanced communist/socialist countries and a reluctance, if not outright refusal, on the part of the capitalist countries to share their accumulated expertise. Thus the industrial revolution has occurred not once but twice, with the same consequences in terms of, for example, urbanisation and environmental degradation. Further, because of large, rapidly growing populations the pressures to industrialise and to increase agricultural production demanded a much faster response, and in much greater volume, than was the case a century or more ago in the core of the capitalist world economy.

Despite these pressures, it could be argued that the demands on the environment in socialist countries should be less because of the absence of the drive to create surplus value for the accumulation of wealth, regardless of people's 'real needs'. Production in socialist societies occurs in order to meet socially defined needs, and although these go well beyond subsistence to high material standards of life, nevertheless there are no pressures or use of the mass media to convince people that they 'need' certain consumption goods and 'want' to replace those that they have – which are still serviceable and perform their function – by new models. So why were paths to 'development' followed which created ecological disaster on such a scale? Komarov suggests that in part it was a consequence of the failings of centralised planning and the nature of the giant bureaucracies in Russia, where the most powerful individuals and agencies were those whose continued power depended on delivering high material standards to the population and whose ideology was very much based on growth, on investing in economic development in order to 'obtain strategic advantage over the United States' (Komarov, 1981, p. 135). Furthermore, he argues, there was major ignorance of the extent of the ecological disaster. The majority of the population was denied information, while the affluent 15 per cent of the Soviet population enjoyed high standards in clean environments, insulated from the ecological problems by 'the green fences around their suburban houses' (p. 134). Meanwhile, the

> majority willingly suffers from the noise, the smog of those cities where they can find better paid jobs, where they can find some products to buy, let alone worrying about the carcinogens, allergens, or substances causing chromosomal mutations present there.

Government experts knew the extent of the ecological disaster, Komarov claims, but the power-elite used their positions to ensure they were relatively untouched by it.

> Five to six per cent of our society has access to natural products . . . , special drinking water, and special swimming pools with filtered sea water (without oil and phenol) . . . Hence for us everything will always be ecologically all right. In fenced wild forests there will be enough 'wild boars' to hunt; in lakes screened by underwater nets there will be fish for anglers. And no matter how Baikal is degraded, they will try to keep a few bays in virgin splendour, with pines on the high banks and the purest water . . .

The anti-alienation component of communist ideology should have ensured a different approach to the processes of industrialisation, with regard to relationships with the environment, what Blaikie and Brookfield (1987d, p. 208) call a 'distinctive socialist environmental management'. This has certainly not happened, and all of the evidence suggests that environmental despoliation has been as extensive in the 'East' as in the 'West'. Part of the reason for this was the pressure on the authorities in the East to achieve the aimed-for high material standards rapidly, in order to maintain the loyalty of the population and to prove to the 'West' that it could be done. Further, there was little accumulated capital available and the industrialisation programme (including the industrialisation of agriculture) had to be achieved as efficiently (i.e. as cheaply) as possible; the extra costs of industrialisation without negative environmental externalities could not be afforded (even if they were appreciated). Finally, since industrialisation and urbanisation necessarily have substantial negative impacts on the natural environment, so any programme of increased commodity production, whether capitalist or socialist, is bound to affect not only the store of stock resources but also the nature of flow resources.

## IN CONCLUSION

A first conclusion to be drawn from this chapter is that any form of social organisation is going to have substantial impacts on the natural environment and the equilibrium of the systems that comprise it. With some modes of social organisation, their primitive technology means that the environmental impact is likely to be relatively limited, as people are very much subject to the perceived environmental constraints within which they live. But as technological advances occur, so the potential for significantly altering those environmental systems increases, perhaps at an even greater rate than the technological advances themselves. Alongside the faster rate of change has come the increased spatial scale: current concerns about ozone layer depletion and global warming indicate that it is the earth as a whole which is under threat, not separate countries within it.

Marx was aware of this a century ago, as made clear in his brief remarks on the changing relationships between people and nature, quoted at the beginning of this chapter. He saw the penetration of agriculture by capitalism as replacing 'old-fashioned' methods by scientific ones, and noted that, as a consequence,

> it disturbs the circulation of matter between man and the soil, i.e. prevents the return to the soil of its elements consumed by man in the form of food and clothing; it therefore violates the conditions necessary to lasting fertility of the soil . . . all progress in capitalistic agriculture is a progress in the art, not only of robbing the labourer but of robbing the soil; all progress in increasing the fertility of the soil for a given time, is a progress towards ruining the lasting sources of that fertility. (Marx, 1977, pp. 474–5)

That robbery can be limited to some extent, through the application of human ingenuity and technological expertise. But, as has been argued here, the pressures to allow those alterations to proceed, in order to facilitate the advance of the mode of production, are very strong, and the limitations have been relatively ineffective. To bring them about needs a collective determination to succeed, and it is to the discussion of the nature of collective action that we now turn.

# 5  Collective Action and the State

> Free and open markets may be the key to financial success. But if they are to operate fairly and honestly, someone has to write the rules and to see they are rigidly enforced. (Queen Elizabeth II, speaking at the Guildhall, London, and reported in *The Independent*, 11 February 1989)

Two major arguments have been advanced in the preceding chapters. The first is that because the environment comprises a vast complex of interlocking systems and sub-systems, environmental problems must be countered collectively, rather than individually. The externality effects of environmental use, over both space and time, are such that their generation can only be effectively tackled by society at large. Thus, although individual initiative in the attack on environmental problems is desirable there are major limits to it, especially within competitive modes of production (see Johnston, 1986a, Chapter 2); viable approaches to both the solution of existing environmental problems and preventing the creation of others must involve collective action. The second argument is that the creation of environmental problems is not only a consequence of the human struggle for survival, but also increasingly a product of the predominant mode of social organisation (capitalism) through which that struggle is co-ordinated collectively.

These two arguments lead to a somewhat paradoxical situation. Collective control of the environment is necessary if it is to be kept in a condition capable of sustaining human life at high material standards; this requires mitigating the demands made on the environment under the unceasing quest for greater profitability in the production and circulation of commodities. But if that quest is constrained, the mode of production may well decay, with negative consequences for the levels of individual well-being. Profitability must be promoted, which means promoting environmental stress, unless ways can be found of simultaneously reducing environmental stress and expanding the production of surplus value. The promotion of profitability is also a collective concern, as will be argued here. Thus, it would seem, we at one and the same time need collective action to promote profit-making and collective action to promote environmental protection. Whether the two are compatible is a major concern; within it, the goal here is to appreciate the basis of collective action, with particular reference to the role of the state.

Collective action can be brought about in three ways.

(1) *Voluntary*, ad hoc *agreement.* This category includes all agreements where a group of interested parties come together, develop an appreciation that collective action is necessary, and then undertake such action. This

occurs very frequently, in almost all aspects of human life, and at all spatial scales; examples range from sporting bodies agreeing on the criteria for eligibility for selection to a national team to members of a family deciding to share the costs of residential accommodation for an elderly parent. Three features characterise all such agreements: (a) they are entered into voluntarily; (b) they are *ad hoc* only, developed for a specific purpose and with no explicit influence on any other activity; and (c) they need not be entered into by all interested parties.

(2) *Voluntary acceptance of a central power.* This comprises all agreements made by a single body which cover a wide range of topics, and are binding on all constituent members of the body. People accept the standing of that body to legislate in certain areas, and agree – perhaps grudgingly, and probably without formally registering their acceptance – to abide by its proposals. By far the most important example of such a body is the state, an institution with sovereign power within a defined territory. It may be accountable to the residents of that territory in a variety of ways, for example through the process of election for the right to run the state and through a constitution which limits the state's powers and reserves all other power to the people. Within the state apparatus, decisions are made in a wide area of activities, and separate decision-making fora do not have to be established for each issue, as is the case with the first category.

(3) *Imposition from without.* In this form of collective action, the majority of those involved have no say on whether action should be taken on an issue, or in what direction. There is an individual or body of individuals which has (assumed) the power to impose rules of behaviour on others, and also the power to ensure that they obey those rules. Such bodies range widely in size and scope. Our concern here is with bodies that have the power over large populations. Most are known as states, but they differ from the states described in the previous category in that the constituent members have no guaranteed influence over those who exercise power there; accountability is weak.

The state, and especially the state as defined in the second of these three categories, is the focus of this chapter. Thus appreciation of the nature of the state, and of its necessary role in the capitalist mode of production in particular, is central to the discussion. This requires an initial understanding of why the first of the above categories is not workable in many circumstances, so that a state is necessary to ensure that the required collective action occurs.

## THE LOGIC OF COLLECTIVE ACTION

The basis of the case for a state, or at least some independent body that insists on people taking certain actions, is the work of a number of theorists on the logic of collective action. They argue that people acting separately will not necessarily do that which is in their individual best interests; they need others to impose rules which ensure that they do act consistently with those interests, in ways which are also in the collective best interest. Some suggest that this is not a general conclusion, but it is sufficiently important as an underpinning of the theory of the state to be allocated substantial coverage here.

## THOMAS HOBBES AND *LEVIATHAN*

The classic statement of this position was provided by the seventeenth-century philosopher, Thomas Hobbes, in *Leviathan* (first published in 1651). He argued that we are all concerned with our own survival but that some people's success will be to the detriment of others, because their search for the means of survival could well involve their imposing their power on others. Because all want to survive, all will want to be powerful over others; the result is that everybody is wary of everybody else and everybody feels insecure. To quell this insecurity, everybody then seeks to increase his/her individual power over others, which in turn only heightens the insecurity. In a market society, this power is sought through that mechanism with the results, as Macpherson (1968, p. 38) expresses it, that

> everyone can and does continually compete for power against others. Every man's power resists and hinders other men's search for power, so pervasively that any man's power is simply the excess of his above others' . . . Everyone seeks to transfer some of the powers of other men to himself, or to resist the transfer of some of his to others. And he does not do it by open force but by a market-like operation which sets every man's value at 'so much as would be given for the use of his Power'.

Hobbes's analysis of this continuous search for power over others concluded that it would be destructive, or, as he put it, there would be

> no place for Industry; because the fruit thereof is uncertain: and consequently no Culture of the earth; . . . no Knowledge of the face of the earth; no account of Time; no Arts; no Letters; no Society; and which is worst of all, continuall feare, and danger of violent death: And for the life of man, solitary, poore, nasty, brutish, and short. (Macpherson, 1968, p. 41)

To avoid lives that were 'solitary, poore, nasty, brutish, and short', he argued, individuals should be prepared to give up some of their natural freedoms: 'the right to do or take anything and invade anybody – provided everyone else would do so at the same time' (Macpherson, 1968, p. 43). In other words, people would be prepared to enter an implicit contract with a sovereign power, which would restrain the competition for individual power that was in the end going to destroy that which people were seeking to achieve from it –

high material living standards. They would accept the power that the state exercised, and the sanctions that it applied to those defying its power, because they realised that such obedience was for both their own individual long-term good and for the general good. The nature of that obedience was laid down in 19 'laws of nature', and the state's role was to enforce those laws.

## RATIONAL ACTION AND GAME THEORY

Hobbes's work has been carried forward in recent years by several theorists. Seminal among them is Olson's *The Logic of Collective Action*, which begins with the observation (1965, pp. 1–2) that:

> It is often taken for granted, at least where economic objectives are involved, that groups of individuals with common interests usually attempt to further those common interests . . . But it is *not* in fact true that the idea that groups will act in their self-interest follows logically from the premise of rational and self-interested behavior. It does *not* follow, because all of the individuals in a group would gain if they achieved their group objective, that they would act to achieve that objective, even if they were all rational and self-interested. Indeed, unless the number of individuals in a group is quite small, or unless there is coercion or some other special device to make individuals act in their common interest, *rational, self-interested individuals will not act to achieve their common or group interests.*

Olson hinted that one can deduce from this proposition, as did Hobbes, that a coercive power is needed to ensure that individual and general interests are promoted, and also that rational individuals will accept this power. Rational people should therefore be prepared to enter into a social contract with the state as the coercive power established to further that end.

The validity of Hobbes's and Olson's proposition is frequently illustrated by a simple 'game' in the mathematics of game theory known as the *Prisoner's Dilemma*. Laver (1981, pp. 47–50) gives a clear introduction. Two men suspected of committing a serious crime are apprehended committing a less serious one. The police have no conclusive proof of their guilt in the more serious crime, and so want them to provide it by each implicating each other. They are interviewed separately, and the police do not allow them to meet and confer. The deal that the police offer to each is as follows:

> If you implicate your accomplice in the serious crime, and he is convicted, you will go free; if you do not, you will be convicted of the lesser crime in any case, and will go to jail.

The arrested men know that if both stay silent, both will be convicted of the lesser crime, for which the punishment is one year in jail. They also know that if one implicates the other, the squealer will go free and the convicted man will get ten years for the serious crime. Finally, they estimate that if both squeal, each will get eight years. This produces what is known as a payoff matrix, which indicates the likely consequences from each of the alternative actions for each individual – stay silent or squeal; these combine to produce four possible outcomes.

|  |  | **Prisoner B** | |
|  |  | *Stay silent* | *Squeal* |
| --- | --- | --- | --- |
| **Prisoner A** | *Stay silent* | 1,1 | 10,0 |
|  | *Squeal* | 0,10 | 8,8 |

The numbers in the four cells of this matrix indicate the outcome for each of the suspects, according to their decision whether to stay silent or squeal; the first number indicates the sentence that prisoner A will get, and the second indicates that for prisoner B. Thus, according to the top left hand cell, if both stay silent each will receive one year's imprisonment for the lesser crime. If prisoner A stays silent and prisoner B squeals, however, then, as the top right-hand cell shows, prisoner A will get ten years and prisoner B will go free. Similarly, if A squeals and B keeps silent, A goes free and B gets ten years (bottom left-hand cell). Finally (bottom right), if both squeal both get eight years.

What should they do? They face a dilemma, hence the name of the game. They would be best off collectively if both remain silent, because each then will get one year in prison. But each has to gamble that the other will stay silent too; if he does not, then the one who does keep quiet gets ten years. For each, the best thing to do is to squeal, whatever the other does. Thus if Prisoner A squeals, he will get off free if B stays silent, which is better than getting one year if he (A) stays silent too; if Prisoner B squeals, A will get eight years, which is better that the ten if B squeals and A stays silent. Exactly the same calculations hold for B: whatever A does, B will be better off if he squeals. So both squeal, and both get eight years. If both had stayed silent, both would have got one year, but because they could not trust the other not to squeal they had to take the course that assumed that each would. And so, as Laver (1981, p. 49) puts it,

> both do time for . . . [the more serious crime], despite the fact that both
> would be better off staying silent and simply doing their time for . . . [the
> lesser crime]. The pursuit of individual rationality inevitably leads to an
> outcome which is deplored by both criminals.

What if the police had allowed them to confer; would not they have made a pact to remain silent? Perhaps, but each still might have been uncertain whether the other would break the agreement and go for the police deal (i.e.

squeal). Mutual co-operation would be to their individual benefit, but unless that co-operation was enforced in some way, neither could trust the other to stick to the agreement. Contracts have to be enforced, and neither has any power to ensure that the other complies with their agreement.

The general conclusion drawn from this simple example is that mutual co-operation, which will benefit all of the parties involved, will not be the strategy chosen by people acting individually. It is in their self-interest to co-operate, but the rational pursuit of that self-interest as individuals leads to the decision not to co-operate. Only enforced collective action will lead to the optimum outcome.

That general conclusion has been applied to a wide range of situations, and used both to make the case for the state, thus developing Hobbes's ideas, and to show the limitations of the state. Regarding the former, the Prisoner's Dilemma has been applied to develop an argument for the provision of what are known as public goods – state-supplied goods and services which are made available to all and for which all pay out of their taxes. For example, it may be in the interests of all employers within the territory of a state that every employee be literate; illiterate people cannot do any of the available jobs. Thus the first thing that any employer would have to do is train each new employee in the skills of literacy. But why should an employer take on this cost; why not leave it to other employers to do the training, and then, given the freedom of individuals to sell their labour to whom they wish, offer jobs to people once trained? (Employers might even offer a small premium to them in their wages, which would still cost less than the cost of the training.) As a consequence, no employers would offer literacy training. All want literate employees, but none would be prepared to pay for the training because the others might not. Those who did not pay for training would gain a competitive advantage (their production costs would be cheaper): such individuals, who benefit from the expenditure of others while making no contribution themselves, are known as *free-riders*. All would accept the situation whereby compulsory universal literacy training was provided by the state, however, and all employers would agree to pay a 'fair' contribution for that training through their taxes; alternatively, they could be required by the state to provide the training themselves, rather than pay for public provision. Whichever means is chosen, they would know that, because of the obedience owed to the state, all would be contributing the same: there would be no free-riders, no employers letting others bear the costs but reaping the benefits.

An illustration of the Prisoner's Dilemma showing the limits of the state is Brams's (1975) example of two countries involved in an arms race. The payoff matrix used earlier applies: for 'Prisoner' read 'State' and for 'Keep silent' and 'Squeal' read 'End the arms race' and 'Continue the arms race', respectively. For each state, the best solution is for both to select the 'end the arms race' option, because the ultimate consequence of that path (war) might then be avoided and each would have more resources available to devote to other state activities (or to return to its citizens, through lower taxes). But neither can afford to select that option unless it trusts the other to. Trust is crucial; the countries may enter into a treaty on arms limitation, in the same way that the prisoners might have agreed when they conferred, but how can they be sure that the other party will keep the treaty, since there is no 'superstate' to insist that this is done? Thus, as Brams (1975, p.34) argues, states will be very reluctant to opt out of the arms race; if there is no certainty that an adversary will do the same, then 'the nation that disarms will relinquish control over its fate and thereby suffer its worst outcome'.

Some states do opt out, of course; Switzerland took a neutral stance during both of the world wars and has not joined any military alliances. But to do that means trusting that the neutrality will be observed, which was not the case with every state that adopted such a position in the Second World War. Swiss neutrality was of value to the adversarial powers then, and so was observed; Norway's claimed neutrality was not. Many that opt out do so knowing that their security is protected, or at least guaranteed, by other countries that remain in the arms race. But what about those latter countries; do not they sometimes seek *détente* and indicate a willingness to trust the others to opt out with them? Geopolitical analysis (e.g. Kennedy, 1988; Taylor, 1989a) suggests that such a willingness to negotiate is most likely to occur at times when the adversaries are under fiscal and other stress. In a two-nation arms race, for example, if both are suffering budgetary problems because of the costs, then one may be prepared to respond to the other's overtures with regard to reducing the pace of, if not ending, the arms race. But the problem of trust remains; if, as a consequence, one becomes economically stronger than the other, it can then reinvest in the arms race if it wishes.

The Prisoner's Dilemma has been presented here as a 'two-person game', which oversimplifies the situation in most circumstances. But it can be extended to involve many players, thereby becoming much more complex. The basic message remains the same, however. If anything, it is enhanced; where large numbers of individuals are seeking rational personal outcomes, their inability to be sure that their competitors will not take decisions that are for neither the collective nor their own individual good, and will not involve free-riding, will mean that rational decisions lead to sub-optimal solutions. This is well illustrated by an argument of direct relevance to the study of environmental issues.

## THE TRAGEDY OF THE COMMONS

'The tragedy of the commons' is the title of a classic, though some believe flawed, paper by Garret Hardin (1968), which has been developed by several authors as a paradigm example of the Prisoner's Dilemma (e.g. Taylor, 1976; Laver, 1981 ). Taylor introduces it with the simple example of two users of a water supply, who also pollute it. They could cease pollution, at a cost, but is it in their individual interests to do so? The payoff matrix (expressed in thousands of pounds) is as follows:

|  |  | **User B** | |
|  |  | *Not pollute* | *Polute* |
| --- | --- | --- | --- |
|  | *Not pollute* | 2,3 | 1,4 |
| **User A** |  |  |  |
|  | *Pollute* | 4,1 | 3,2 |

This shows that it is in the interests of each user to pollute, because the returns from doing so exceed those from not doing so, whatever the other does: if B does not pollute, for example, then the return is £4000 if A does, compared to £2000 if A does either; if B pollutes, then the return to A from polluting too is £3000, compared to £1000 if A does not pollute. Thus each user prefers to pollute, whatever the other does. In addition, each prefers the other not to pollute, because there are externalities involved. B's pollution spills over on to A, for example. Thus whereas A's return is always greater when polluting, it is greater when B is not polluting. Thus although pollution may not be desirable, especially in the long term, it is in neither's interest not to pollute, even if it is guaranteed that the other will not: voluntary co-operation does not seem sensible, so if pollution is to be ended it must be an imposed solution.

Hardin's paper generalises the point that Taylor draws from it, for a game involving many players, and also develops a moral message: the paper's subtitle is 'The population problem has no technical solution; it requires a fundamental extension in morality'. His source is an earlier portrayal of the same problem (Lloyd, 1833), and is argued as follows. There is an area of common land, on which herders can graze cattle. Each herder will graze as many cattle as possible. Eventually, the carrying capacity of the common land is reached. This should result in stability, but instead 'the inherent logic of the commons remorselessly generates tragedy' (Hardin, 1968, p.1244), because all herders are seeking to maximise the returns from their cattle. Since the positive returns of an additional animal being added to the commons go to the herder owning the animal, whereas the negative costs are felt by all herders, the result is a net gain to the individual who increases herd size. Assume that when the common land is at its carrying capacity, each animal produces a return of £100. An additional animal gives an average return of only £99, because the amount of grazing to be shared by all the animals is slightly less. The value of each animal declines very slightly as a consequence, because the negative costs of going above the carrying capacity are incurred by all. If herder A adds an animal above the carrying capacity, therefore, increasing her herd size from 20 to 21, the additional income is £99. The loss of income from the reduced value of the other 20 is £20 (i.e. £1 each), so the net outcome is that A's returns increase from £2000 to £2079. It is thus in A's interest to add that twenty-first animal. If the others do not also increase their herd size, they will suffer a loss of income – £1 for every animal owned – as a consequence of the depletion of the grazing resource.

It is thus in every herder's interest to increase herd size, even though this takes the common land above its carrying capacity, means that every animal is worth less, and will stimulate the degradation of the commons. As Hardin (1968, p. 1244) expresses it,

> the rational herdsman concludes that the only sensible course for him to pursue is to add another animal to his herd. And another; and another . . . But this is the conclusion reached by each and every rational herdsman sharing the commons. Therein is the tragedy. Each man is locked into a system that compels him to increase his herd without limit – in a world that is limited. Ruin is the destination toward which all men rush, each pursuing his own best interest in a society that believes in the freedom of the commons. Freedom in the commons brings ruin to all.

Hardin claims that there is much evidence supporting this conclusion, as in the continued depletion of fish stocks, so that 'species after species of fish and whales [are brought] closer to extinction' (p. 1245).

The tragedy of the commons provides Hardin with an example of the general argument that in a finite world individual rational action fails to recognise that finiteness, with tragic consequences for all. (The tragedy of the commons can also be expressed as a Prisoner's Dilemma game, with herder A against the rest, and each herder playing herder A in turn.) Hardin used the 'tragedy' to develop a wider (Malthusian) argument regarding the carrying capacity of the earth itself, that the breeding habits of the human population are exceeding the earth's capacity to sustain the additional numbers, and that if this growth is not controlled the ultimate tragedy will be upon us – genocide. Human history shows, he argues, that, at any period of history, land treated as such in a previous period is no longer treated as a common resource. Initially the land from which food was gathered was treated as a commons, but in most parts of the world it is now enclosed and its use restricted. The commons was also used as a place for waste disposal, but increasingly we are realising the perils of polluting those commons and restricting the previously unconstrained dumping of wastes into the environment. As Hardin (1968, p. 1248) puts it:

> Every new enclosure of the commons involves the infringement of somebody's personal liberty . . . But what does 'freedom' mean? When men mutually agreed to pass laws against robbing, mankind became more free, not less so. Individuals locked into the logic of the commons are free only to bring on universal ruin: once they see the necessity of mutual coercion, they become free to pursue other goals.

This leads him to conclude that just as societies agreed to reduce access to the commons in terms of both food-gathering and pollution, so they will agree to

> the necessity of abandoning the commons in breeding. No technical solution can rescue us from the misery of overpopulation. Freedom to breed will bring ruin to all . . . The only way that we can preserve and nurture other and more precious freedoms is by relinquishing the freedom to breed, and that very soon.

This solution has been recognised by the Indian and Chinese governments in recent years, but the evidence that it is widely accepted by the people there is equivocal; there are many claims that China's 'one-child family' policy is failing. Furthermore, many governments in the periphery of the world economy claim that the pressure for birth control from core states involves the unequal exercise of power: the core states have stimulated the tragedy of the commons, and are now asking the poor states to meet the costs.

How might the tragedy of the commons be avoided, both in specific instances and in the generality of Hardin's final argument on population control, given that 'If everyone would only restrain himself, all would be well; but it takes only one less than everyone to ruin a system of voluntary restraint' (1974, p. 562)? Hardin's answer to the question 'How to legislate temperance?' is a policy of 'Mutual coercion mutually agreed upon'. He equates coercion not with its popular usage as 'arbitrary compulsion imposed by distant, non-accountable decision-makers' but rather as mutual consent to do what may be considered undesirable in itself, because the alternative is much worse (Hardin, 1968, p. 1247):

> we are not required to enjoy it, or even to pretend we enjoy it. Who enjoys taxes? But we accept compulsory taxes because we recognise that voluntary taxes would favor the conscienceless. We institute and (grumblingly) support taxes and other coercive devices to escape the horror of the commons.

In other words, we accept the necessity of a state, which will require us to obey policies framed to avoid the tragedy of the commons, but we do that because we have been convinced of it through rational argument. This means the use of education to promote an ideology that will sustain the environmental commons: 'One of the major tasks of education today is to create such an awareness of the dangers of the commons that people will be able to recognize its many varieties, however disguised' (Hardin, 1974, p. 562).

In his second paper, Hardin (1974) takes the lifeboat metaphor as a key to develop his theme; the lifeboat is unable to support all on board, and so unfortunate decisions have to be taken on who should survive. To him,

'Spaceship Earth' is equivalent to the lifeboat, requiring decisions to be made at that scale. Thus he concludes that

> so long as there is no true world government to control reproduction everywhere it is impossible to survive in dignity . . . Without a world government that is sovereign in reproduction matters mankind lives, in fact, on a number of sovereign lifeboats. (1974, p. 568)

This raises a major problem with regard to environmental policies, to which we return later in this chapter.

## IS A STATE NEEDED?

The conclusion to be drawn from the argument so far in this chapter is that a coercive sovereign institution (a state) is necessary to ensure the future of the natural environment; without it, people, acting rationally in what seems to be in their own best interests, will put such pressures on the environment that its quality will be degraded. But is this necessarily so?

In a book on rational ecology, Dryzek (1987) identifies nine different ways of co-ordinating human societies, each of which can be applied to environmental use. He evaluates each according to five criteria: (a) negative feedback, defined as returning to a desired status quo in the case of changes, as with the action of a thermostat; (b) co-ordination across all parts of the ecosystem, so that solution of a problem in one place does not merely transfer it to another; (c) robustness and (d) flexibility, to cope with the (perhaps unexpected) spatial and temporal variability in ecological circumstances (robustness and flexibility are substitutable, according to Dryzek); and (e) resilience, so that if there is a major shift in environmental circumstances, the system can be steered back to its initial operating range. His evaluations of the nine are as follows.

(1) *Through the operation of markets, and the use of prices.* These are characterised by consumer sovereignty and the unconstrained pursuit of self-interest, producing the results so starkly laid out by Hardin. As Dryzek (1987, p. 86) concludes: 'Private enterprise, consumer sovereignty markets may have their good points, but . . . ecological rationality is not one of them'. People will not as a rule willingly pay for environmental protection measures which threaten their potential profits.

(2) *Through commands issued from an administration.* These may be satisfactory for dealing with 'familiar, routine and static problems' (1987, p. 108) and are well suited for the rapid mobilisation of resources to meet an immediate problem within those categories, but 'Highly structured

organizations are at a loss . . . when it comes to dealing with high degrees of uncertainty, variability, and complexity'.

(3) *Through a set of formal rules (laws), to which all adhere.* Laws can be robust, and can co-ordinate, thereby meeting two of the criteria. But robustness may be at the expense of flexibility, so that laws cannot perform well under the other criteria.

(4) *By the promulgation of desirable values, through moral persuasion.* Dryzek finds this procedure wanting in practice and unlikely to succeed in theory, again because success on some of the criteria is likely to lead to failure on others (substantial flexibility makes co-ordination difficult, for example).

(5) *Through what he calls 'partisan mutual adjustment' via a mechanism of 'polyarchy'.* The latter term is used as a synonym for what most term 'democracy' in which collective choices are made by the majority view of a large number of actors with competing interests to promote. Dryzek has more faith in such a system than in either markets or administrations, because its negative feedback and co-ordination devices are superior, but the polyarchies that exist are, he claims, 'far better at responding to signals from General Motors or the *Daily Mirror* than to messages from ecosystems' (1987, p. 131), because of their association with market economies. (Sen, 1981, argues that famines very rarely occur in poor countries which are democratically governed, such as Botswana, but are characteristic of non-democratic countries, such as Ethiopia.)

(6) *Through formal negotiation, with co-ordination achieved via bargaining.* But this mode fails on the other criteria, for reasons stressed by the game theory arguments; what sanctions require people to stick to bargains?

(7) *Through force.* War might be an efficient way of achieving negative feedback, as Malthus suggested, but could it produce global co-ordination, and would it not call forth a large administration, with all the problems thereof? (Furthermore, the idea of war as a way of solving environmental problems appears to be contradictory, given the ecological impact of some recent wars, such as Vietnam in the 1960s.)

(8) *Through radical decentralisation, or the promotion of anarchy,* with societies lacking formal administrative structures. This is the argument developed in Schumacher's influential book *Small is Beautiful* (1973); if societies are locally self-reliant, they will need to develop closer harmony with their environments than is the case with modern global society, and thus promote ways of living that meet the criteria of negative feedback, flexibility, resilience and co-ordination (the last through co-operation, to the mutual benefit of all). But Dryzek finds that such anarchic solutions fail on the robustness criterion; in the face of states with strong repressive apparatus, anarchic societies are doomed to failure, so unless there can be a global revolution, the solution will not work. Others argue against the 'small is beautiful' case: Beckerman (1995) claims that 'small is stupid'.

(9) *Through discussion and practical reason,* which would take place in an open society where interest groups are unable to structure the decision-making agenda and deny people full, unbiased access to relevant knowledge. An open society is an emancipated one, in which people have control of their own destinies, but alone, Dryzek feels, it will not lead to the solution of environmental problems, in part because it will be pragmatic in its approach to problems and will therefore lack co-ordination. However, an open society with its problem-solving mechanisms is attractive if practical reason is introduced, because this will lead to agreement on common interests, purposes and values. Once that has been achieved, the solution of problems can be set within a firm framework; if that framework promotes ecological values, then small-scale, open societies may ensure equilibrium between human societies and their environments.

Dryzek provides an agenda for tackling the problems of surviving within and sustaining the earth's physical environment in which the 'most prominent items are decentralization in the form of substantial local autonomy and self-sufficiency, open and discursive "communicatively rationalized" social choice, and (perhaps) limited bargaining'. Clearly, achievement of the items on this agenda will involve major shifts in both the organisation of production, distribution and exchange and the nature of political institutions. Such may be attainable long-term goals. In the meantime, however, we face the problems of living in societies characterised by markets, administrations, laws, polyarchies, bargaining, and some use of force. The argument so far in this book has been that market operations lead to environmental degradation, but states might prevent that. In the absence of any alternatives, we must then turn again to a consideration of the state.

## ALTERNATIVE GAMES

Might not people adopt the practices that Hardin says are necessary of their own free will; might they not act altruistically, because in the end that is in their self-interest too? This issue is faced by Taylor (1976), who argues that such behaviour might be forthcoming in certain circumstances. Laver (1981, p. 50) describes those circumstances in the following way. Assume not one game of the Prisoner's Dilemma but a sequence of several, involving the same participants, as in the arms race. Each player may take the following position: 'I'll start off by co-operating. Thereafter, I'll do whatever you did in the previous game. If you co-operated, I'll co-operate; if you damaged me, I'll damage you.' In this situation, if you choose a damaging strategy you become worse off. If your adversary declines to increase arms in a given period, but you do invest, then in the next period the adversary will do too, and you will need to respond; you are both damaged in the long term, even though you individually may have gained a short-term advantage. But if you do not invest either, a status quo is maintained: as Laver (1981, p. 51) says: 'If none are armed, or if all are armed, there is a stand-off. Clearly an unarmed stand-off is preferable to an armed stand-off, since it is cheaper'.

People might therefore be prepared to enter into agreements not to increase stock on the commons beyond the proven carrying capacity, for example, not to breed beyond a certain level, or not to pollute a water supply. But, Laver goes on to argue, Taylor's analyses suggest that such co-operative strategies are only likely to emerge when the number of individuals involved is small; the larger the group, the greater the probability of a 'wildcat' defection and the greater the problems of monitoring adherence. (Examples of small-scale successful agreements are given in Ostrom, 1990. See also Ostrom, 1995; Snidal, 1995; Young, 1995.) Further, the individuals involved must perceive that the immediate benefits to be gained from defection are small relative to the long-term gains of continuing to adhere to the agreement. The more 'future-oriented' people are, the greater their likely commitment to the bargain. But how 'future-oriented' are people with regard to environmental issues, especially when their decisions to limit profits may affect not only immediate returns but also long-term survival (in a competitive market, not in an ecological sense)?

In an arms race, of course, one defector out of a small number of countries involved in an agreement to limit investment on weapons would almost certainly be sufficient to lead others to abrogate the treaty. But in the sorts of situations illustrated by the tragedy of the commons, the defection of a few out of a very large number might not be fatal – assuming that the few were not extremely strong relative to all others. Thus if 1000 herders had access to the commons, and all had approximately the same number of animals, if one or two increased their herds slightly and the carrying capacity was breached (we assume that this is known) the degradation would probably not be very severe. A few free-riders can be accommodated, just as the London Underground does not become non-viable if a few fare-dodgers succeed; the problem is how to ensure that there are only a few!

Before turning to a fuller discussion of the nature of the state, we need to look at two other games that Taylor (1988, p. 10) has introduced. Both, he points out, involve the existence of a privileged sub-group within the group under study, such that there is 'at least one subgroup whose members collectively find it worthwhile to provide some amount of the public good by themselves.' If the public good is action either to solve or to avoid environmental problems, then these games suggest that individuals will act without the sort of coercion that a state would impose, through self-interest and not altruism.

Taylor's presentation of these games involves classifying the individuals involved into two groups, those who co-operate (C in the payoff matrices) and contribute to the costs of environmental programmes, and those who defect (D) and fail to contribute. The first game they are involved in is

Chicken (whose name is taken from the 'real' games, played by both children and adults) in which the payoff matrix is:

|               |   | Individual 2 | |
|               |   | C | D |
| --- | --- | --- | --- |
| Individual 1  | C | 3,3 | 2,4 |
|               | D | 4,2 | 1,1 |

Each individual gets a greater return from co-operating than not, irrespective of what the other person does; individual 2, for example, gets a return of 3 units from contributing towards the costs of the environmental programme (i.e. option C) if individual 1 contributes also, which is better than a return of 2 units if individual 1 defects.

To illustrate the relevance of Chicken, Taylor gives two examples. In the first, there are two neighbouring cultivators whose cropping activities depend on the maintenance of drainage ditches which divide their properties. Either can do all of the work, but would prefer to share it with the other; the consequences of neither doing it are so dire, however – involving the almost complete loss of the crops (the D,D option in the payoff matrix) – that one would do it even if the other did not. Thus both will contribute, without being forced to – although it could be argued that one might gamble on the other doing it and decide to free-ride. The latter involves what Ward (1987, p. 23) identifies as a reputation for toughness,

> a reputation for sticking to commitments not to co-operate . . . Tough players are often able to force the other player to bear the costs of providing some public good all by himself and are therefore themselves able to enjoy the benefits of free-riding upon his actions.

If toughness worked, then clearly some coercion would be needed to ensure that the free-rider met a fair share of the costs; Ward concludes that a toughness strategy will work in certain circumstances only, however. (For another example, see Dufournaud and Harrington, 1989.)

Taylor's other example involves two factories which emit polluting wastes into a lake. If only one pollutes, the lake survives, but if both do, a critical threshold is crossed and the lake 'dies'. Each factory-owner can either co-operate by not polluting or defect by polluting. Each would prefer to defect, and free-ride on the other, but the potential catastrophe if both defected is such that each will unilaterally decide to co-operate. This is an example of what Taylor calls a 'lumpy good', in which there is a discontinuous relationship between the amount of pollution and the consequence (as suggested by bifurcation theory – p. 36). Again, however, it is possible for one individual in the game to 'act tough', and gamble on the other not doing so, a situation that led, according to the Taylor and Ward (1982), to the virtual extinction of certain species of whale (though note that Taylor and Ward suggest that the experience with the commercial extinction of the blue whale because of 'toughness' by both Japan and the USSR was a learning experience which ensured that a similar fate did not befall other species). Where the Chicken situation occurs, Taylor and Ward are more optimistic that at least some of the individuals involved (in a game of $n$ players) will co-operate than is so where the Prisoner's Dilemma is operative: 'the only convincing possibility under which none of the public good will be provided in Chicken games is that of risk-loving players pre-committing themselves simultaneously to non-cooperation' (1982 p. 370).

But this is not to say that all of the costs of the needed environmental programmes will be met. Further, it is often in people's short-term interests to adopt non-co-operative strategies, not just to free-ride on others but also, in the ideology of the technocratic fix that underpins much of capitalism, to assume that if one resource is exhausted another will be found ('invented') to replace it.

The other game introduced by Taylor (1988) is *Assurance*, which has two payoff matrices for separate situations. In the first (case I), neither of the players can provide the public good alone, perhaps because it is too expensive; in the second (case II), either can provide some of the public good, giving benefits to each, but the one who does co-operate and make a contribution receives less in return than the costs. In both cases, if neither contributes, there is no benefit at all. The two payoff matrices are:

| Case I | | 2 | | | Case II | | 2 | |
|---|---|---|---|---|---|---|---|---|
| | | C | D | | | | C | D |
| 1 | C | 2,2 | -2,0 | | 1 | C | 2,2 | -1,1 |
| | D | 0,-2 | 0,0 | | | D | 1,-1 | 0,0 |

In both cases, the cost of contributing to the public good is 2 units and the benefits are 4 units, so that the total net gain available is 2 units. In case I, if both contribute, both make the maximum net gain; if only one contributes, that person loses 2 units of investment, and neither has any gain. Thus for any gain at all, co-operation is essential. But people will only co-operate if they perceive the benefits, implying that all must perceive the public good as desirable. If some do not, then they have no stimulus to contribute, and will only do so if coerced, presumably by a state which has accepted the arguments of those who favour the public good. Taylor's example of case II involves two individuals sharing a vegetable patch; one person cannot control the weeds entirely, but enables some crops to be grown by both, so the return from only one person weeding is just one unit. Thus if one person weeds but the other does not, the former suffers a net loss and the other a net gain. The implication would seem to be toughness again, and a free-riding benefit. But for both players there is a better return from co-operating, whatever the other does, than from not doing so, which suggests that each should undertake weeding, to their mutual benefit.

Although in some situations it seems that individual and collective goals coincide, so that people will co-operate in the provision of public goods which include those that sustain the environment, nevertheless in many cases this may not eventuate, at least initially. After a period of learning people might come to appreciate the benefits to be gained from voluntary co-operation (although Ward, 1989, concludes that to obtain the needed reassurance that others will co-operate individuals may have to take risks), but during that period the environment may be irrevocably degraded (as with the extinction of the blue whale). The conclusion must therefore be that, in environmental issues involving a complex, interacting set of global systems, individual action will not prevent the problems of resource deterioration from emerging, and that whatever the attractions of Dryzek's agenda its achievement in the foreseeable future is unlikely. Thus, following Hardin, a state appears to be a necessity.

## UNDERSTANDING THE STATE

The state is a universal phenomenon of the contemporary world, which suggests that neither the capitalist nor the advanced communist/socialist mode of production could operate without one. Why is this so? And why is it that the modern state is so large and apparently all-powerful, implicating itself throughout the daily lives of people, in the spheres of both production and consumption? Such questions have increasingly concerned social scientists, leading to a substantial number of examinations of the nature and function of the state (e.g. Alford and Friedland, 1985; Dunleavy and O'Leary, 1987). The following section draws on those sources to develop an appreciation of the role of the state, particularly in capitalist society, which is necessary to later attempts at understanding how it might operate to resolve environmental problems.

At the outset, it is necessary to be clear what is meant by the state. Dunleavy and O'Leary (1987, p. 2) give the following comprehensive definition, identifying the state by five characteristics.

(1) The state is a recognizably separate institution or set of institutions, so differentiated from the rest of its society as to create identifiably distinct public (i.e. state) and private spheres.
(2) The state is sovereign, or the supreme power, within its territory, and by definition the ultimate authority for all law, i.e. binding rules supported by coercive sanctions. Public law is made within the state apparatus and backed by a formal monopoly of force.
(3) The state's sovereignty extends over all individuals within its given territory, and applies equally, even to those in formal positions of government or rule-making. Thus sovereignty is distinct from the personnel who occupy a particular role within the state at any given time.
(4) The modern state's personnel are mostly recruited and trained for management in a bureaucratic manner.
(5) The state has the capacity to extract monetary revenues (taxation) to finance its activities from its subject population.

These five characteristics make it clear that the state's sovereignty is territorially defined. What they fail to stress is that the state is necessarily a territorial body, that it could not operate if it were not, and that its territoriality is part of its power base (Mann, 1984).

Dunleavy and O'Leary's definition of the state clarifies what it is, but not why. States perform many functions, not all of them in the same way – just as there are different ways of seeking to make profits in the sphere of production and of organising civil society, so there are different ways of doing what the state has to do, and the state may do other things that it does not have to do. Clark and Dear (1984, p. 43; following O'Connor, 1972) collapse the many activities of the capitalist state into three basic operational objectives:

(1) to secure social consensus by guaranteeing acceptance of the prevailing 'contract' by all groups in society;
(2) to secure the conditions of production by regulating (a) social investment to increase production in the public and private sectors, and (b) social consumption to ensure the reproduction of the labour force; and
(3) to secure social integration by ensuring the welfare of all groups, but especially the subordinate classes.

These are placed in a clear priority order. Unless stability can be maintained, by whatever methods, those operating the state will almost certainly be relatively unsuccessful at the other two objectives.

States differ one from another, and individual states vary in their characteristics over time. This is because the state is not a pre-given in society, there at the outset. Nor is there any particular form of state which is necessary to achieve the general objectives set. Individual states have developed through conflict and accommodation, as various interest groups have contested for power within society (Painter, 1995); such contests continue, and states change accordingly. Thus the capitalist mode of production needs states or similar institutions if it is to survive, but within that constraint particular states may vary widely in their detailed composition and means of acting; they have to meet the three objectives, but are given no directions on how that must be done!

## THE STATE AND THE SPHERE OF PRODUCTION

Capitalist society is founded on the creation of saleable commodities, from which profits can be realised. Both the creation of the commodities and their sale for profit involve market-place transactions. Why does the state need to be implicated?

Part of the answer to this question is provided by the Prisoner's Dilemma analogy. Buying and selling in market systems involves taking things on trust. Individuals agree to sell their labour against a contract that they will receive a wage at the end of a given period of work, usually a week or a month. Manufacturers buy a machine from another manufacturer against a contract of sale which guarantees that the machine will be able to do certain tasks, if properly used, and should last a certain (usually only vaguely specified) time. But what if these undertakings are not met, if the labourers' wages are not paid, or the machines fail to perform satisfactorily? What recourse do the injured parties have if contracts are not honoured? The honouring of contracts is one of the nineteen 'Laws of Nature' identified by Hobbes in *Leviathan* – 'That men performe their Covenants made' (Hobbes, 1968, p. 201). But, in his terms, it needs a Leviathan to ensure that they do. If there is no available recourse to redress from broken contracts, then it may not be in the interests of people who enter them to keep them. They may suffer in the long term – a manufacturer whose machines fail to satisfy may get no further custom from the dissatisfied customer, who in turn may encourage others not to purchase from the same source – but the short-term benefits of not providing what was agreed may outweigh those other considerations. With the contract for labour, the sanctions within the market-place may be less severe, especially if the supply of labour exceeds the demand, so that it is a buyers' market; failing to meet the terms of one contract is then unlikely to prevent others coming forward to sign new agreements (as illustrated by firms which break strikes by sacking all of their employees and taking on new, non-unionised, labour).

One way to try and counter the failure to honour contracts is for those affected to act collectively. In the case of the machinery sales, for example, if all manufacturers of a certain product joined together in an organisation and agreed to co-operate on issues of mutual interest, the experience of one of their members might lead them to initiate a collective boycott of a machine manufacturer who failed to meet the specifications set out in a contract of sale. But individual manufacturers may decide not to join, and even having joined may decide not to participate in the boycott, because it is not in their interest so to do (they might get preferential treatment from the machine seller). With regard to the labour example, the individuals concerned could combine in a trade union and bargain for collective rights; employers might then be more bound to honour contracts entered with a stronger bargaining body than a single individual, but there may be those prepared to work outside those bargains. In both cases, the groupings are voluntary (although compulsory union membership has characterised some capitalist countries – such as New Zealand – at certain times), and there is still no requirement for the contract to be honoured.

The honouring of contracts can only be achieved if the alternative to not doing so is a substantial enough punishment that it is not attractive to break them. (For example, newspaper editors may implicitly enter a contract not to libel individuals, because the law requires them not to. But they may be prepared to break that law, and commit a libel, because the costs of so doing – the redress they are required to make to the injured party – are less than the additional income obtained from selling the libel through their papers' increased circulation.) There must be an institution which can create rules of contract compliance that hold for all contracts entered into within the territory where that law holds; it must also have the power to hear cases against accused malefactors and impose punishments if the accusations are found to be valid. That institution, with sovereign power over the population of a defined territory, is the state.

This example of contract compliance is but one of a very large number of issues which relate to the successful operation of a market economy. More generally, that market economy needs an infrastructure within which it can operate. In part, that will be a physical infrastructure – markets cannot function unless there is a transport system, though it is not a necessity that the transport network be state-provided. In part, it will be an abstract, facilitating infrastructure. Transactions in a market economy are almost all negotiated in a common currency and in a common set of weights and measures, for example. People signing contracts which involve payment at a future date want an assurance not only that they will be paid on the due date but that the value of what they are paid will not be less than they expect in real terms (i.e. in the purchasing power of the currency). Thus stability of the currency is highly desirable (as is stability of one currency relative to others for international trade), and ensuring this is a major task for the state; as in many capitalist countries in recent years, the British state has placed control of the rate of inflation (the rate by which money loses its value) very high in its priorities, in order to facilitate profit-making. People, it is argued, are much less prepared to invest in a capitalist venture which will be profitable at some date in the future, if the size of that profit is uncertain. An as-far-as-possible inflation-free future is thus a requirement for successful attempts at wealth accumulation, and if such investments are not forthcoming the health of the population involved is jeopardised, as eventually is their potential for survival.

The provision of this facilitating infrastructure is an example of what is widely known as the provision of *public goods* by the state. Their need is often stimulated by 'market failure', whereby private producers fail to provide for themselves that which they need. In some cases they could not provide it. It would be impossible, for example, for individuals to provide themselves with the security that a modern national defence system gives, yet without that security they may not be prepared to make a long-term speculative investment in a territory; similarly, it would almost certainly be unworkable for many different currencies to be circulating in a country. In other cases, it might be possible for the private sector to provide the needed good or service, but for some reason (usually related to profitability) it fails to do so, even though it needs it. The earlier example of the provision of literacy training illustrates this; all employers want literate workers but none is prepared to pay for the training voluntarily, for fear that competitors may steal a march on them by free-riding. But if all are compelled to meet the costs of the training, then they are content. And so the state is an acceptable body to ensure that the market failures are rectified, by requiring all to meet the necessary costs.

The longer-term problems of the capitalist mode of production are linked to its in-built crisis tendencies associated with overproduction and underconsumption. Such crises affect not only those who suffer directly, such as the manufacturers of goods for which the market is no longer expanding, but also indirectly all others in society, through the multiplier processes; fewer people have money to spend, less goods are consumed, smaller profits are obtained, investment is reduced, and so on. It is in no one's interest for this to happen, and yet it is within no one's grasp to prevent it. Prevention might be achieved collectively, however, via the sovereign power of the state. For example, the profitability of certain groups of manufacturers might be enhanced if they could gain access to cheaper sources of raw materials. The state can assist this by subsidising their search for such sources; examples include the monopoly that the British government gave organisations such as the East India Company and the Hudson's Bay Company over trade in certain parts of the world, monopolies that were backed by the state's domination of the use of armed force, and, even more so, the colonisation of areas to ensure uninterrupted access. This involved the state in the creation of the core–periphery structure of the world. Alternatively, the state might assist in a restructuring of the economy, by helping investors to write off redundant stock and fixed capital while investing in research which might lead to the invention of marketable new products. Or the state might become a large-scale purchaser – as happened at the end of the 1930s when many states invested heavily in rearmament programmes and stimulated demand in their economies.

This imperative stretches beyond the regulation of what Clark and Dear term 'social investment' in the sphere of production to the sphere of civil society, involving what they call 'social consumption' expenditure to ensure the reproduction of the labour force. Labour is a necessity, and so it must be reproduced. This requires shelter. The provision of housing can be undertaken through the market, with people investing in home construction, either to sell or to rent. If they are to be sold, then there must be buyers with either substantial sums of money available for the purchase of an expensive product with a long life expectancy (including the land on which it is built, which has an infinite life expectancy, and is in fixed supply) or the ability to borrow the money needed to finance such a purchase. If neither is available, the homes for purchase may not be built. With regard to homes for rent, the returns on the investment come slowly, over the long life of the building; alternative investments may generate quicker profits, and mean that houses are not built. This is yet a further example of market failure to provide a necessity – homes for the needed workers. The state may then be called upon to remedy the failure, either by creating the conditions that will encourage the provision of housing – subsidising its construction, perhaps, or subsidising the purchase and/or rental in some way – or by providing the housing itself.

Employers want healthy workers, because they are more productive. They may be able to obtain a continuous supply, because of an excess of labour available over that demanded, in which case they may be prepared to do little about their employees' health and may discard them when their productivity declines. But if that strategy is not available, they may have to spend on keeping their workers healthy. As with the training example quoted earlier, they may not be willing to do this unless required to, which involves the state in either enforcing health expenditure by employers or ensuring a health service for all, so that potential as well as actual workers are healthy. Similarly, state activity may be the only way of ensuring that the products on offer are safe for the population to consume, hence the legislation of minimum standards for the preparation of foodstuffs, for example. The state must ensure there is investment in civil society as well as in the sphere of production. If it demonstrably fails to meet these needs, it faces a potential crisis which may lead either to replacement of those currently operating the state apparatus or to its replacement by a new state apparatus, usually after conflict (as in *coups d'état*).

## THE STATE AND SOCIAL INTEGRATION

As well as the in-built tendencies to crisis inherent in capitalism because of the problems of overproduction and underconsumption, there are further problems caused by antagonisms between the buyers and sellers of labour –

what Marx terms the class conflict. Each category is dependent on the other: if they cannot hire satisfactory labour, employers cannot produce commodities and so realise profits that can be translated into wealth; if they cannot find employers to purchase their labour power, potential employees cannot obtain the income with which to purchase the means of reproduction and survival. This interdependence means that in the long term the two parties must reach agreements, otherwise all will lose. But in the antagonisms that precede such accommodations, the employers invariably have the greatest power. Those selling their labour have little to fall back on if they are out of work, and any savings they might have are rapidly depleted; the stock of wealth held by most employers means that they are better able to weather periods without income, and so can hold out longer (in a strike, for example). Or they can reinvest that wealth elsewhere, and obtain surplus from putting other people's labour to work; capital is more readily switched than labour in many circumstances.

The nature of this unequal relationship between the two categories means that the employed group are potentially hostile towards the capitalist mode of production, and hence could be mobilised to support political and other programmes designed to bring about its downfall. Capitalism can be presented to them as an exploitative system in which, although their absolute living standards may rise in certain circumstances of high productivity and buoyant markets, their position is always relatively insecure. To counter that potential mobilisation, and its threat to the social order of capitalism, the state is called upon to legitimate the mode of production, and win the grudging support of those who ostensibly stand to gain least from it. This can be done in a variety of ways, many of which are associated with what is popularly known as the 'welfare state'.

This legitimation function involves the state acting to protect the interests of members of the employee category, therefore, basically by guaranteeing them a minimum level of welfare below which no individual and family will be allowed to fall. In particular, welfare programmes are designed to give assistance to those who have fallen on hard times through no fault of their own. In Britain, for example, programmes of unemployment and supplementary benefit are used to provide subsistence-level incomes for those unable to obtain work, and a range of other benefits is provided for those whose earned incomes are lower than a prescribed level deemed necessary for basic subsistence; special attention is paid to those who either cannot earn themselves but are dependent on others, such as children, or may have nobody on whom to depend, such as childless old people.

Alongside those aspects of the welfare state that are provided to protect the weak in periods of hardship, but may be so structured to ensure that people do not become dependent on them and lose the incentive to work, there are other aspects designed to assist all people in the search for better life chances. The public education service is a good example of this. Most capitalist societies have a strong meritocratic ideology, which argues that success comes to those who earn it and is equally available to all with the right qualities and attitudes. In a meritocracy, potential ability to succeed in a wide range of occupations is associated with educational attainments; the better educated are those fitted for the more demanding, and thus better-paid, jobs. Thus if access to the relevant education is equally available to all, then all are being given equal chances to compete and succeed in the meritocratic rat race. A public education system is thus promoted among the population as being provided by the state for all irrespective of background, class or place; it is part of the legitimation function, since it allows the state to present itself as the champion of the relatively underprivileged. A public health service can be similarly presented as in the interests of all.

Payment for these public services comes from the state's exchequer, which obtains its income from taxation. To the extent that the taxation system is progressive – the higher people's earnings, and the greater their wealth, the greater their tax contribution – the rich pay more. To the extent that the benefits of the public systems are provided either equally to all or biased towards those in greatest need, the poor receive more. Thus the welfare state can be justified as redistributive from the rich to the poor, thereby once again presenting the state as the champion of the relatively underprivileged in capitalist society.

Acceptance of this role for the state involves the poor seeing the state as their protector; while it does that, and they are relatively satisfied with the outcome, they are prepared to accept the mode of production, or at least not to question and challenge a system that produces wealth by exploiting them and continually demanding greater productivity from those who have work. The more affluent, who are in most cases either employers or managers whose incomes come from ensuring that capitalist enterprises operate successfully, accept that they pay a higher proportion of the costs of the welfare state, in order to achieve the needed quiescence; they may question the level and range of welfare spending, but not the principle on which it is based. If the state fails to convince people that it is acting in their interests, however, then it faces a legitimation crisis.

There is something of an apparent contradiction between the two roles of the state discussed so far – the promotion of accumulation and the legitimation of the mode of production. Expenditure on the latter comes to a considerable degree from what would otherwise be profits. But those who would receive those profits are convinced that it is sensible to have the welfare state, for two reasons. First, it is in their interests to have a quiescent labour force which accepts the nature of capitalism and is prepared to work within it, particularly when its costs are being met by everybody. Secondly, many of the aspects of the welfare state are public goods which it is necessary for the state to provide because of market failure. The public education system is a good example of this; as well as being a part of the state's legitimating role, it subsidises the training of skilled employees for the capitalist enterprises. Thus employers may question the level of expenditure, and perhaps the detail of how it is used (they may not, for example, like the teaching of social sciences that call the legitimacy of capitalism into question), but they will not challenge the provision in principle, because they benefit from it too. (Increasingly, however, states are calling into question the provision of free higher education, arguing that those who benefit from it, and obtain higher incomes than the average as a consequence, should pay at least some of the costs themselves.)

## SECURING SOCIAL CONSENSUS

The education system plays a part in the third state function, too, since it is involved in state activity designed to ensure social consensus. In order to operate successfully, a society must be orderly, stable and secure. To achieve those ends, all members must accept a set of laws and rules within which they will act. They must submit to a rule of law, a system for arbitrating between opposing claims and making decisions, including determining punishments that will be accepted; and they must be prepared to serve, if called upon, to defend that system and its members from outside aggressors.

Part of this function thus involves establishing a set of laws and a legal system, a policing system, and a defence force, to provide the needed order, stability and security. The laws, for example, will define the nature of property ownership, what individuals can own, what they can and cannot do with their property, and under what circumstances they can be required to yield part or all of their property to others, including to the state. Those legal, police, defence and security systems must enjoy the support of the population (or at least not be challenged by them) in order that they can operate, and it is a function of the state to ensure that such support is forthcoming. This is best achieved by obtaining acceptance of the systems by people during their most formative years of socialisation – their childhood and early adult years. This can be done in two, linked ways. First, the state-provided or state-sponsored education system can be used to promote an ideology that is entirely supportive of the systems, presenting them in a positive light as operating in everybody's individual and collective good and ensuring that people accept the disciplines of obeying the legally given orders of the various components of the state apparatus. Secondly, this socialisation can be bolstered by ensuring that it is backed up in people's homes, where many of the disciplines have to be put into operation, and in the various media (popular and otherwise) which circulate within the state.

Failure to perform these various functions satisfactorily can stimulate crises of the state, as argued by O'Connor (1972). If operations in the sphere of production are unsatisfactory, with poor profit levels and low investment, the state may face a rationality crisis; capital will be moved either to other uses or to other places, with significant consequences for the quality of people's lives within the state's territory. And if it fails in the sphere of social integration, so that people feel that the state is not meeting their needs, then a legitimation crisis may follow, generating social disorder which in turn threatens the stability of investments by the creators of wealth and jobs. Thus those operating the state face a continual series of decisions regarding which group to favour by which policies – straying too far in either direction can risk a backlash from the disadvantaged group. Either a rationality crisis or a legitimacy crisis may always be looming, therefore: what the state has to avoid is a combination of the two – creating an accumulation crisis – which threatens revolution and a recomposition of the fabric of the state.

## WHY THE STATE?

Why is it the state that undertakes these tasks, rather than some other body that is independent of neither the sphere of production nor civil society? Many of the things that the state does would not be accepted by at least some of the individuals affected if they thought the state were acting for particular interest groups only. Thus, for example, if the state were part of civil society and dominated by members of the employee class, the latter might accept its activities but the members of the employer fraction, whose wealth is derived from success in the sphere of production, might not; the latter might feel that the state is biased towards one group only and might either direct their investment elsewhere or seek to take the state over themselves. On the other hand, if the state were dominated by members of the employer class, then its attempts to legitimate the mode of production for the members of the other fraction could be seen as presenting one group's interests only; the employee class, in turn, would be less prepared to accept the rule of law that the state represents.

The state must be presented as objectively neutral with respect to the interests of any groups within the population, therefore, and instead seen as working in the interests of all. If it is explicitly 'owned' by one section of the population, its legitimacy is open to resistance and challenge – as occurred in South Africa during the decades of apartheid. Further, the state must be seen as independent of those in positions of power within it. In democratic states these comprise two groups of people. The first are those employed to run the state, to operate its laws but not to enact them. Often known as the 'bureaucracy', they are engaged, as Dunleavy and O'Leary's definition of the state makes clear, for their managerial capabilities and are accountable to the other group of powerful members of the state, and hence to the population at large. They should not be seen as promoting the interests of certain groups over others, but merely as administering the state efficiently. The second group are the politicians, those elected by the population at large to define the parameters within which the state will be run, and to be answerable to the electorate for that definition and its perceived successes and failures. Thus the state in such circumstances does not 'belong' to either group; it 'belongs' to the whole population, who determine collectively how it will conduct itself and fulfil the tasks that are set (usually only implicitly) for it.

This independence of the state is seen by some as a charade, for a variety of reasons. Some argue, for example, that the employer and managerial classes clearly do dominate the state, and even if they do not 'own' it their power is so disproportionate that they in effect have complete control, with the electoral process no more than window-dressing and the meritocracy so manipulated that the ideology of equality of opportunity is really a myth. (On this, see Dunleavy and O'Leary, 1987, Chapter 4.) More fundamentally, others argue that since capitalism is an unequal, exploitative mode of production, structured to advance the interests of the wealthy few to the (relative) detriment of the majority, then if the state is promoting capitalism it is necessarily promoting the interests of the few over the rest. To them, the only way to alter that situation is to capture the state and, through a socialist programme, change the mode of production so that there is no class division and all are indeed treated equally.

## THE LIMITS TO THE STATE

As stressed in the earlier discussions of the spheres of production and civil society, capitalism is not a determinate mode of production in which a certain behaviour pattern is required in order to promote the underlying dynamo, the accumulation of wealth. The driving forces can be taken forward in many ways. In the sphere of production, for example, there are many options open to those who make investment decisions – what type of commodity production to invest in, how to organise the production, and where to make and to market the product. In civil society, similarly, there are many options available for the conduct of life away from the workplace. And the same is true of the state. A state is necessary to capitalism, and it must play the three roles discussed above. But how those roles should be played and how the script should be interpreted is a matter for the personnel who run the state and, to the extent that they are accountable to an electorate, for the population at large.

The degrees of freedom of the state personnel extend beyond the necessary roles of the state as defined here. Those roles must be played, and the state must ensure the health of the mode of production within its territory. But its actions are not confined to those roles alone, and if the personnel involved wish to take on additional roles then they can, as long as playing them is acceptable to those to whom they are accountable and does not significantly impede the necessary activity. Thus those in charge of the state may bring to that task certain imperatives that they wish to carry through other than their economic-political functions, or they may be convinced by others that certain additional roles are desirable and would be widely supported – many of the agenda items of the so-called 'New Right' in the 1980s and 1990s (such as anti-abortion laws) exemplify this freedom.

What other roles might the state personnel adopt? In a major essay on the nature of power in society, Mann (1986, pp.2–3) suggested that organisational power, 'the capacity to organize and control people, materials, and territories', can be categorised in two ways, according to its use. He distinguishes first between *extensive* power, which is 'the ability to organize large numbers of people over far-flung territories in order to engage in minimally stable co-operation', and *intensive* power, which is the 'ability to organize tightly and command a high level of mobilization or commitment from the participants' (1986, p.7). Secondly, he distinguishes between *authoritative* power, which involves obedience to commands emanating from the state elite, and *diffused* power, which is spread though a population without necessarily any commands but rather 'an understanding that these practices are natural or moral or result from self-evident common interest' (1986, p.8). This leads to the following typology of what he terms 'forms of organizational reach':

|              | *Authoritative* | *Diffused*      |
| ------------ | --------------- | --------------- |
| *Intensive*  | Army command    | General strike  |
| *Extensive*  | Military empire | Market exchange |

Thus power is intensively used in an army command, and is authoritative; it is limited to the troops being commanded, however, whereas in a military empire there is wide general control but the command structure does not penetrate far into everyday life. In the two examples of diffused power, the general strike is intensive, concentrated on a particular group only and diffused since it is accepted by those involved as the thing to do, not enforced upon them. And the system of market exchange is both extensive, since it penetrates most aspects of life (as described in Chapter 2), and diffused, because again it is accepted as the way of doing things, not imposed by a command structure.

Extensive, diffused power is typical of modern capitalist states, especially those in Western Europe and North America. The state influences very many aspects of daily life in both of the other spheres; it does so not through the issuing of commands that must be obeyed but rather by developing understanding about what should and should not be done. Understanding about what? According to Mann, there are four sources of power involved – economic, ideological, military and political. Economic power is involved with the organisation of production, distribution, exchange and consumption, and is the foundation of the capitalist mode. The state exercises economic power in order to facilitate the operation of the capitalist system. Ideological power involves the transmission of a set of ideas that allow people to give meaning to their existence; it provides the concepts and categories with which to appreciate that which is perceived. These norms are in part related to economic power, since capitalism requires a state-backed ideology to sustain it. But they can extend well beyond the economic sphere, to cover all other aspects of life; they usually have a moral base in a religion, and many states promote a particular set of religious norms, either explicitly or implicitly. In so doing, the state influences life way beyond the basic structure of market exchange. Military power involves the application of organised physical force; it too can be used to promote the market system (as in colonialism) but it may be used by the state personnel in other ways, to promote ideas and goals that are independent of the economic sphere – as in Britain's defence of the Falkland Islands in 1982 and the Argentinian invasion of the Malvinas to help promote a national identity. Finally, political power involves centralised organisation of social relations, which again may not be a necessary adjunct to the economic sphere, as with state involvement in the organisation of commercial sport.

The personnel who control the state apparatus have available to them an organisation that can be used to structure life within the state's territory in a whole variety of ways. In deciding how to exercise that power, those involved draw on the four sources itemised above, and in so doing benefit from the experience of those who preceded them and acted similarly. They are part of the process whereby a culture is reproduced, culture being defined as the entire corpus of ideas that underpin life in a society. That culture must incorporate and facilitate the mode of production, but it will almost invariably extend well beyond that task. And it can be changed, if the state personnel are determined enough and what they propose is acceptable to the population. Such culture change may well involve changing attitudes towards the environment. A society's culture, as described in Chapter 1, certainly embraces such attitudes, and so the state can be used to change them.

## STATES AND TERRITORIES

The arguments developed in this chapter demonstrate the necessity of a state for the capitalist mode of production. But they say nothing about either the number of states or the size of individual states. Is it necessary to have more than one? Is the present system of states a desirable configuration?

The state is necessarily a territorial body; in order to function as it does it needs a clearly defined territory over which its sovereignty holds. The reasons for this are relatively straightforward. The state exercises power, which involves influence (if not control) over people. It does that largely by setting norms and enacting laws to which all of the people over whom it has power must conform, with the sanction that they will be punished if they do not. How then is that power efficiently exercised; what strategies can be used to ensure that the laws are obeyed, that the norms of behaviour are accepted, that the ideology is absorbed, and so on?

Territoriality, according to Sack (1983, p. 56), is a widely used strategy involving 'the attempt by an individual or group (x) to influence, affect, or control objects, people, and relationships (y) by delimiting and asserting control over a geographic area'. Sack suggests ten 'tendencies' that explain why territoriality comes to the fore as a strategy for obtaining control. Among them are: the ready classification that territory provides, since a person or object is either inside or outside the territory; the ready identification of the territory, through a boundary marker; the fact that territory provides a means of reifying power, through a link with an inanimate object which thereby displaces attention from the real objects in the power relationship (you obey 'the law of the land', not what somebody directs you to do); the apparent neutrality of territory, and the impersonality of relationships which use of the territoriality strategy thus involves; and the ability to engender identification with a territory, which thereby legitimises the control.

Although territoriality is not the only strategy available to the state in its exercise of power it has been almost universally adopted, which suggests that it is probably the most efficient. Thus associating a state with a defined territory enables it to exercise power, especially its military power; it could well be argued that such power could not be exercised over a population without a territorial identity. The state's exercise of economic power is similarly facilitated by its association with a territory; regulatory and other policies apply to all economic activities within that defined area. Because those two types of power are so readily exercised through a territoriality strategy, this gives additional strength to the state elite in their exercise of ideological and political power; they have a firm base within which to influence the culture of a people, and since their economic performance is an important criterion in electoral judgements, this gives substantial freedom for the other activities, which may include promoting ideas about and policies towards the environment. In Mann's (1986) terminology, the state in a market economy penetrates most aspects of economic and social life. To facilitate that penetration, it is involved in a wide range of surveillance activities (Giddens, 1989), which are much eased by a territoriality strategy; defined borders enhance surveillance operations very considerably.

Territoriality has a further advantage, because it enables people to identify with a defined locale and promote their collective interests accordingly, which might not be impossible but certainly would be difficult using other strategies. Harvey (1985b), for example, has discussed the value of what he calls 'regional alliances'. Members of particular interest groups in a defined area collaborate through the state in what he terms a 'spatial fix', to promote the interests of all those resident within the area against people from elsewhere. This stimulates geopolitical strategies which associate the state with promoting its citizens' interests beyond its borders.

The association of the state with a territory is probably a necessity, therefore; it is unlikely that its roles could be conducted otherwise. But what territory, what set of containers (Taylor, 1994, 1995)? Clearly the present set of states is just one of an almost infinite number of possible configurations, and there is nothing either 'natural' or 'desirable' about it. It has evolved out of pre-capitalist and other formations and from the geopolitical rivalries of those exercising the four types of power. It continues to evolve, as new states are created and others consider whether to submerge their separate identities (as in the European Union). The collapse of the USSR and of the communist system in eastern Europe stimulated attempts at rewriting the political map, a number of which have been successful while others continue. Most have been based on nationalist claims, whereby members of cultural groups (usually characterised by a shared language and attachment to a defined locale) seek self-rule within a claimed territory, from which they may try to remove members of rival nationalities (as in Bosnia-Herzegovina), forcibly if necessary. Territorial states thus provide a firm framework within which economic, political, military and ideological power can be exercised, because they are units within which sovereignty is exercised and with which people identify.

## REGULATING THE SYSTEM OF STATES

Division of the world into a set of territorial states is therefore efficient in many ways. But it is inefficient in others, because many state boundaries are artificial and interrupt the operation of systems that have a wider spread. This is becoming ever more apparent as the organisation of capitalism becomes increasingly global in scale, and the economic roles of individual states are restructured as a consequence (Johnston, 1986b). It is also becoming increasingly apparent in the field of environmental policy, and recent work has illustrated the problems caused.

Environmental systems, as stressed from the outset of this book, are global in their interaction; no part of the earth is independent of all others, and no system or sub-system is constrained by 'artificial' political boundaries. Thus tackling environmental problems requires inter-state collaboration in many situations (on the difficulties, see Dufournaud and Harrington, 1989). In a large number of cases global solutions appear to be required; as Hardin argued (p. 139), global government is needed to attack global issues.

International law has evolved over the centuries, and especially during the twentieth century, either to provide the needed order in inter-state relations over issues that are international in their scope or to cope with problems which occur outside individual states' jurisdiction (as on the high seas). It involves states agreeing to co-operate, if necessary through a regulatory body which they establish, and accepting the decisions of an international court on issues of disagreement. Two types of co-operation are characteristic. Treaty law is binding on the signatory states only, which may involve not only governments agreeing to sign but also in some cases, such as the UK, such documents being ratified by national parliaments (Churchill, 1991). Where treaty law does not apply, general (or customary) international law prevails. Its operation depends on 'custom and practice', so that a state can be deemed subject to a rule's operation unless it can show that 'it has consistently rejected the rule since the earliest days of the rule's existence: dissent expressed after the rule has become well established is too late to prevent the rule binding the dissenting state' (Akehurst, 1977, p. 38) – although there may be difficulties in requiring a state to operate within a rule which it no longer accepts. Much international law is of such a customary type, reflecting the operation of sensible rules – as with the control of air and shipping lanes.

The tragedy of the commons and Prisoner's Dilemma metaphors once again illustrate the problems of international agreement. In this application, the individual actors are states. Each state is making a demand on the world's environment, treating it as a commons, and may be degrading the environment, not just within its borders but globally. Thus it is in the interests of every state to agree to environmental controls, but it may well be that in certain circumstances some states at least are not prepared to impose such controls – either because they do not see it as in their interests to do so, whatever the others may do, or because they do not believe that an agreement can be effectively monitored, so that some might break it.

Laver has illustrated these problems with two examples. The first analyses international co-operation in outer space, what he terms the 'tragedy of the celestial commons' (Laver 1986). Outer space can in some ways be treated in the same way as land resources on earth, but unlike terrestrial land it is outside any state's recognised jurisdiction; it comprises what is known in legal terminology as *res communis humanitatis* (RCH) – territory which is not only beyond national state claims but is also recognised as the common property of all humanity (Johnston, 1992). Like terrestrial land, it is a scarce resource that can be destroyed by exploitation:

> Whether we are talking about the use of the Moon as an ultra-clean research laboratory or as a source of raw minerals, whether we are talking about orbital space stations as providing vital communications nodes or surveys of scarce terrestrial resources, we are talking about a set of problems with essentially the same underlying structure, (Laver, 1986, p. 361)

which is that of the tragedy of the commons. But there is one crucial difference; the actors in outer space are states, and there is no 'international government' that can regulate what those states do there (through the use of effective sanctions).

In the absence of such an international body, the only way of obtaining protection for extra-terrestrial environments is via international co-operation through treaties and other agreements. Two of these have been formulated by the United Nations Committee on the Peaceful Uses of Outer Space (COPUOS) – the Outer Space Treaty and the Moon Agreement. The first defines outer space as a commons – the legal term is *res extra commercium* (REC); under international law it cannot be claimed as part of a state's territory but can be treated as a commons on which any state can 'graze' (Johnston, 1992). The second defines the moon as a collective territory (i.e. RCH), using phrases such as

> equitable sharing by all States Party in the benefits derived from [lunar] resources, whereby the interests and needs of the developing countries, as well as the efforts of those countries which have contributed either directly or indirectly to the exploration of the Moon, shall be given special consideration.

The Moon Treaty has not been ratified by either the USA or the former USSR, however, and so is an agreement between countries which lack the ability to exploit the moon's resources. The two countries which have the proven technological capability of exploiting those resources refuse to recognise the moon as the common property of all because, according to Laver (1986, p. 368):

> 'Public' appropriation of common resources by all, the potential solution under treaty law, can be resisted by the strong, who anticipate that they can dominate the anarchy that results if neither public nor private appropriation is possible.

Since none of the states which are signatories to the Treaty can exercise its theoretical right of equal access to the resources, the two that are exercising that right feel no obligation to conform and share their gains.

In his other example, Laver (1984) focuses on two cases of the use of 'inner space'. The first concerns radio broadcasts, which use particular frequencies within the spectrum that cannot be polluted but which are easy of access and fixed in amount. As the demand for broadcasting increases, so the possibility of exhaustion of the available frequencies increases too, which leads to calls for co-ordinated collective action to achieve optimal use. This has been in operation since 1906 through the International Frequency Regulation Board (IFRB), whose decisions governments respect and operate, because it is in their interests so to do. ('Free-riding' is not feasible, because 'pirates' can have their use of the frequencies 'jammed'.) The benefits of belonging to the IFRB are perceived by all governments, which are prepared to implement its rules; there is no need for an international regulatory body in such cases, because all are members and all members respect the rules. This solution to a potential tragedy of the commons requires both the absence of gains from free-riding, however, and the necessity of the resource.

The second case refers to the placing of satellites into geostationary orbits around the earth, access to which is currently limited to those states which are able to afford the expensive technology and which are therefore obtaining a monopoly over a limited resource – such satellites must be located 36 000 km above the equator. As yet, no international action has been proposed to regulate that limited commons, but many states see that they are being effectively, and potentially permanently, excluded from a resource by those which already have access to it and see no benefits in agreeing to share it with others. Their relative affluence allows them to be potential free-riders, and to reserve the major gains of access for themselves.

Two further examples illustrate the relevance of Laver's arguments to the use of terrestrial environments. The first concerns the resources of the Antarctic continent. To date these have not been exploited, apart from the fishing, whaling and sealing activities around the shores, so that although several states have claimed sovereignty over parts of the continent they have not been concerned to enforce those claims strictly, since there are no perceived benefits from doing so. In 1959 they all signed the Antarctic Treaty, along with other countries which have no territorial claims in Antarctica but are prepared to support its general principles. Under that treaty, the continent is not to be used for military purposes and is to be freely accessible to all for scientific work. The signatories have agreed to share the commons but conflict resolution, should it be called for, may not be very effective. Article XI of the Antarctic Treaty sets out the agreed framework for enforcement:

> 1. If any dispute arises between two or more of the Contracting Parties concerning the interpretation or application of the present Treaty, those Contracting Parties shall consult among themselves with a view to having the dispute resolved by negotiation, inquiry, mediation, conciliation, arbitration, judicial settlement or other peaceful means of their own choice.
> 2. Any dispute of this character not so resolved shall, with the consent, in each case, of all parties to the dispute, be referred to the International Court of Justice for settlement; but failure to reach agreement or reference to the International Court shall not absolve parties to the dispute from the responsibility of continuing to seek to resolve it by any of the various peaceful means referred to in paragraph 1 of this Article.
> (Kiss, 1983, p. 152)

Thus disputing parties are encouraged to seek mutually acceptable resolutions, but there is no sanction available if they fail, and no absolute requirement to submit the dispute to the International Court of Justice (Johnston, 1992).

The Antarctic Treaty contains no reference to economic exploitation, particularly of the known extensive mineral resources, because at present it is either not technologically feasible or economically desirable to exploit them (the winning of oil in the Arctic suggests it is probably the latter rather than the former). Thus an attempt was made to extend the treaty by adding an Antarctic Minerals Convention, to ensure that when such exploitation is proposed it will be judged against strict environmental standards, thereby preventing a scramble for resources and the likely degradation of the environment that could ensue. Nine countries signed the convention in Wellington, New Zealand, in November 1988, but four more merely indicated that they would sign soon (including the United States and the United Kingdom). The chapter on disputes procedures in this convention is stronger than that in the treaty itself, however; all signatory parties must declare in writing whether they wish disputes to go to the International Court or an arbitral tribunal, but neither body has jurisdiction over territorial sovereignty claims. Furthermore, the environmental advisory committee established under the convention has no independent decision-making authority, and would not necessarily receive all details of proposed exploration or mining; prospecting did not require any prior authorisation (Elliott, 1994). For conservation groups this was unsatisfactory, not least because it gave the same body powers over both environmental conservation/preservation and resource-use regulation. Thus, according to Elliott (1994, p. 262) the convention had basic flaws:

> a lack of integration, insistence on voluntary compliance and resistance to any kind of institutional framework that might have been able to facilitate monitoring both of compliance and of cumulative environmental impacts.

Pressure to remedy these was organised by the Australian and French governments, and in 1991 a Protocol on Environmental Protection was agreed in Madrid, with the USA (under George Bush: see p. 229) agreeing to sign at the last minute. This designates the Antarctic as a 'natural reserve, devoted to peace and science' within which the signatories agree to comprehensive protection of the environment and its ecosystems, and there are binding, compulsory dispute settlement procedures (although the needed inspectors can only be appointed by consensus). Despite this, Elliott is only cautiously optimistic about whether the Antarctic case indicates willingness on the part of states to yield sovereignty for the long-term protection of the environment: will they be prepared to invoke binding dispute resolution procedures?

But do countries always honour the conventions and treaties that they sign? Experience with the United Nations Universal Declaration of Human Rights suggests not (Johnston, 1989). It may be, however, that states will enforce policies to prevent the use of CFCs in aerosol sprays and refrigerators, because of the potential dire consequences of not doing so. (This may be a good example of an Assurance game; see p. 144.)

Laver's examples and the evidence of the Antarctic Treaty lead to doubts regarding the probability of international collaboration over certain types of environmental problem, therefore. These are backed up by the second example, recent attempts to reach international agreements on oceanic resources. There have been several conferences on the law of the sea since the Second World War, convened under the auspices of the United Nations as a response to the growing technical ability to exploit maritime resources and for states to defend coastal waters against outside users. Until that time, the *de facto* operating law was that of 'the freedom of the seas', and only a small coastal zone, a few miles wide, was claimed by states as the 'territorial waters' over which their sovereignty held (see Schachter, 1986). But in 1947 Chile claimed a 200-mile zone to protect its fishing industry (especially whaling) from competition with other fleets, two years after President Truman of the United States had expressed concern over the exploitation of both fish stocks and hydrocarbons from the zone of the continental shelf, the relatively shallow area of sea around most coasts. These stimulated the search for global agreement over the exploitation of resources within and beneath the oceans.

The work on these agreements was done in the series of United Nations Conferences on the Law of the Sea (UNCLOS): the first was held in 1958, the second in 1960, and the third, which continues, began in 1973. A major problem faced was to decide whether the sea bed was just unclaimed territory which could, like the land surface, be claimed by states which wished to establish sovereignty there, whether it was a 'commons' open to all and which no state could appropriate (REC), or whether there was no relevant custom and practice so international law had to be written *de novo* to cover the sea bed. Agreement was eventually reached with regard to the definition of sovereign limits: states could claim exclusive economic zones, within which they have rights to the resources of the sea bed, up to 200 miles wide. (This led to many definitional problems and legal cases, as fully illustrated by Prescott, 1985.)

Much more difficult to handle was the ownership of and access to resources beyond those exclusive economic zones, in the area known as the 'high seas'. This became particularly relevant as technological advances made it potentially possible to exploit the mineral resources on and beneath the sea bed, although as yet it is not economic to do so: according to Dubs (1986, p. 95) 'the seabed resource is there in munificent abundance – but there are no miners who will exploit that resource in the next two or three decades'. To date, the proposed treaty to govern that exploitation has not been supported by all states although, according to Schachter (1986, p. 54), the non-signatories remain committed to the concept of treating the sea-bed resources as a common heritage whose exploitation should be organised through international agreement (i.e. as RCH). The treaty proposes that the resources should be treated as common and their exploitation governed by an international authority which would receive a large share of the net proceeds of the operations. That income would be distributed among all countries by an elected council of 36 states (for fuller details, see Prescott, 1985, pp. 124ff.)

The United States was among the countries which declined to sign the treaty. Its reasons were given by President Reagan in 1982, and covered five problems (Dubs, 1986, p. 113–14).

(1) The provisions would deter exploitation of the resources, because of the appropriation of a large part of the net proceeds by the authority.
(2) The constitution of the council would not accord the United States and other countries 'a role that fairly reflects and protects their interests'.
(3) Amendments could be passed even if the United States disapproved, since no veto was allowed.
(4) There was the possibility of national liberation movements and other 'undesirables' benefiting from the distribution of the net proceeds.
(5) The absence of assured access in the future discouraged states from investing in the necessary technology for exploiting the resources (see also Clingan, 1986).

As with the Moon Treaty, therefore, the powerful states in the world have been unprepared to sign a treaty which recognises certain resources as a 'common heritage' because that would involve them renouncing some of their power. They refuse to adopt what others see as the optimal way of using and protecting those resources and achieving the optimal outcome of a Prisoner's Dilemma game; through the process of uneven development that characterises the capitalist mode of production these powerful states have obtained a position whereby they can protect their interests and potentially hasten the tragedy of the commons.

These examples refer to environmental issues affecting a large number, if not all, of the current mosaic of states on the earth's surface. As argued in Chapter 2, the nature of environmental systems is such that a problem generated in one place is likely to have at least indirect effects on most others. Nevertheless, in many cases the impacts of environmental problems are small for the great majority of states and only a few are directly involved. In such situations, while it may be desirable to have an international court which can adjudicate between rival claims, and whose decisions would be accepted as final by all parties and in all states, negotiation between the states concerned could allow resolution of many problems if they recognise the benefits of co-operation, as illustrated by the Assurance game (p. 144).

Canada and the United States have established a mechanism within which to resolve shared environmental issues. In 1909 they signed a Boundary Waters Treaty which constituted an International Joint Commission, comprising three members from each country. It can only consider issues referred to it by the two federal governments together, and it makes recommendations only (see le Marquand, 1986); its major function is as a fact-finding body, with the perceived quality of its work giving its pronouncements high status, but it can also act as a facilitator, helping conflicting parties in the two countries (which may include state/provincial as well as federal governments and also private sector concerns) to reach accommodations. The Commission's utility entirely depends on its standing and the willingness of the parties to disputes to accept its advice, and some observers (e.g. Carroll, 1986; Sewell and Utton, 1986) believe it an inadequate mechanism because of mutual distrust in the two countries. Wherever this is the case, the absence of a supranational state will mean that local as well as global environmental conflicts involving two or more separate sovereign jurisdictions will have the characteristics of Prisoner's Dilemma rather than Assurance games.

## THE STATE IN ADVANCED COMMUNIST/SOCIALIST SOCIETIES

The discussion throughout this chapter has either explicitly or implicitly focused on states in capitalist societies. But much of what has been said applies to advanced communist/socialist states as well. States are clearly necessary to the economic activity there, as already suggested (p.72); they are also involved in the exercise of political, ideological and military power; they are actors in the international negotiations over the environment; and they need a territorial identity in order to achieve their goals.

Where the advanced communist/socialist states differ is in the absence of large numbers of separate economic actors to be regulated within their societies. Regulation involves central planning, which determines what shall be done where, and in what quantities, and provides the resources to enable the plans to be achieved. Thus the tragedy of the commons and Prisoner's Dilemma metaphors do not apply to activities within those states (except that most have some residual private land, much of which is farmed in the same way as tenants farmed under feudalism), and issues of environmental use do not require state involvement in the regulation of individual activities. Instead, it is the state plans themselves which are the sources of such environmental degradation as may occur, and the attitudes of the state personnel towards the environment are crucial. They must weigh up the environmental consequences of their plans against the economic and social objectives set, and determine to what extent they are prepared to commit resources to ensure relative harmony with nature. They too are seeking to ensure the production of an increasing range of commodities, with all the implications of this for environmental use, although the decisions on what to produce are made on utilitarian rather than profit-making criteria. That difference apart, the pressures on the state regarding environmental use are similar to those in the capitalist world; they must balance the imperatives of their mode of production against the damage that they do to environmental systems.

The extent of the damage done – and thus an implicit evaluation of the balance selected – by four decades of central planning in eastern Europe is illustrated in a collection of essays edited by Carter and Turnock (1993c). They argue that the urge to develop national economies rapidly and so eliminate material underdevelopment led to

> a proliferation of large-scale programmes of mining and heavy manufacturing which increased the risks of environmental damage by alarming proportions. Adoption of the Stalinist model of economic development led to emphasis on heavy industry, including cement, chemicals and metallurgy, along with the drive to exploit all available energy resources through domestic thermal power-stations, which all helped to take their toll on the environment. Moreover, the Marxist concept of regarding natural resources as 'free goods' has only added to the problem by encouraging waste. (Carter and Turnock 1993a, p. 1)

Carter (1993a, p. 38) extends this by claiming that Bulgaria's communist leaders believed that environmental degradation was a characteristic of capitalist countries only.

To illustrate the volume of pollution generated, Carter and Turnock (1993a, pp. 4–5) cite the city of Leipzig, which was covered in 400 000 tonnes of sulphur dioxide annually, had a life expectancy six years below the national average for the GDR, and where 80 per cent of children aged under 7 suffered with either chronic bronchitis or heart problems or both. Elsewhere, the emission of pollutants by a hydrolysis and yeast fodder factory and a pulp and paper mill contributed to a 14-fold increase in respiratory infections between 1970 and 1984 in the Razlog valley of Bulgaria, where reported nervous disorders increased by 171 per cent over the same period (Carter, 1993a, p. 51). Poland was one of the worst-affected of the countries (the most polluted in the world according to Timberlake, 1981), and in 1988 the Polish Academy of Sciences reported that there had been 'a complete breakdown of the state of natural balance' in 27 districts covering one-tenth of the land area and containing one-third of its population (Carter, 1993b, p. 109). In 1964-7 32 per cent of the country's rivers were graded as class I (fit for human consumption); by 1978–83, this had fallen to only 7 per cent, largely because of the emission of municipal and industrial wastes into water courses: Carter (1993b, p.114) reports that by the late 1980s 18 per cent of industrial enterprises discharging wastes into surface waters did so without any purification (the Vistula at Cracow contained a higher concentration of salt than the Baltic Sea), that 366 towns and cities (including Warsaw and Łódź) had no municipal sewage treatment plant, and that of the 459 such plants in existence two-thirds worked inefficiently.

Public appreciation of the problems has created pressure for change, especially so following the collapse of the centrally planned communist states. By 1990, Romania had two green political parties which contested the elections then: they won 4 per cent of the votes cast overall, and performed especially well in Bucharest and other urban areas (at over three times the national average in the country's ecological blackspot of Copsa Mica, for example), securing two places in the Senate and 20 in the Chamber of Deputies (Turnock, 1993). Governments have reacted positively to these pressures (whereas under communist regimes they ignored the concerns expressed by academics and others) but, as Carter and Turnock (1993b, p.188) express it: 'faced with economic problems such as inflation and unemployment it is difficult to judge where sufficient capital for environmental enhancement will come in the pecking order of priorities'. Furthermore, eastern Europe's competitive advantage in the capitalist world economy is assisted by its attitudes to the environment:

> Attempts at reducing atmospheric and other forms of pollution depend not only on technical and economic issues but also on changes in outlook and ideas. Industrialized countries have to recognize the need to make their socio-economic activities and lifestyles environmentally sound. Unfortunately, in a spatial sense Europe is far from united in this approach; Eastern Europe consists of countries with unregulated industries and cheap sources of labour which can undercut more environmentally conscious West European competitors. (Carter and Turnock 1993b, p.218)

That competitive edge could be easily lost if strict environmental controls are introduced.

## IN SUMMARY

The present chapter has explored the nature of the state, and its necessity to the health of the capitalist and advanced communist/socialist modes of production. Although the state is a necessary institution, and must perform certain roles, there is no necessity for it (which means the people who control it) to act in particular, predetermined ways – just as a Shakespeare play requires certain roles to be filled and lines to be delivered, but leaves it to those directing and acting in the play to interpret those roles and lines, so an advanced economic system requires a state, but leaves it to the people involved to interpret the state's necessary tasks. It is to that interpretative role, and the ways in which others can influence it, that we turn next.

# 6 State Operations and Environmental Problems

A nation that destroys its soil, destroys itself. (Franklin D. Roosevelt)

No generation has a freehold on this earth. All we have is a life tenancy with a full repairing lease. (Margaret Thatcher, speaking to the Conservative Party Annual Conference, September 1988)

The degrees of freedom available to the state within the mode of production mean that if environmental attitudes occupy a central place in a national culture, then relevant policies to promote those attitudes can (and should) be implemented by the state apparatus. Thus those seeking to promote pro-green policies must ensure that the relevant attitudes have a place within the national culture. To appreciate the extent to which this is feasible, we need to understand how the state works.

## DEMOCRACY OR NOT

Most people in the English-speaking world live in democracies, briefly defined as countries characterised by rule of the people, for the people, by the people. If a particular goal is desired by a majority of the population, then this should be reflected in their state's policies; if it is not implemented, then some groups must exercise veto power within the state, which negates the concept of democracy. However, no state has democracy in the true sense. Many have little or no democracy at all; the rest have representative democracy, with rule by a small group acting on behalf of everybody, because involving the entire population in the everyday running of a highly complex operation is not feasible. It is necessary to explore these two caveats in a little more detail.

### THE GEOGRAPHY OF LIBERAL DEMOCRACY

Representative democracy, according to Berg (1978, p. 156), is 'an ideal type of national decision-making system whose members (above some minimum age level) enjoy equality of self-determination'. Berg (1978, p. 167) defines this self-determination as follows:

> An individual has self-determination to the extent that he is not excluded from making decisions that are relevant to him and to the extent that he makes or effectively participates in the making of such decisions.

This is translated into the concept of liberal representative democracy, according to which, as stated in Article 21 of the (unanimously adopted) 1948 United Nations Universal Declaration of Human Rights:

> Everyone has the right to take part in the government of his country, directly or through freely chosen representatives.

Furthermore:

> The will of the people shall be the basis of the authority of government; this will shall be expressed in periodic and genuine elections which shall be by universal and equal suffrage.

These statements of principle lead to accounts of the institutional guarantees necessary for the existence of liberal representative democracy, set out by Dahl (1978) as follows.

*Necessary Condition I – The Formulation of Preferences*
    Institutional guarantees required:
        freedom to form and join organizations;
        freedom of expression;
        the availability of alternative information sources; and
        the right to vote and to compete for votes.
*Necessary Condition II – Signifying Preferences*
    Institutional guarantees required:
        all of the above, plus
        free and fair elections; and
        the freedom to stand for public office.
*Necessary Condition III – Equal Weighting of Preferences*
    Institutional guarantees required:
        all of the above, plus
        institutions which ensure that government policies depend on voting
        and other popularly-expressed preferences

How many countries meet these criteria?

Several recent studies have portrayed aspects of the geography of liberal democracy (for reviews, see Johnston, 1989; Taylor, 1989a). A single variable frequently used to indicate the existence of a democratic regime is the use of free and fair elections to produce a government, whereby no political parties are proscribed, transfers of power are orderly and occur only as a consequence of electoral outcomes, all of the seats in the parliament can be contested by all parties, there is a universal, adult franchise, there is a fixed timetable for holding elections, campaigns are open and free from intimidation, and voting is secret. Strict observance of these criteria would see very few states qualify. (Does the existence House of Lords disqualify the United Kingdom? Does the gerrymandering and other manipulation of the electoral system disqualify the

United States? Was the Federal Republic of Germany disqualified when a minor coalition partner 'switched sides' and produced a change of government without an election?) Allowing some small deviations from the ideal, however, still produced a list of only 28 countries with more than 3 million inhabitants which qualified as liberal representative democracies in the late 1970s, according to Butler et al (1981). Since then, a number of other countries – most in South America and eastern Europe – have joined the list.

The countries which have long been considered democracies are, with very few exceptions (India is the most obvious), concentrated in the core of the capitalist world economy. This suggests to some that liberal democracy is a 'natural' consequence of the process known as 'modernisation', as specified in Rostow's (1971) classic study of *The Stages of Economic Growth*. Correlation studies show that level of modernisation and level of democracy are closely linked (e.g. Coulter, 1975), and that the core–periphery structure of the world economy has liberal democracy concentrated in its core (Bollen, 1983). From this it is inferred that as modernisation spreads into the periphery, so liberal democracy will follow. Hence the widespread adoption of representative democracy in the 1980s and 1990s is associated with the triumph of capitalism and its associated political form (Fukuyama, 1992).

There are several critiques of this argument (Taylor, 1989b, calls it the 'error of developmentalism'). Here we concentrate not on arguments whether there can ever be economic equality in a capitalist world (on this, see Hirsch, 1977) but rather on the 'achievement' of liberal democracy. Implicit in the arguments of Coulter and others is that liberal democracy is a 'natural' consequence of modernisation; once a certain level of modernisation has been achieved, then the democratic guarantees will be fulfilled. But in all of the countries in which liberal democracy now exists it has been yielded, slowly and grudgingly, by an elite, as the price to pay for social consensus within the state and to sustain the legitimacy of the mode of production. (A few of the British settler colonies, such as Australia, Canada, New Zealand and the United States, are partial exceptions to this. Their establishment came after the granting of substantial democratic freedoms in Britain, and these were immediately implemented in the new countries; the struggle for some democratic rights – notably the universal suffrage – continued, however.)

This struggle for democratic rights is well illustrated by the slow spreading of power in the United Kingdom: first, the transfer from the absolute monarch to the major landowners; then, the incorporation of the urban bourgeoisie; and, following this, the battle for universal suffrage and the removal of all qualifications other than adulthood and citizenship. Even with the achievement of universal franchise, there were claims that the electoral system was 'rigged' in some places to devalue the votes of certain groups relative to those of others, as in Northern Ireland up to the 1970s, and even today Scotland and Wales are overrepresented in the House of Commons relative to England. In the United States, too, there has been a similar struggle to enfranchise groups implicitly excluded from the democratic process despite explicit statements in the country's constitution. For many years, for example, southern state governments employed a literacy qualification to prevent blacks from registering as electors (before the Civil War, slaves counted as possessions and as only a fraction of a free person in the counting of the population for determining the number of representatives a state was entitled to). In addition, the process of registration was made difficult, to dissuade blacks from exercising their civil rights.

The struggle for civil and democratic rights is now taking place in many parts of the world. It appears to have been successful in some; most South American countries currently have elected governments, for example, though this may be temporary. As in several African and Asian countries too, these countries have experienced periods of democracy punctuated by episodes of autocratic rule, usually by the military or with its clear support following an 'irregular' transfer of power (i.e. a transfer not agreed by the population in a free election). This alternation of democratic and non-democratic rule can be linked to the situation of those countries in the periphery of the world economy.

An ideal-type representation of the sequence suggests the following. A non-democratic government is in power, which denies citizens at least some of the civil rights agreed in the United Nations Declaration. There is popular agitation for those rights to be granted, and the strength of the mobilisation of opinion is such that the stability of the regime is under threat and maintenance of order is difficult. Those in power decide to yield it to the population, and a democratic regime is established. This not only grants civil rights, in order to generate consensus, but also seeks to advance the general welfare of the population through legitimation policies (see p. 151). As a result, the costs of capitalist operations in the country increase, and outside investors may question whether to leave their capital in the country, especially if there is any possibility of some form of state takeover of their assets (as in Chile under the Allende regime). If withdrawal occurs, then the policies of the state are undermined, general prosperity is threatened and the welfare policies begin to fail, because they cannot be afforded without punitive levels of taxation, which in turn further discourage investment. This can lead to popular protest, and demands for government action which cannot be met; the economy stagnates, inflation may become rampant, and the maintenance of law and order becomes difficult. Eventually, a non-democratic solution may be imposed by the military and its allies (usually the local capitalists, whose profits are threatened, plus the middle classes who prosper under them). This is presented to the population not as a permanent situation but as a way of restoring stability and prosperity, after which there will be a return to democracy. The latter may eventuate; just as likely is a failure of the military government to deliver prosperity and general welfare, stimulating popular protest and demands for a return to democracy and freedom (as in Chile in the 1980s).

The small number of countries in the core of the world economy have escaped this sequence through their achievement of high levels of prosperity (though, of course, relatively few have experienced no deviation from the ideal model of democracy in the last four decades, as in France in the 1950s). That prosperity has, at least in part, been achieved through creation of the global capitalist economy with its core–periphery structure, and it is doubtful whether the core could be substantially enlarged – though its membership may change over long periods as new members (e.g. Japan) enter and others slide into the semi-periphery. According to this argument, only a small number of countries in the core of the capitalist world economy are likely to qualify as liberal democracies conforming to the criteria laid out above. In the remainder of the world, democracy is a luxury that cannot be afforded for long, and civil rights, welfare state policies and self-determination (the hallmarks of what Taylor, 1989c, calls liberal-social democracies) must take second place to the maintenance of a fragile stability based on an exploited situation.

Liberal representative democracy remains fragile outside the core of the world economy. In several eastern European countries which adopted it after the collapse of communism in the late 1980s, for example, the failure to deliver widespread economic prosperity is now threatening democratic stability, and there is considerable popular support for a return to power of the (slightly refashioned) communist parties. At the same time, in a number of South American countries presidential powers over elected parliaments have been substantially increased. As *The Economist* (6–12 May 1995, p. 19) expresses it: 'To most West Europeans and North Americans, the clash of parties is integral to democratic government. To many voters in Latin America, it is a pain in the neck'. Prosperity matters much more to many of the latter than do the civil rights enshrined in liberal representative democracy. They are prepared to accept semi-dictatorial presidents (or *caudillos*). In an ideal world, their demands might be met through

> the mills of party politics and the other mechanisms of democracy, such as free and honest media and courts. In real Latin America, and not only there, elected presidents have to decide how to do what the voters want, and sometimes what they need but don't want, and then get it done; democracy means action as well as the expression of multiple opinions.

The green agenda partially fits this model: many greens are more concerned with 'ends' (saving the earth from ecological disaster) than with 'democratic means', which often imply painfully slow progress at best.

Liberal representative democracy as described here is very much a Western conception. There are substantial variations within it, and also different conceptions of democracy in non-Western countries which nevertheless accept the basic principle of accountability which underlies the Western conception. A number of east Asian countries give less emphasis to individual freedom and more to collective responsibilities and citizenship, for example, which contrasts with the ultra-libertarian views characteristic of some New Right positions in the West. Thus whereas a British prime minister could state firmly that 'there is no such thing as society, only individuals and families', shared values take pride of place in Singapore's formulation of democracy: the first of its five values is 'Nation before community and society before self'. The latter view permits a form of democratic 'developmental authoritarianism' in which 'the state intervenes to dampen political opposition in the declared interest of social order and economic development' (Leifer, 1995, p. 16). Such restrictions on human rights are justified there by the rapid economic growth achieved by the governments involved; theirs is a culture which stresses respect for authority and strong individual obligations to the group, and which is currently succeeding economically, whereas those in the West which stress individual rights are weakening the powers of governments and leading to slower economic growth. The implications for environmental policies in both types of regime are profound.

## TYPES OF NON-DEMOCRATIC STATE

The great majority of states in the world are classified as non-democratic, therefore, but with considerable variation within that category. All are run by a bureaucracy, an administrative class with its own culture; democracies are run by bureaucracies too, but with the major difference that their bureaucracies are subject to political, and hence popular, control. Among the non-democratic states, the nature of the group to which the bureaucracy is responsible is the criterion used to differentiate them into five main types.

### The Military Dictatorships

Power in these is vested in the armed forces, which provide the ruling elite from within the military and without consultation with the population at large. There may be conflicts within the military, and occasional transfers of power, bloodless or otherwise, from one faction to another, and there may be consultation with outside bodies and powers, some of which may strongly influence, if not 'control', those in charge of the state apparatus. In most cases, military control is the result of a takeover at some stage from a civilian, frequently a popularly elected, government. The military sees its main task as maintaining law and order, if necessary by repressing opposition to its policies and the denial of civil and human rights. Strongly linked to those law and order goals will be economic policies designed to facilitate capitalist accumulation, and thus to benefit a small civilian elite and sustain its support; that elite, and the associated middle class, will provide senior members of both the military and the bureaucracy. (In a few cases, as described below, the military may promote other modes of production.)

### The Semi-feudal Dictatorships

Power in these regimes is held by the major landowning families, with no tradition of popular participation in running the state. Civil rights are largely disregarded, at least in the context of liberal democracy, and authoritarian rule is common. The senior ranks of the bureaucracy are drawn heavily from the families of the ruling elite.

### The Self-sustaining Bureaucracies

In these regimes, groups from within the population win control of the bureaucracy, and rule with military support and little accountability as it is understood in liberal democracies. Access to the bureaucracy, especially its senior levels, is carefully controlled by those in power, to ensure no challenges to their rule.

The best examples of this type of rule come from the advanced communist/ socialist states, where the bureaucracy is controlled by the Communist Party (or some close equivalent). Only members of the party qualify for powerful positions, and membership is closely vetted to ensure that those who join accept the attitudes of the ruling elite. Most of those states originated through either popular revolt, led by an elite who were to become the bureaucratic class, or military imposition of such rule by another state where it already existed; the particular form of rule was then legitimated by the ideology of the people's democracy.

In a classless society there is no split of the population into mutually antagonistic groups, and so no need for alternative parties which compete to run the state; there is just one party, which reflects the popular view as expressed through its deliberations, and the legitimacy of that approach is secured through elections in which only the one party fields candidates. Clearly, then, the degree to which it represents the popular wishes and enacts them through the bureaucracy is a function of the party's openness. To the extent that it can control the flow of information and the agenda of what political debate there is through the bureaucracy, so the party acts as a self-perpetuating autocratic body.

Such party-run bureaucratic states need a strong and loyal police-cum-military in order to sustain their legitimacy and to avoid challenges to the imposed social consensus. Where the state has recently been created, therefore, probably replacing either a liberal democratic state, a military dictatorship, or a retiring colonial power, the military presence may need to be large and the armed forces may play a major role in the operation of many parts of the state apparatus, as in several African and Asian countries in recent decades. The military dominance should, ideally, be a temporary stage prior to the development of a state ideology which will achieve popular legitimation of a people's democracy. If it is not, it might become too expensive to sustain, with consequences for the regime's stability.

## Nation-Based Part-Democracies

In regimes of this type, control of the state is reserved to one group within the population, and other groups either play a subsidiary role only or have no say at all in the operation of the state apparatus. Most of the examples of this type of government occur in countries that have several national groups within their borders, of which at least one is denied equality of civil and political rights. The clearest example is South Africa, where one small racial group seized control and for nearly 50 years gave limited rights to two other small groups, while denying any power to the largest of all (which forms a substantial majority of the population). The powerful group operated a carefully manipulated part-liberal democracy, designed to ensure continued support for the ideology and dominance of the bureaucracy. Eventually it failed, because it was economically unsustainable and strongly opposed externally, and the entire population was enfranchised in 1994.

Avoidance of possible conflict between racial and other groups in new, post-colonial states has led to constitutions being written to ensure situations whereby all national groups participate in the state and none feels the need to impose itself on the others. The Fijian Constitution sought multi-cultural harmony, mainly between the (larger) Indian and native Fijian populations, but when elections in 1986 produced a government in which the Indians were in a majority the Fijians, who controlled the military, overthrew it and insisted on a new constitution that would ensure their dominance of the state apparatus (Lawson, 1988).

### Colonial States

Power in this type of regime resides in another country, which has occupied the territory and imposed itself on the native population. It controls the military and the bureaucracy, in association with a local elite which allies itself to the colonial power in order to promote its own interests: senior positions in the military and the bureaucracy not occupied by citizens of the colonial power are filled from that comprador elite.

## INFLUENCING THE STATE

Two basic types of state have been identified, therefore, the liberal-democratic and the bureaucratic. If policies to solve existing environmental problems and to avoid the creation of others are to be promoted, there is a need to understand how those states operate and how they can be influenced. Most attention is focused here on the liberal-democratic states.

## THE POLITICS OF LIBERAL-DEMOCRATIC STATES

The freedom to organise and campaign within liberal-democratic states means that people with different views can form political parties which present their programmes to the electorate. In complex societies, where frequent recourse to the population is not possible and so methods of representative democracy have been evolved, it is argued that such parties are necessary to the running of the state, for two reasons. First, they allow the election of blocks of representatives to the legislature, who can be relied upon to vote together on most, if not all, issues, and so give some stability to the allocation of power within that body. Second, they allow the electorate to be presented with coherent programmes for the conduct of the whole of the state's business, and not *ad hoc* policies for particular, perhaps transitory, issues. Together, these form the cornerstone for the adopted method of running most parliamentary democracies ruled by a government accountable to a deliberative assembly. After an election, power to run the government, and hence control the bureaucracy, is allocated either to that party which has a majority of the members of the legislature or to that coalition of parties which is prepared to work together and which has majority support in the legislature, as expressed through votes of confidence. (In states with a legislature consisting of two houses, as in Australia, constitutional arrangements determine which has primacy if the majority party is not the same in both. Other states have power distributed among several parts of the state apparatus – as in France and the United States, where both the president and the legislature are separately elected and may be in conflict over the direction of policy; constitutional arrangements there determine which has ultimate power, and under what circumstances.) Thus the representative system of liberal democracy involves the population granting power to political parties according to their relative importance in the legislature. This is especially so where parliament is a deliberative assembly which considers and passes legislation and is the forum for the conduct of government business (as in the UK), as against a consultative assembly, which discusses issues separately and has no exclusive legislative powers.

A major task of the political parties is to mobilise support among the electorate around their political programmes. Such mobilisation could start anew at the time of each election, when the parties have to go to the electorate for their approval. This would not be in the parties' interests, however, for it would mean they had no stability of support. What they want is as many voters as possible committed to their political programme, and then for those voters to express that commitment in the ballot box. This they achieve through processes of political socialisation, whereby people are raised in milieux within which the political parties, either directly or through associated agencies (such as trade unions), seek to educate them continuously and so win their strong support, if not even greater commitment to the cause as expressed through membership of the party and willingness to act for it in a variety of ways.

How are the political programmes around which parties seek to mobilise support formulated? Each country has unique features that have influenced its development, but in an important essay two political scientists suggested a general model of the emergence of what they term 'electoral cleavages' (Lipset and Rokkan, 1967). An electoral cleavage is a division of a society on electoral grounds; those on one side of the cleavage are mobilised to support one party, whereas those on the other side are mobilised by a further party, which both presents an alternative political programme and opposes that of its rival. Lipset and Rokkan's major contribution was their classification of such cleavages into four major types.

From a comparative analysis of western European political systems, Lipset and Rokkan suggest that electoral cleavages have developed as a consequence of two major periods of revolution. The first was the national revolution, when the nation-state, associated with a centralised state apparatus, emerged as necessary to the promotion of capitalism. This generated two major cleavages, of which only one might be present in some states. The first was between dominant and subservient national groups, with the former taking control of the increasingly centralised state apparatus and the latter being relegated to a subsidiary position, creating what is frequently termed a 'core–periphery cleavage'. The relative importance of this cleavage depended on the degree to which different national groups existed within the state's territory, or were later incorporated within it as part of the process of nation-building, and also on the degree to which the dominant nation was able to impose itself on the others and erode their identity. The second cleavage was between the supporters of the new focus of ideological power, the centralised state, and those of the old, the Church. If the first of these cleavages were present, parties would develop to represent the interests of the different national groups and to promote political programmes which favoured them; similarly with the second, parties emerged to promote respectively the secular and the religious control of the state and its ideology. If both were present, there could be at least four parties (one representing the secular dominant nation, for example, and another representing the religious subsidiary nation).

Following the national revolution came the industrial revolution, which substantially changed the contours of most societies. Again, Lipset and Rokkan suggest that two major cleavages may have emerged. The first was between the two major economic interest groups – the landowners, whose wealth was obtained from agriculture, and the industrialists, whose wealth was based on manufacture. To the extent that these two groups wanted different political programmes (protection for one, free trade for the other, for example), so they could be mobilised to support different parties, producing an electoral cleavage that was basically a division between town and country (or the urban bourgeoisie versus the rural gentry).

The final cleavage in Lipset and Rokkan's schema followed the industrial revolution, and particularly the enlargement of the franchise. As an increasing proportion of the population joined the electorate, there arose the potential to mobilise voters across what has become known as the 'class cleavage', with those who sold their labour power on the one side (often known as the working class) and those who bought or managed it on the other (the middle class).

Lipset and Rokkan argued that the relative importance of the first three cleavages depended on the nature of the different societies which provided the matrix into which the fourth was set following franchise extension. The class cleavage virtually eradicated all others in some countries (Great Britain is usually presented as a paradigm example of this), whereas many others have remnants of at least one of the preceding three (as in the Netherlands and in Switzerland). In a few other countries particular local circumstances saw the development of cleavages outside the model's orbit. In the Republic of Ireland, for example, the main cleavage has been between two parties which had opposing views on the validity of the 1922 settlement with Britain, but class issues have increasingly intruded (O'Loughlin and Parker, 1989). In the United States, federal politics was long dominated by regional differences, which in part reflected a core–periphery division (Archer and Taylor, 1981) but also resulted from the wish of southern whites to sustain their assumed racial superiority. Nevertheless, class differences are also present, and have been observed in voting at state and local scales (Hodge and Staeheli, 1989).

Further 'revolutions' have taken place more recently, which have either introduced additional cleavages or led to the replacement of the preceding ones (Harrop and Miller, 1987). The first is the 'welfare state revolution'. As political programmes designed to ensure the legitimacy of the capitalist mode of production among the 'working class' were advanced, so a growing proportion of the electorate became dependent on welfare state provision and were mobilised to support its continuance, against those who promoted free market operations (on this in Britain, see Dunleavy and Husbands, 1985; on its possible demise, see Johnston, 1993). Secondly, there was the growth of what some see as a 'post-industrial' stage of capitalism, in which affluence is widespread, material concerns are less important, and class politics is replaced by 'value politics' (Harrop and Miller, 1987, p.175). This 'value politics' may include support for environmental causes, and is the focus of more detailed examination below.

## THE CONTEST FOR POWER

Each liberal democratic state has one or more electoral cleavages, therefore, whose nature reflects the history of conflict within its political system, the major social divisions within both its sphere of production and its civil society, and the activities of the political parties in mobilising voters around particular causes and programmes. Each party's goal is to establish a core of support on which it can rely in all electoral circumstances; from that core it extends its campaign to others either less committed to any particular party or apparently prepared to switch parties. The larger the core the better, of course, but the larger the core the greater the probability that it will be heterogeneous in composition and thus difficult to hold together.

Whereas political parties would ideally like voters to be committed to them without question, such undying loyalty is unlikely (increasingly so given the greater social and spatial mobility within society). Citizens must be socialised to support a broad-based programme which leads them to identify with the party and its attitudes towards the particular issues of the day; mobilising voters around specific issues may generate substantial support in certain circumstances while the issue is salient, but may make it difficult to sustain that support when the issue is of less importance to most people. Thus parties develop a general ideology, based for example on an appeal to people in a particular social class (with the party perhaps making a substantial contribution to the development of that class identity, so that class and party go together). From the core of support that this provides, they can then develop policy agenda relevant to issues that may be localised in both time and space.

Having created an identity on one side of an electoral cleavage, a party then has to compete with others for electoral support. The goal is to win as many votes as possible, so that it obtains a majority of the seats in the legislature and can form the next government. This competition for votes means, as a seminal analysis by Downs (1957) showed, that to some extent the parties must conceal their separate identities in order to capture sufficient support. Downs's analysis assumes that members of the electorate are arranged on an attitudinal scale from left to right; the closer they are to the ends of the scale, the more 'extreme' they are in their views. The cleavage is between right and left, so each of the two parties has its core of identifiers to one side of the median point on the scale. In order to win power, each party must be supported by at least half of the electorate. If more than half are closer to it than to any other party, then a party's success is ensured; the problem is for the other party, which would seem to have no chance at all of winning majority support. Whatever the distribution of attitudes on the scale, the parties will come close together as they compete for votes.

Assume the distribution of voters on the attitudinal scale shown in Figure 6.1A. Assume also that electors are rational, and vote for the party closest to them on the scale. To win majority support a party must place itself closer to over half of the voters than its opponent. The two parties start somewhere to the left and the right of the centre respectively; both have the support of about half the electorate, but neither can be sure of winning a majority. Party L starts the strategy by shifting slightly to the right on the scale, and therefore putting itself closer to more than half of the electorate (Figure 6.1B); it 'invades' some of R's territory. Party R responds by moving towards L (Figure 6.1C), thereby not only 'regaining' territory but also 'invading' some of L's. As this strategy continues, so the parties approach each other, until both occupy a position in the middle ground (Figure 6.1D), fighting for votes

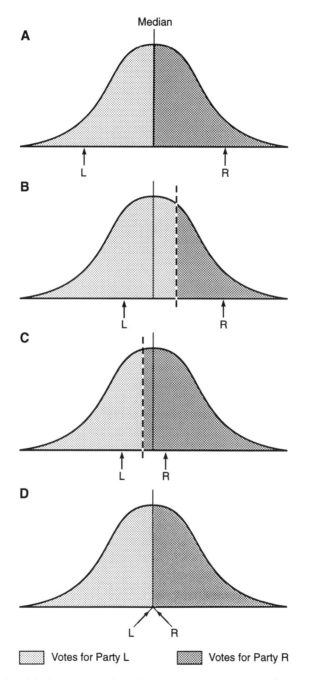

**Figure 6.1** Graphical representation of Downs's argument regarding the nature of party competition

on election programmes that are very similar because they want the support of the same voters.

This argument makes a number of potentially unrealistic assumptions about voter and party rational behaviour, but as a general picture of party competition it bears considerable similarity to the situation in many liberal representative democracies (as suggested in Butler, 1960; see also Johnston, 1979a). Moving to the centre carries with it the possibility of alienating support at the extremes, where voters either abstain or support a party established to win their backing; to avoid either possibility, each party must keep contact with its 'wing'. But not to move towards the 'middle ground' opens up the possibility of a 'centre party' occupying it, and (if a majority of the electorate is 'middle of the road') garnering a large number of votes as a consequence.

Many societies have more than one cleavage, but Downs's analysis works in a multi-dimensional attitudinal space as well as the simple one-dimensional attitudinal scale shown in Figure 6.1. In such situations, however, it is often hard for any one party to come close enough to sufficient of the voters to win majority support, in which case it has to be content with a substantial legislative presence, in the realisation that no other party will have a majority of seats either. The formation of a government then involves the creation of a coalition of parties based on their power within the legislature and their willingness to co-operate with other parties (and thereby perhaps bargain away some elements of their programme in order to win support for others in the joint government programme). The larger parties usually have most power in such bargaining, but mathematical analysis has shown that small parties may 'hold the balance of power' and have more bargaining resources available to them in the coalition-formation process than they have seats (see, for example, Johnston, 1982c; 1995).

Downs's analysis treats the electorate of a country as a whole, and each party's task is to win as many votes as possible. This implies that the number of seats which a party obtains in the legislature is a function of the number of votes it obtains, a situation generally termed 'proportional representation'. The relationship between votes and seats won is frequently far from perfect, however, as a consequence of the particular form of electoral system used. Each country practising liberal representative democracy has its own electoral system which differs in some details from all others. The basic features of those systems can be related to three main characteristics, however.

(1) *Constituency size.* The main difference is between systems of single-member constituencies, such as those for the UK House of Commons and the US House of Representatives, and those which use multi-member constituencies, such as the Irish Dáil. Israel and the Netherlands each has a single constituency, the entire country.

(2) *Method of voting*. Systems differ between those in which electors only indicate a single preferred candidate or party and those in which they are required to rank-order their preferences for some if not all of the candidates/parties.

(3) *Method of distributing seats*. On this characteristic, electoral systems differ in the way that they translate votes won into seats to be occupied. With some, such as the list systems of several western European countries, the differences are relatively minor and relate to the formula used for allocating seats. In others, the method depends upon the other two characteristics. Both Australia and the UK have single-member constituencies, for example: in the UK a plurality system is used, whereby each constituency is allocated to the candidate winning the largest number of votes, which may well not be a majority; in Australia a preferential voting system – the Alternative Vote – is used to ensure that more people prefer the elected candidate than any of the others.

These three characteristics make for an interesting diversity of electoral systems, especially when they are combined into hybrids (as in Germany and, from 1995, New Zealand). Our concern here is not with their details (see, on this, Taylor and Johnston, 1979), but rather their political implications.

It is sometimes claimed that a country's political system is very much determined by its electoral system, a claim refuted by detailed analysis (as in Bogdanor and Butler, 1983). Nevertheless, Rae's (1971) comparative analyses showed that whereas plurality, single-member systems such as the British are likely to produce legislatures in which a single party has a majority of the seats despite not having a majority of the votes (what Rae calls a 'manufactured majority'), in systems where the seats are distributed proportionally to votes majorities in the legislature are rarer and coalition government is common (see also Taagepera and Shugart, 1989). Further, systems such as the British favour a political milieu dominated by two parties only (Gudgin and Taylor, 1980), especially where a single electoral cleavage dominates too; 'third parties' find it difficult to win seats in such situations.

## THE CONTEST FOR VOTES

This discussion of electoral systems is important to an appreciation of the use of the state in the attack on environmental problems. Before turning to that topic explicitly, however, it is necessary to look at the bases of political competition.

In the contest for votes at national elections in the liberal representative democracies, almost all of which are in the core of the capitalist world economy, parties offer themselves to the electorate as willing and able to operate the large and complex state apparatus and sustain it in its basic functions of securing social consensus, promoting capitalist accumulation, and legitimating the mode of production. They do not campaign on those terms, but nevertheless they are clearly the basis of the appeal, which is more popularly expressed in slogans such as 'Life's Good under the Conservatives: Don't Let Labour Ruin It' and 'Britain Is Great Again: Don't Let Labour Wreck It'. Thus the salient issues at most elections relate to the three basic functions. Different aspects of the functions may take precedence at different elections, however. At the 1979 UK general election, for example, law and order was high in many voters' minds and in the party campaigns, following the 'winter of discontent' and the many strikes in the preceding months, whereas at other recent contests the rates of inflation and unemployment have been crucial issues. Sarlvik and Crewe (1983, p. 272) used survey and polling data to identify four major 'issues that counted' during the 1970s in the UK: strikes, unemployment, rising prices, and law and order. At the 1983 general election, attitudes and policies towards the welfare state and defence were salient too (Dunleavy and Husbands, 1985), and in both 1987 and 1992 the main focus was on individual and national prosperity.

The importance of a small number of general issues related to accumulation, legitimation and consensus has been demonstrated by a substantial volume of research by political scientists and others on the relationships between these and voting/party support. (A general review is given by Weatherford, 1986.) In the United Kingdom, for example, work on the four general elections won by the Conservative Party in 1979, 1983, 1987 and 1992 provides clear evidence that those satisfied with their current and forthcoming financial situations were much more likely to vote for the incumbent government's return than were those who were dissatisfied and pessimistic (Johnston and Pattie, 1989), thereby accounting to a substantial extent for the growing spatial polarisation of the British electorate (Johnston et al, 1988). Indeed, economic voting explanations now dominate psephological debates (see Sanders, 1994) – in particular, governments' re-election prospects are believed to be closely aligned with what is known as the 'feel-good' factor. That factor is multi-dimensional, comprising elements of both individual self-interest (egocentric voting) and community interest (sociotropic voting). On the first, people will reward governments under whose policies they have prospered, especially if they are optimistic about the future, whereas pessimists are more likely to punish them by voting for opponents. On the second, people will reward governments which deliver national (or regional: Johnston and Pattie, 1995) prosperity, whatever their individual situations, and punish those which do not.

These analyses suggest that certain sets of issues are likely to dominate the electoral agenda because of the functions of the state in capitalist societies. The dominant issue at a particular election may not be directly linked to the three main state functions, either because it is of immediate importance to the electorate or because the parties do not differ on the salient issues (as was claimed in the UK after the 1992 general election, when all three main parties embraced expansion of the European Union). This is rare, however, and it is difficult for parties to manipulate the electoral agenda away from issues of general concern, as exemplified by the Australian general election of 1978, which followed the Governor-General's dismissal of the Whitlam government; Whitlam sought to focus the electorate's attention on the constitutional issue raised by the dismissal, but the opposition won because of its attack on Whitlam's economic policies.

## BRINGING ENVIRONMENTAL ISSUES IN

How can environmental policies be brought to the forefront of the political agenda? How can parties and governments be forced to give priority to solving existing environmental problems and preventing others being created? For the moment, we assume that the existence of the problems is not controversial, and focus on the political process of promoting policies.

### Convincing an Existing Party

One strategy available to those seeking to promote environmental policies is to convince one of the existing parties – preferably a major one that is likely to win electoral power either on its own or as a major partner in a coalition – to adopt, and be committed to implementing, a range of environmental policies. In this way, the environmentalists would be allying themselves with a party that already has a core of support among the electorate and has a programme in place that covers the salient issues in the electoral contest. Such a party would have to consider whether adoption of environmental policies would make it more difficult to extend its electoral support, and whether it might even lose support from among its core as a consequence of embracing green causes. Environmentalists would need to consider what would happen if the party lost power, and the green policies were then dropped by the new government.

### Convincing All the Major Parties

A second strategy is to convince all of the major parties that they should adopt environmental policies, because of their importance to future prosperity, and thus to the long-term promotion of accumulation. Success with this strategy should ensure a prominent place for environmental policies, whichever government is in power, and the threat of withdrawal of support from the pro-environmentalists should those policies not be promoted vigorously might be an effective sanction. The viability of that sanction, however, would depend very much on whether environmental issues are salient to the electorate, so that they would withdraw support from a party on those issues, even if they were satisfied with its performance on others, notably the economic.

Parties can partially outflank this strategy by all adopting a pro-environmental stance, and thereby effectively removing it from the political agenda; if all parties agree on an issue, then it cannot be used to discriminate between them, unless evaluation of their performance on that issue is salient when they next approach the electorate for support. This has been the situation in the United Kingdom in recent years, as both Brotherton (1986) and Owens (1986) have shown. With regard to conservation, for example, Brotherton provides quotes from each of six parties published in 1983 which are 'interchangeable: any of the six parties could have made any of the six statements' (1986, p. 151). But his analyses led him to conclude that:

> although all six parties view conservation as a desirable goal, it is, for all but one [the Ecology Party], subordinate to more important aims and ideals. As a result, conservation policies are not always framed in terms of what is best for conservation. At the very least they must be compatible to the party's ideology; and, if possible, they will positively promote this. Conservationists may not like it. But conservation policies reflect party ideals, not conservation commitments. (1986, p. 159)

Thus, for example, of greatest concern to Labour and the Scottish National Party are the inequalities of wealth that are the consequence of land ownership, while Conservatives are really interested in championing the freedom of farmers, along with other individuals, to use their property as they wish. The commitment to conservation would seem to be of only 'fringe importance' to the parties, and is included to ensure that they cannot be accused in electoral debates of 'not caring'. This conclusion is illustrated by studies of voters' attitudes. Analyses of responses to eight environmental issues among the British electorate in the late 1980s, for example, showed that they differed in three separate ways (Pattie et al, 1991; for similar findings from a multinational survey, see Rohrschneider, 1991). There were those who were for and against nuclear power (with varying degrees of strength of opinion), those who were for and against countryside conservation, and those who approved or disapproved of 'modern' farming methods. The anti-nuclear group were strongly pro-Labour, whereas those favouring countryside conservation were pro-Conservative: the Alliance had most support among those opposed to modern farming methods.

Owens (1986, p. 200) also identifies a 'greening' of the positions of all parties, producing 'a striking similarity in the rhetoric across the political spectrum'. She argues that this is because the parties are accommodating their positions to changing social values, without making any major commitment to action:

> all parties have tried to accommodate the new concern without confronting any fundamental contradictions between their own values

and ideology and those of 'green' politics. The result is a certain blandness of environmental policies across the board.

Nevertheless, she suggests that accusing politicians of blatant opportunism may be an oversimplification, in part because there are few votes to be gained in green issues, relative to economic and other concerns. Rather:

> An alternative explanation is that environmentalists have been presented with a 'window of opportunity' by a particular combination of circumstances: a new party [the SDP] seeking 'untrodden' policy grounds; a handful of prominent 'single issues' (lead in petrol, green belts, acid rain, nuclear waste); and the significance of some of these issues in marginal seats. Recognising the opportunity, committed individuals within the Alliance have actively colonised environmental ground and other parties, fearful of losing votes, have followed suit. (1986, pp. 200–1)

Thus when the Prime Minister, Margaret Thatcher, made a major speech promoting pro-environment attitudes in autumn 1988, and followed this with a conference aimed at ending the use of CFCs, the other parties could not condemn the policies and rhetoric, but only suggest that her conversion was 'too little, too late', that her policies were not going to work because they clashed with her government's ideology, and that they (the other parties) were much 'greener than she'.

### Launching a New Party

A third strategy involves launching a new party that will have environmental issues as its major concern. This has been done in several countries in recent decades, led by the West Germans and the French: as Porritt and Winner (1988, p. 212) express it, the Green Party in West Germany (Die Grünen) has 'seized hold of the imagination of all those even remotely interested in green matters. They have been a beacon of hope' (though they continue by observing that 'they have in many important respects made an appalling mess of things in their own country').

The success of a green party depends on two factors. First, it must convince electors that, of the many issues on the political agenda, environmental problems are the most salient and that other parties do not give them the highest priority in their manifesto commitments and likely policy directions. Voters should therefore opt for a party whose manifesto makes it clear that environmental issues are the most important facing society and their resolution must be the highest priority in any legislative programme. Second, on the assumption that it will not win a legislative majority, the green party must be able to influence government policies and thereby ensure action against environmental problems.

The West German electoral system was particularly suited to the emergence of such a party with regard to both of these issues, which is not to imply that it is necessarily either the only place for a relatively successful green party to emerge, or that it had to be successful there. (According to Hay and Haward, 1988, p. 435, the first 'green party' was founded in Tasmania in April 1972, one month before the inauguration of the Values Party in New Zealand.) Each person has two votes in the German electoral system, one for a constituency member (elected as under the British system) and one for a regional party list; the final composition of the *Bundestag* is proportional to the distribution of the second set of votes. Thus electors can vote for both one of the major parties (usually in the constituency contests) and the Green Party (on the regional list), a possibility not available in most other countries, where to vote green means voting for no other party. It is easier to convince people to vote green at least once in Germany, and indicate their support for environmental policies, since by doing so they are not effectively disfranchising themselves from influencing the process of government formation, which they would be doing by voting for the greens (or any other minority party) in other electoral systems.

In the UK, on the other hand, electoral support for the Green Party can be interpreted, as it is by members of other parties, as a 'wasted vote': some are prepared to 'waste' their vote because of their commitment to the party and its principles; others may do so in constituencies where their vote is likely to be 'wasted' anyway, because the constituency is a safe seat for one of the major parties. In 1989, the Green Party won over 15 per cent of the votes cast in the United Kingdom at the European Parliament elections. Some perceived this as a major breakthrough, but others (rightly so, in retrospect) were less optimistic. The government party was extremely unpopular, both major opposition parties were in some disarray, the election had low salience with the electorate, and turnout was very low. A strong Green campaign won support from those prepared to express their environmental concerns when no other issues were to the fore; by the time of the next general election (1992) most voters were influenced by economic issues and the Green Party's share of the poll fell to about 1 per cent.

The importance of the electoral system in the development of green party politics is stressed by a number of authors. Rudig and Lowe (1986, p. 277), for example, argue that:

> The British system makes it relatively easy to form a political party and to field a small number of candidates. The financial threshold of the deposit makes it difficult for small parties with limited resources to mount a larger electoral challenge, and the first-past-the-post system makes it very difficult for new parties to achieve any representation.

Their analysis of the British Ecology Party (as it was then called) is largely pessimistic; their article's title is 'The "withered" greening of British politics'.

Apart from the problems presented by the electoral system, they concluded that the stimulus for radical green politics had been weak in Britain in the 1970s and 1980s because:

> low economic growth and industrial inefficiency have constrained the development and the expansion of environmentally controversial projects . . . [which in any case] were sited in a way which reduced the potential for local opposition. Where strong resistance to particular projects did arise, the authorities were relatively quick to withdraw the plans. (1986, pp. 281–2)

The focus of green politics in Britain has been on particular, usually localised, projects rather than a general mobilisation around environmental themes, therefore; governments are adept at limiting political damage when such a local project is strongly countered; and the British economy was in such a condition that few projects were being launched in any case. (Rudig and Lowe might also have noted that the British electorate appears to be convinced that economic issues, and especially personal economic issues, are those on which they should judge the performance and promises of political parties.) Green politics will flourish in periods of relative prosperity only, it seems, when the affluent will vote for policies to limit the creation of environmental problems. Similarly, in their analysis of a Tasmanian campaign, Hay and Haward (1988, p. 445) conclude that:

> Little can be claimed beyond the obvious: that the green vote flourishes in areas where both blue collar workers and the very affluent are comparatively *under*-represented . . . green values have little attraction to either the conspicuously affluent or the traditional working class.

This limits those who can be mobilised around environmental issues to the 'humanistic intelligentsia' (the term is Gouldner's, 1979) who are 'tertiary educated, urban, relatively affluent, professional and employed in those parts of the public sector not engaged in provision of the production infrastructure' (Hay and Haward, 1988, p. 445; they thereby exclude what they and Gouldner term the 'technical intelligentsia', who are directly involved in production). Hay and Haward optimistically note that the humanistic intelligentsia is rapidly growing in its relative size, however, and has interests very different from those of the 'traditional middle class'.

Rudig and Lowe (1986, p. 283) suggest that in order to succeed environmental parties will need to broaden their appeal:

> environmental parties will thrive to the degree that they can absorb other issues and cleavages. Where the New Left, regionalism, or agrarian interests have failed to form their own strong organizations or promote their demands successfully by other means, they might become attracted to the idea of a green party.

They note, in particular, the failure of the British Ecology Party to embrace the anti-nuclear movement, many of whose members remained active in the established parties (especially Labour and Liberal). To advance their argument, they quote the West German Grünen, which occupied political ground made vacant by the failures of the New Left, and which when in the *Bundestag* represented the peace movement and campaigned for the welfare state, as well as promoting green issues.

Whether green parties can act elsewhere in the way Rudig and Lowe describe for West Germany depends on the legislative context. In some situations, their votes may be crucial because no party has an overall majority and therefore the greens may be wooed into a coalition; to achieve this, they will undoubtedly be required to bargain away some of their proposed policies (if not their principles) in order to have others accepted and enacted. To what extent should they be prepared to bargain? Should they bargain at all? These questions were raised within Die Grünen, and led to substantial public intra-party differences. The main split was between those who recognised the need to reach an accommodation with the other parties in order to achieve any of their goals (hence they are termed the realists, or *Realos*, who aim to achieve radical reform through bargaining within the system – their programme, according to Papadakis, 1988, is one of 'self-limiting radicalism') and those who prefer to stand by their principles and not compromise (they are thus the fundamentalists, or *Fundis*). Each faction faced a major problem. The fundamentalist strategy may fail, because the group becomes isolated within the legislature and has no impact at all on policy; it may attract publicity for its members and their cause by their legislative presence, but if they deliver nothing they may then be punished at the next election by all but their staunchest supporters. The realist strategy may fail, too, because the stronger parties are able to accommodate most of the green policies, probably in a watered-down form. Further, unless the party holds some 'balance of power' in the legislature, so that its votes are crucial to the government parties, its long-term influence is likely to be slight.

The German situation has been favourable for Die Grünen since the late 1980s, however, especially in some of the *Länder* rather than the national *Bundestag* (see *The Independent*, 13 March 1989) and in this context the *Realos* appear to have won the debates within the party (*The Independent*, 6 March 1989). In May 1995, the small centrist Free Democratic Party (which has frequently held the balance of power in Germany) was ejected totally from the legislatures in Bremen and North Rhine-Westphalia, whereas Die Grünen doubled their vote share (from 5 to 10 per cent) and forced the Social Democrats to negotiate over coalition arrangements. As *The Economist* (20–26 May 1995) expressed it, the Greens'

> long campaign to turn a corner from sandals-and-beard radicalism seems
> to have paid off: Germany's mood seems to be turning their way.

The Greens are no longer right out of tune with German industry, especially since industry itself has turned environmental protection into big business. It was perhaps no coincidence that the Green surge in North Rhine-Westphalia came at a time when new environmental industries in the Ruhr (clean-up technology, recycling and so on) provide more jobs than coal and steel put together.

The Social Democrats are increasingly willing to work with the *Realos*, with their leader pointing to 'a massive difference between the Greens' often weird and woolly musings within their own circles and their national leaders' more urbane images', an observation which implies a potential conflict within Die Grünen.

## Influencing Individuals

A fourth strategy is to influence individual members of the legislature, irrespective of party. In most legislatures, party organisations are strong and dominate the conduct of business. Individual members have few degrees of freedom but may be able to achieve substantial gains acting individually, by promoting legislation that wins sufficient support to be enacted; the abortion legislation piloted through the UK House of Commons by David Steel in 1968 using a Private Member's Bill is an excellent example. So lobbying individual members may generate particular successes, but major policy changes (such as outlawing nuclear power generation) are unlikely to be achieved in this way.

One electoral system where the party organisation is weaker than elsewhere is the American, in part because of the division of powers between Congress and the President. Individual members of Congress can promote measures that particularly concern them (and/or their constituents), and can mobilise the support of other members by promising to support their pet measures in return. Support is most likely to be forthcoming in this logrolling process for measures that are local in their impact – i.e. affect the individual member's constituency only. A widespread practice which has developed there is known as the pork barrel, whereby individual representatives and senators promote the interests of their home districts and states, thereby hoping to advance their own re-election chances by winning favour 'back home': pro-environmental groups could promote local interests through this channel, and win environmental improvements (as illustrated in Ferejohn, 1974; Johnston, 1980a). Further, they could extend the American system of pressure groups 'rating' the performance of members of Congress (in particular their voting records on salient issues) and indicating whether they endorsed candidates' re-election campaigns, especially in the primary elections within their own party. The endorsed candidates are those whose records are consistent with the pressure group's own programme, and the goal is to have as many candidates as possible from each of the two main parties who are acceptable to the group's position.

### Influencing the Population

A fifth strategy is to influence the population at large. This can have two components. One is the general process of influencing attitudes, whereby the local culture changes; that is the topic of later discussion, and here the focus is on the second only – influencing the population at large in ways that can be expressed through the electoral system.

This strategy is especially important where the political system involves consulting the electorate on specific issues, outside the more general one of electing a government; in some cases the electorate can insist on its opinions being considered. Such routine consultation usually involves the use of the referendum or a similar device. Referendums are virtually unknown in some political systems, such as the British, but are widely used in others. In Switzerland, for example, referendums on certain issues are compulsory (the government cannot act without first obtaining popular approval) whereas on others they are optional, and are usually only held if a fixed number (currently 100 000) of citizens demand that the electorate be consulted. Whatever the origin of the referendum, its result is binding on the government, though in some cases this means that support for the referendum must be given not only by a majority of the electorate but also by a majority in a majority of the 22 cantons (Aubert, 1978). Environmental groups have required referendums on a range of issues in recent years, including control of pollution from cars and 12 car-free Sundays a year: most have failed, however, because such 'initiatives are usually over progressive issues . . . and the majority of the people, are even more conservative than the parliament' (Aubert, 1978, p. 46).

Referendums are not used by the federal government in the USA, but are in several of the states, with the facility for citizens to require ballots on certain issues, whose results are binding on the state or local government. As in Switzerland, they have been used by environmental groups, but with limited success (Ranney, 1978). The facility is frequently used in California, where it became widely known through the success of 'Proposition 13' in 1978, which limited the tax-raising powers of local governments. Several environmental proposals were placed on the ballot papers in the 1970s and 1980s, with only limited success (the main success was the measure that introduced protection of the coast from further development). Failure to carry most initiatives in part reflects the same conservatism among the electorate as noted in Switzerland by Aubert, but it is also a consequence of the nature of the campaigning over the issues. Many of the proposals could, if enacted, severely impact on the profitability of individual enterprises, which have spent very large sums campaigning against them (Lee, 1978). Such campaigns are frequently successful, especially since the proponents of the policies usually have fewer resources available. Issues are often polarised as between protecting the environment and protecting jobs and prosperity, and when they are presented in that light, large numbers of people vote for the latter. They are, after all, socialised into societies in which the dominant ideology is pro-accumulation.

## ENVIRONMENTAL ISSUES, POLITICAL PARTIES AND THE ELECTORAL SYSTEM: A SUMMARY

The conclusion to this section is very largely pessimistic regarding the promotion of policies designed to protect the environment through the electoral system. Elections are conducted in liberal representative democracies in the context of a dominant ideology created and upheld by the state into which people are socialised, and around salient aspects of which (accumulation, legitimation) they are mobilised by the major political parties. As suggested here, some successes have been achieved in getting green policies adopted and green influence in the legislatures, but these have been relatively limited and the prospects for more are not great.

The general failure to advance the green cause within the political and electoral systems of core world-economy countries reflects the incompatibility of that cause with the underlying ideology in those countries. It is certainly not the case that large segments of their populations are against much that the greens argue for. Indeed, Inglehart (1995) has used the 1990/91 World Values Survey to show that a majority of respondents in 32 of the 43 countries surveyed 'strongly approved' of the ecology movement. (Interestingly, the countries with support below 50 per cent included Great Britain, the United States, Sweden, Finland and Norway. The greatest support – over 75 per cent – was expressed in former communist states of eastern Europe and in Argentina, Brazil and Chile.) Alongside this general expression of support (62 per cent overall strongly supported the movement and a further 34 per cent expressed support), other questions tapped people's willingness to implement ecological programmes. Nearly two-thirds indicated willingness to pay higher taxes in order to prevent environmental pollution (70 per cent in Great Britain: eastern Europeans were least willing, and Nordic country residents most) and Inglehart (1995, p. 61) concluded from all of the evidence that

> public support for environmental protection in a given country tends to reflect that country's objective circumstances: the more severely polluted, the greater the public concern . . . Perhaps the most striking finding here is that the publics of three Scandinavian countries (Sweden, Denmark and Norway), together with the Netherlands, show the greatest willingness to make sacrifices for environmental protection. The point is clear: support for environmental protection is not limited to those

countries with the most serious pollution problems – for these four are prosperous countries with relatively pristine environments. It is also no coincidence, we believe, that these are four of the most advanced welfare states in the world . . . [which] suggests that cultural changes associated with prosperity and security have an important linkage with support for environmental protection.

Those prosperous countries with strong welfare states show the greatest development of what Inglehart (1977) calls 'post-materialist' values: this cultural shift involves not only attitudes towards the environment but also 'orientations towards work, fertility, and consumption patterns' (p. 62), as a consequence of the receding threat of severe economic deprivation. Post-materialists, who are increasing in number throughout the more 'developed' countries, are not only more concerned about the environment but also more likely to have done something about environmental issues. This last finding is confirmed by a separate study of 'willingness to pay' for environmental protection in a range of countries. Brechin and Kempton (1994) also found the Japanese much less willing than is the case in all societies with comparable national wealth. Like Inglehart, they believe that this is probably because Japan has fewer post-materialists than other core countries.

Given these conclusions, why are green parties not more successful in the electoral contests in countries with well-developed post-material attitudes? The answer probably lies in the disjuncture between their philosophies and those of their wider political milieux. The philosophy of most green parties is ecologism rather than environmentalism, and while many people may support environmentalist causes (especially local ones relating to conservation) far fewer endorse those promoted under ecologism. The difference between the two is fundamental. Dobson (1990, p. 13) claims that whereas environmentalism

> would argue for a 'managerial' approach to environmental problems, secure in the belief that they can be solved without fundamental changes in present values or patterns of production and consumption

ecologism

> argues that care for the environment (a fundamental characteristic of the ideology in its own right, of course) presupposes radical change in our relationship with it, and thus in our mode of social and political life.

In other words, most green parties' programmes are much too radical for most electors (as the British Conservative Party sought to make very clear after the 1989 European elections, fearing that voters might shift their support more permanently to what was a fundamentally anti-capitalist programme).

This point is illustrated in Pepper's (1993a; 1993b) classification of British political philosophies and their environmental components (see also Harvey, 1993). Thus traditional conservatism focuses on conservation of 'traditional' landscapes and social orders, and believes that enlightened private ownership is the best means of conserving them. Market liberals are even more convinced about the beneficial role of 'market forces' in achieving environmental protection, whereas welfare liberals, also technological optimists, accept the need for state regulation. Many democratic socialists promote green issues within a decentralised society, whereas revolutionary socialists seek to advance environmental concerns as part of the class revolution; the emancipation that will result from their success will end the alienation of people from nature observed by Marx (see p.123). Mainstream green ecologism promotes change in values, attitudes and behaviour and criticises 'old politics', but in its programmes seems to 'straddle the categories of welfare liberalism and democratic socialism' (Pepper, 1993a, p.51). Adherents of green anarchist ecologism, on the other hand,

> generally reject class politics, seeing social change as consequent on the action of individuals in forming spontaneous, mutualist, non-hierarchical groups to live out their politics (e.g. in communes), setting an example for others to follow. . . . the British eco-anarchist's vision [is] of an ideal society involving small-scale, collective, decentralised commune-ism, participatory democracy, low-growth (or no-growth) economy, non-hierarchical living and consensus decisions and the rest . . . (Pepper, 1993a, pp.53–4)

Pepper (1993b) makes clear the distinction between socialist and anarchist analyses of capitalist society and blueprints for the future. Socialists see injustice and exploitation as an outcome of the class structure of the world economy, and call for central planning by states to remove this; anarchists, on the other hand, locate the origins of injustice in hierarchical power structures, which are not peculiar to capitalism, and argue for their removal through stateless societies. Pepper's preference (1993b, Chapter 5) is for ecosocialism, based on common ownership, democratic control, and production to meet needs (see also Ryle, 1988): such socialism can be green, and is both attainable and viable, whereas ecoanarchism is not.

These strands of anarchism and utopianism are very much out of line with mainstream politics, which is strongly focused on material concerns. To ecosocialists, according to Eckersley (1992, p.183), ecoanarchists are 'ultimately marginal and ineffectual' in promoting programmes that can resolve the impending ecological crisis. Their dominant focus on the state as the institution for resolving the crisis is also criticised by Eckersley (1992, p.185), however, who sketches

> a broad-brush picture of what an ecocentric polity might look like. Such an ecocentric polity would be one in which there is a democratic state legislature (which is part of a multilevelled decision-making structure that

makes it less powerful than the existing nation State and more responsive to the political determinations of local, regional, and international democratic decision-making bodies); a greater dispersal of political and economic power both within and between local communities; a greater sharing of wealth both within and between local communities; a far more extensive range of macro-controls on market activity; and the flowering of an ecocentric emancipatory polity . . . I do not assume that handing over more power to local communities will necessarily make them Green, like-minded and 'good'. Higher-order legislative assemblies, institutional checks and balances, the protection of basic political freedoms (e.g. of speech and assembly), and the rule of law are essential to prevent excessive parochialism and the abuse of power.

But is this 'middle-way' between the stateless society of the anarchists and the predominant state of the socialists any more likely to come into being? Does it offer the proponents of ecologism a realistic framework for achievement of their goals, or is it equally likely to be rejected by electorates, even if they have strong environmental concerns? And if it is rejected by electorates, how can it be achieved?

## ALTERNATIVE MODES OF INFLUENCE IN LIBERAL DEMOCRACIES

The 'classic' model of liberal representative democracy has the state steered by a representative body, accountable only to the electorate. Governments are elected to achieve certain goals, and are evaluated on their performance at the next election, relative to the potential of other parties who wish to form the next government. Thus the voter is sovereign, in the same way that in a market-place the consumer is supposed to be sovereign.

This theory of voter sovereignty only partially represents the real situation, just as the theory of consumer sovereignty is only a partial representation of the situation in capitalist markets. In the latter, the producers and sellers of goods not only respond to the consumers' preferences but also seek to mould those preferences, to make buyers want certain goods, and prefer certain brands to others. Similarly, in an electoral system, the 'sellers' (the political parties) seek to mould the opinions of the 'consumers' (the electorate). What is the nature of the mould that they use, and how is its construction influenced? As already discussed, political parties seek to mobilise support around particular versions of the dominant ideology (we thus exclude parties which challenge the dominant ideology). That is not done in a vacuum; the parties are promoting sets of attitudes that are relevant to various interest groups within societies and, as the theory of electoral cleavages illustrates, most political parties emerged to represent major interest groups within society – Church versus state; town versus country; farmers versus manufacturers; workers versus employers; state tenants versus home owners;

and so on. Some of those parties remain tied to particular, relatively narrow, single-issue interest groups only, but the great majority have developed broad programmes presented as representing the interests of major groups within the society, if not society as a whole.

Two questions follow from this outline sketch of the nature of political parties. How do they respond to changing economic and social circumstances? And how do they respond to conflicting claims from within the major interest group(s) they serve? On the first, the normal mode of response is to listen to cases presented by the interest groups affected by the changes and to respond with altered policies where these are deemed necessary; such alterations, if they are to be credible to the electorate over the long term, should be consistent with the party's general ideology. (Though developments in the New Zealand Labour Party after it won power in the 1984 general election indicate that this is not an inviolate rule; increasingly, the parliamentary party, and especially an inner group within the Cabinet, distanced itself from party policy, arguing that it was elected to govern and it knew best. See Johnston and Honey, 1988; James, 1992.) With regard to the second, the parties may either listen to the conflicting claims (from different groups within manufacturing industry, for example, or from both industrialists and trade unionists) and decide on balance which to support, or they may prefer to listen to certain groups only, because they are more sympathetic to their views.

There is a very great range of interest groups, large and small, within a complex capitalist society, and any party has to be selective in deciding which it pays attention to; it may well employ its own advisers to hear the detailed arguments and evaluate the claims, and the civil service bureaucracy also exists to give advice. Thus achieving goals within such a society through political action means having access to and being able to influence those with political power. Such access and influence can be obtained in a variety of ways. One is to treat it as a commodity, to be bought (and sold) like any other. Those wanting influence obtain it, for example, by contributing to a party's funds and promoting it and/or its candidates at election time. Many countries regulate this, to ensure that political parties, and thus governments, are not entirely in thrall to those with money in society, but most parties depend to a greater or lesser extent on donations from those who expect to get benefits (in a general sense if not specifically directed at them) from the party's actions when in power. Thus members of the US Congress may find that success in 'pork-barrel politics' generates substantial local donations to their re-election campaign funds.

Such direct 'buying' of influence is supplemented, very substantially in many cases, by other modes of achieving particular policy directions. For example, political parties strongly committed to the free operation of markets will be prepared to consult those interest groups which share that commitment. The consultation may be formal and organised, but in many situations it need not be. The members of such parties are likely to have many interests in common with those who will benefit from such policies, and they are likely to come from the same backgrounds and residential areas. Informal contacts between acquaintances and friends thus supplement, if not replace, the formal processes of consultation, and are often crucial in obtaining a particular goal.

Given the important function of the state in promoting accumulation, interest groups representing capitalists and their close allies are likely to want to ensure that government policies do not threaten profitability. Thus it is sometimes a surprise to observers that whereas the British Labour Party has a substantial number of its MPs drawn from trade union backgrounds, relatively few Conservative MPs are drawn from the world of business (most are from the professions, especially law and accountancy). The paradox is in part answered by the links between many members of the professions and the operations of capitalism, and also by the common backgrounds of many of the Conservative MPs and the business men and women whose interests they serve. The latter do not need to bother with politics, it is argued, because members of the Conservative Party are well aware of the general interests of business, and are readily accessible informally to make sure that particular points are brought home.

The nub of this argument is that whereas elections *produce* governments, interest groups *influence* them. This mode of operation is termed 'corporatism'; 'corporations' (the representatives of particular fractions of workers, professions and business) seek, and frequently achieve, major influence on the actions of governments. It involves, as Dunleavy and O'Leary (1987, p. 193) describe it, non-elected elites (frequently called 'policy communities') seeking power over elected elites. The result is government via elite collaboration, in which the process of elections plays only a small part.

Corporatism involves more than elected governments being strongly influenced by interest groups, for those groups may also undertake some of the tasks of government. Thus, according to Cawson (1987a, p. 154), it involves not only situations in which

> organizations representing socio-economic interests are permitted a privileged position by public authorities in a bargaining process over public policies which takes place in usually informal institutions outside the reach of formal democratic controls such as parliamentary scrutiny or ministerial responsibility,

but also an 'abdication' of power by the state, so that (Cawson, 1987b, p. 105)

> In exchange for favourable policies, the leaders of the interest organizations agree to undertake the implementation of policy through determining the co-operation of their members.

The result is what O'Sullivan (1988, p. 9) terms a neo-corporatist state, involving both the decentralisation of state sovereignty and the replacement of the 'command–obedience' method of government by one of 'consultation–commitment' (the terms are Ionescu's, 1975). Middlemas (1979) associates this with both the failure of the established political parties to convey popular demands to governments and the relative stability of British politics during much of the twentieth century.

Each political party will accord certain interest groups more influence than others, and work with and through them to ensure that the state functions are performed satisfactorily, both for the interest groups and for the segments of the electorate to whom the party will have to appeal again in a few years. Clearly, given the economic and, in some cases, ideological power of some of the corporate interest groups, it is in the interests of those controlling the state apparatus to collaborate with them, since the alternative is conflict that might be to everybody's disadvantage. If the state does not collaborate with the major economic interest groups in contemporary society, for example, the consequence may well be that the latter withdraw their investments from the state's territory, with obvious implications for economic prosperity, social welfare and the popularity of the political parties concerned.

Where interest groups have it within their power to create crises of various types, they can influence those in charge of the state apparatus. If the crisis largely affects the profitability of investment, it is a *rationality* crisis, which can be tackled by policies that promote accumulation more vigorously. If it largely affects the welfare of individuals, it is a *legitimation* crisis. Several interest groups can stimulate a rationality crisis; investors withdrawing capital, for example, and trade unionists generating threats to profitability. Those operating the state have to try to keep both sides content; they may fail, or they may seek to neutralise the impact of one side (the British Labour Party through nationalisation of major industries, for example; the Conservative Party by methods of reducing the power of trade unions). In the end, the interests of capital must prevail. But they must not be given too many concessions, or this may impact on the provision of welfare and other services, and lead to a legitimation crisis, so the state has to balance the two. Where it fails on both, a motivation crisis comes about, with the decline of consensus and the sort of transition from democracy to dictatorship and back again discussed earlier (p. 174).

The capitalist state apparatus is a large and complex structure: most states are divided both sectorally (different departments charged with oversight of different aspects of economy and society) and spatially (regional and local governments operating under constrained delegation). Most of the topics of particular interest to business within a capitalist society, such as macroeconomic controls, are handled by the central state, whereas many of those of particular concern to individuals, such as the detailed operation of welfare state agencies, are either devolved to local governments or delegated to local offices of central agencies. Thus those promoting causes may have to deal with several agencies at different scales. This is very much the case with many issues of environmental concern: the central government will pass legislation concerned with controls over land use, for example, but its implementation may be the business of local politicians and/or bureaucrats.

## TYPES OF STATE ACTION

How does the state exercise power in order to sustain the mode of production? The political parties and bureaucracies which operate the state apparatus bring sets of attitudes to that task which influence their interpretation of the mode of production and the functions of the state. To some extent, those attitudes comprise a blueprint for the future, a statement of the form of society which the powerful wish to see develop. But many of the politicians' and bureaucrats' actions involve not so much implementing a blueprint but rather dealing pragmatically with issues and problems as they arise. Their attitudes suggest how they should act, but they are rarely able to call on accumulated evidence to back their judgements (in the way that physicians do, for example) which indicates that a problem is typical of a certain category of problems and that there is a set procedure available for dealing with it. That may be the case lower down in a bureaucracy, but at the higher decision-making levels it is rarely so. Because capitalism is always evolving, new problems are always appearing; as Harold Macmillan once replied when asked what were the main influences on his actions as Prime Minister, 'Events, dear boy, events'!

Why do those in power face 'new' problems regularly, which call for pragmatic decision-making, in the light of experience with previous problems but needing specific rather than generalised responses? In part it is because capitalism is always changing, in order to counter its own in-built tendencies towards self-destruction: as certain activities become less profitable, so replacements must be sought, and there are no specific rules which tell investors what will be profitable next. They must 'gamble' on the relatively unknown, and in doing so they create new sets of conditions within which the state must perform its functions. The switch from fossil fuels to nuclear power generation created issues which could not have been foreseen long in advance, and so the state had to respond pragmatically with ways of regulating the nuclear industry as it developed. Secondly, the economic systems operating within capitalism are as complex as the physical ones that they wish to manage, and many of the models of capitalist economies which are used to predict the impact of particular policies are extremely large (as the example in Bennett and Chorley, 1978, p.418, shows). Because of the many interactions involved, a large number of which may be nonlinear, the consequences of certain actions can often only be foreseen very generally.

State actions can be characterised using Berry's (1972) classification of planning activities into four types.

(1) *Normative, goal-oriented: planning for the future.* This is the ideal type, in which the state prepares a blueprint for the future and then devises, implements and monitors policies intended to move the society towards the agreed end.

(2) *Ameliorative problem-solving: planning for the present.* This is 'band-aid' action: a problem arises, and an immediate solution is sought, because a rapid response is called for. Many of the problems are relatively trivial, and have been experienced before in slightly different situations, so a fund of expertise should be available to draw upon. But that expertise is usually applied to ameliorate the problem only; a traffic bottleneck is removed by a small piece of engineering, for example, which means that sooner or later another bottleneck will probably emerge nearby. Many environmental problems are treated in the same way, in part because there is no alternative: a drought in an area is tackled by importing water, for example; nothing can be done to prevent another drought occurring, apart from facilitating the transfer of water.

(3) *Allocative trend-modifying: planning towards the future.* This involves identifying trends within society, and then deciding which to promote and which to dampen down, if not eliminate. Society is steered in the way it seems to be going, which should enable some of the problems along the route to be identified and prepared for beforehand. There is no blueprint, as in type (1), but rather an acceptance of the status quo and a willingness to work with it. Thus, for example, a suburbanisation trend may be identified, and the decision taken to accept it as a desirable evolution of urban form to be facilitated by the provision of better transport networks.

(4) *Exploitative opportunity-seeking: planning with the future.* Unlike the previous category, there is little attempt to recognise the problems that might arise from a trend (such as increased traffic requiring better networks) and instead it is allowed to continue, as desirable for the present, and with the future left to take care of itself. Thus, for example, it may be decided that nuclear power generation is cheaper than that involving fossil fuels, and so investment is encouraged; the problem of how to dispose of the waste will only be identified in the future, rather than being foreseen and influencing the decision whether to promote that trend (as would be the case under type (3)).

Of these four, therefore, the first and the third involve some degree of preparation for the future, whereas the other two involve waiting for the future. The latter predominate in many liberal democracies, in part because of the nature of the electoral process. Governments are elected for limited lives – rarely more than four years. Thus anything but a relatively short-term future is of little relevance to politicians who want to be re-elected when they next go to the country for approval. Many parties will take blueprints (or at least partial blueprints) for the future to the electorate, and argue that they involve a long-term programme spanning several legislative sessions; they then return in a few years' time and ask to be re-elected to finish the job. This wish may be granted, but many governments fall because of negative evaluations of their current performance, irrespective of longer-term goals. They may convince the electorate (especially if the opposition lacks credibility) that in a first term they have done the unpleasant things, to prepare for benefits next time; but they may not. Survey evidence suggests that increasingly people are voting according to their evaluation of the recent and forthcoming performance of the party or parties in power, especially with regard to economic policy, so governments must be able to present a favourable image at election time. This suggests a political-economic cycle, in which governments use the year or so immediately before an election to stimulate the economy and win votes from prosperous constituents (perhaps with the aid of tax cuts), and the years immediately after their victory restraining the economic growth they have generated and the problems of inflation that it has caused.

According to this argument, therefore, ameliorative problem-solving and exploitative opportunity-seeking are the types of action likely to dominate political agenda. In addition, many of the problems that governments and bureaucracies face are not soluble. The concept of a solution to a problem implies a question with a right answer. But many of the environmental problems faced have no right answer, or at least no single right answer; each of the parties involved has its own view of what the right answer is. Solution is thus impossible; all that can be achieved is a resolution, a decision that is accepted by all of the parties concerned. The government, in moving towards a resolution, therefore has to weigh up the protagonists' arguments and propose a resolution. (It may be a protagonist itself, as with proposals from one part of the state apparatus to build a new road, which are evaluated by another part of the apparatus alongside the counter-proposals of other interested parties.) In doing this, the power of the interested parties, including their power to affect the government in some way, may be important; a proposal to dump nuclear waste at one of five sites, several of which were in constituencies held by government members (including ministers), was dropped by the British government shortly before the 1987 general election.

Environmental problems are largely created by human interference with natural systems, interference that is promoted because it is in the interests of some individual(s) or group(s). The resolution, if not solution, of those problems requires them to be placed on the agenda by other interest groups, whose advocacy might then stimulate the state action needed to ameliorate, if not eradicate at source, the problem as perceived. Is that consistent with the operation of political agendas as described here?

## ENVIRONMENTAL PRESSURE GROUPS

Bringing items on to political agenda is the role of pressure groups, defined by Ball and Millard (1986, pp. 33–4) as 'social aggregates with some level of cohesion and shared aims which attempt to influence the political decision-making process'. (This definition does not deny that individuals, working alone, can influence the decision-making process, but argues that in most cases it is necessary for influential individuals to show that they have the backing and commitment of others of like mind.) There is a wide variety of such groups. One way of differentiating them separates interest groups, which promote the views of people defined by their role in society (such as manufacturers, farmers, and trade unions), from attitude groups, which comprise people of like mind, irrespective of social and/or economic background and characteristics, and have much more open memberships. Most of the pressure groups concerned with environmental problems are attitude groups, which creates organisational problems since they have no obvious constituency on whom to draw and who might be expected to join (it is hard to promote a 'closed shop' around such problems), and they have no obvious resource base on which they can call to finance their activities; they are dependent on what the members are able and prepared to contribute (which will reflect their commitment to the cause) and what they can raise from sympathetic others. In promoting certain causes, they are often countered by well-organised and well-financed interest groups.

The number of environmental issues and problems generated by human interference with natural systems is immense, providing the opportunity for a large number of pressure groups, whose existence may be counter-productive and whose co-ordination is extremely difficult; the problems of managing individual voluntary organisations are often very substantial, let alone overlapping organisations with slightly different agendas and campaigning styles. In general terms the groups can be classified on two criteria.

(1) *The focus of their activity.* The main difference is between generalist attitude groups, which promote debate about environmental issues over their full range (Greenpeace, Friends of the Earth and the Sierra Club are good examples), and those which concentrate on one sphere of the environment only, such as the Ramblers' Association in Britain and the National Audubon Society in the United States. Many organisations are neither generalist nor specialist, however, but cover a number of (usually related) issues.

(2) *The specificity of their goals.* Some groups are convened for a specific purpose, such as opposing the drainage of a few hectares of wetland; others have a continuing political programme. The former share many of the characteristics of an interest group, because membership is probably concentrated on, though not exclusively constrained to, residents of the local area involved, and thus a group will probably have a limited life; once the

problem is resolved, its *raison d'être* disappears. The latter have longer programmes, and while they may fight particular issues, their remit extends beyond the individual cause. The two types may conflict. A local group may be formed to oppose the construction of a new road through its area, for example, but it may be relatively unconcerned if the road is routed elsewhere. Such an interest group (sometimes termed a NIMBY group, the acronym derived from the 'not in my back yard' focus of their protest) may be opposed by an attitude group that is against new road construction in general.

How do these groups promote their causes? This is often not a problem for the NIMBY groups, since the existence of the proposal they oppose in itself leads to the establishment of a forum within which their opposition can be expressed and a legal procedure through which their case can be channelled, as, for example, with the land-use planning system in the United Kingdom. Similarly, to the extent that such proposals call forth their protests, wider attitude groups can use the same fora and procedures. But the existence of such institutional structures indicates recognition by the state that such conflicts will arise; they do not cater for 'new' problems, for which there is no recognition and no established mechanism for debate. If this is the case, then the pressure groups have to agitate to get the issues not only on to the political agenda (both electoral and corporate) but also high enough on those agenda that responses are forthcoming.

The initial task of those concerned about an environmental problem is creating awareness that a problem exists; only then can means of countering it be discussed. Their strategies to create that awareness include lobbying individuals and groups within the state apparatus, both bureaucrats and politicians, and many countries have a well-established 'lobbying industry' which offers advice and services to groups wishing to contact and influence those with power to act. Such lobbied individuals may be convinced by the case, and decide to act accordingly. Whether their action will be effective depends on their power and the receptivity of the (relevant national or local) government to what is proposed. In addition to lobbying, activists may enlist support through the media, both to bring issues to wider attention and to put further pressure on those they are seeking to influence.

Politicians are particularly receptive to cases brought to their attention if they believe that there are political benefits to be gained from acting, or political costs to be incurred from not acting. They may be prepared to promote those benefits themselves; for example, if a government is convinced that certain aerosol sprays are destroying some component of the atmospheric system, it may be prepared to promote a 'public education' campaign to support its proposal to reduce the production of such sprays, if not ban them altogether, and it may enlist the assistance of influential individuals within society in that campaign. But if it is not convinced, either by the scientific evidence or by the weight of the case that action is needed, then the pressure group may have to act further to convince it, in one of two ways. The first is amassing further evidence to support the case, especially its scientific basis. The second is obtaining public support; public awareness may have to be built up first, which could involve undertaking 'illegal' acts to attract publicity and therefore media treatment of the cause.

In weighing the evidence, a government or one of its agencies may receive alternative information and advice from other pressure groups, many of them interest groups. For example, the case that a pesticide is leading to the eutrophication of waters may be countered both by the manufacturers, who see their profits threatened, and by the farmers who apply it in order to increase the productivity of their land. The case of acid rain production illustrates the problem well (Park, 1987).

Environmental pressure groups face two major difficulties when they present their cases, especially in public fora such as planning and other inquiries. The first is available resources. In many of those inquiries they are opposed by affected interest groups with very substantial resources available to them, including in some cases agencies of the state itself. The pressure groups are rarely rich, and are therefore at a considerable disadvantage (in the ability to employ legal counsel, for example), as demonstrated in a study of a major British inquiry into the case for a further nuclear power station (O'Riordan and Kemp, 1988). The second is that much of the research on which cases are based is inconclusive, by the nature of the complexity of the systems being studied and the lack of any possibility of conducting test experiments (would a trial nuclear explosion be allowed to see what the outcome might be under certain climatic conditions!?). Thus scientific witnesses 'on the stand' may have to admit uncertainty, leaving those sitting in judgment to decide not on the basis of fact but rather on an assessment of probabilities, albeit expressed by experts. (The representatives of opposing interest groups may seek to discredit the evidence of those experts, if not the experts themselves, in order to influence the judgment.) Scientists face major problems when appearing as expert witnesses, especially as many of them advocate particular causes (Clark, 1982). In many cases it is possible to locate experts with opposing views, so the decision may then rest on the standing and plausibility of the experts, rather than on the work on which their evidence is based.

It is easier to stimulate interest in, and concern about, some issues than others. O'Riordan (1987) has proposed two scales relevant to this (Figure 6.2). The first is familiarity. At one extreme are issues, such as hazards of all varieties, which are immediately identified by and familiar to most people. Smoking and skiing are examples; they are well-known activities, the dangers of which are easily evaluated by individuals for themselves, given a limited amount of information. At the other extreme are the unobservable hazards, whose consequences are not well known and whose effects are in many cases

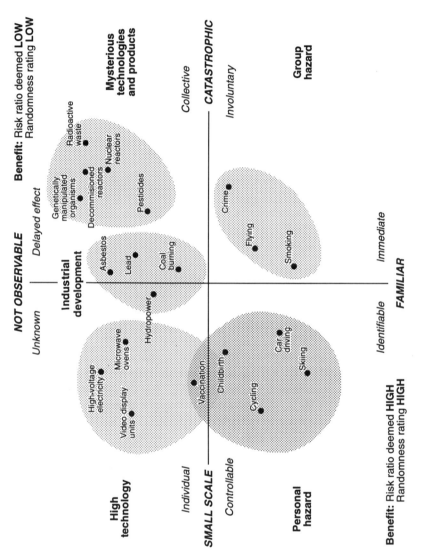

**Figure 6.2** A classification of hazards and risks (redrawn from O'Riordan, 1987)

delayed; asbestos and microwave ovens are cited as examples. The second scale is hazard control. At one pole of the continuum are the small-scale hazards that can be controlled by the individual for her- or himself, while at the other are those whose impact is collective and which cannot be controlled, certainly not by individuals and possibly not by society as a whole. Few hazards fall at the former pole (overeating perhaps?) because in many, such as riding a bicycle on a public road, however careful you are the actions of others can still create hazards over which you have no control. At the other end are 'natural catastrophes', such as earthquakes, against which some collective action can be taken – in the design of buildings for example. Much research on natural hazards, such as floods, has shown that the collective action taken, such as providing insurance, in effect increases the probability of suffering from the hazard (see Burton et al, 1978); people are more prepared to take risks if the costs of failure can be met by a relatively small prior investment (the insurance premium).

O'Riordan identifies five groups of hazards on a diagram with those two axes (Figure 6.2).

(1) The *personal hazards*, which affect people individually, are largely controllable, either by the individuals alone or by one individual and a few others in the vicinity (other car drivers, for example), and involve risks that people can evaluate satisfactorily for themselves without assistance from the state. (This does not prevent the state occasionally insisting on particular actions to protect individuals against hazards in this category, such as compulsory hospitalisation for childbirth in some countries.)

(2) The *group hazards*, which also involve relatively familiar situations for which individuals can evaluate the risks and decide whether to participate, such as flying in commercial aircraft and eating certain foods. Nevertheless, to the extent that the risks are created by others, such as commercial airlines and foodstuff manufacturers, the public may demand state action to minimise the risks by insisting on high levels of safety and protection against human error. Similarly, where the activities have spillover effects, state action may be required to protect the innocent potential victims – such as non-smokers who could be affected by the smoking of others nearby, and the laws against driving when under the influence of alcohol.

(3) *The high-technology hazards*, such as the possible consequences of overexposure to radiation from video-display tubes on office equipment and from microwave ovens, and the believed cancerous consequences of living near power stations and waste tips, and even under power lines. Their impact is usually on individuals and can be controlled accordingly – by the choice of where to live, for example, though the relatively affluent have more choice and are better able to afford to live away from hazards than are others. But the nature of the hazard is often poorly understood, in part because its impact may be delayed, perhaps for years. There is thus a need for public

information and education to mobilise people's concern about the hazards before action can be demanded.

(4) The *industrial development hazards*, which are usually experienced by individuals as members of collectives defined by their co-location, as with the residents of an area affected by the pollution from an industrial plant upwind of it, and the lead pollution from car exhausts that may be experienced by those who live alongside major roads. Again, the impact of many of these hazards is poorly understood, in part because they are slow-acting and the cause–effect sequence is not readily observable (if at all).

(5) The *mysterious technologies and products*, which can have mass, catastrophic effects, as with the failure of safety procedures (the nuclear reactor at Chernobyl, for example), but whose sources are very difficult to appreciate for all but the relatively few who are technologically literate. It is difficult to promote education about these hazards, especially since understanding cannot counter the potential mass devastation; much effort has therefore been invested in creating a fear of the hazards, by pressure groups concerned to limit, if not end, their use, and the existence of that widespread fear has often provoked state action while other, better-understood, hazards are left unregulated.

Many of these hazards involve human interference with the environment, and others could be placed on the two scales. The activity itself may not be hazardous, but its possible consequences are: ploughing land is not a hazard, but the soil erosion that may result is. Many of the activities which lead to environmental degradation are familiar, but their operation may not be observable, either because they are slow-acting or because the impact is felt elsewhere (as with the hole in the ozone layer over the Antarctic apparently caused by the release of CFCs, largely in the northern hemisphere). More importantly, while the actions creating, or at least contributing to, the hazards are individually controllable (we can all stop using aerosol sprays), the impacts of individual use are not limited to those directly involved; it is in the nature of systems that spillovers occur and there can be many 'innocent victims'. Thus, as argued earlier with regard to the Prisoner's Dilemma (p. 132), it requires collective action to ensure individual control.

So how do pressure groups convince those who control collective action through the state of the need for regulation, especially given the time and space delays in the realisation of the impacts of individual action on and in the environment? The hazards in the top half of O'Riordan's diagram need education, of both those who will take the action and those (the general public) who might then demand it of them, if they are to be appreciated. Thus access to education is a major goal of the generalised environmental pressure groups. To some extent it is readily available, because scientists and social scientists from the disciplines involved in the identification of the hazards are themselves involved in the educational systems, especially at the higher education level; they can use research findings to influence their students, and thereby slowly influence others through the formal and informal educational channels. But that is often insufficient, and may be both too slow and too fragmented.

Environmental education, by which all are introduced to the science and social science of the environment, is thus vital to the task of the pressure groups. But they may be opposed by other interest groups, who see such education as potentially damaging through stimulating a set of attitudes within society at large which might threaten their own advancement. Thus the content and style of education are politically contested, especially since education is one of those public goods which the state provides and/or sponsors in order to promote both accumulation and legitimation of the mode of production. In many countries, the content of the educational curriculum is closely prescribed by the state, which therefore has to be convinced of the need for environmental education; this creates a 'catch-22' situation for the pressure groups involved who may have to seek other means of promoting their arguments. The difficulties faced are illustrated by a 1989 report on environmental education produced by the inspectorate of schools in England and Wales, which argued that pupils should be prepared to counter the 'propaganda' of environmental pressure groups: the headline of the story summarising the report in *The Independent* (25 January 1989) was 'Pupils "must know enough to avoid green bias" '!

Even if a policy's desirability has been established by an environmental interest group, it still faces many problems in getting such a policy implemented and monitored. Implementation in capitalist societies frequently involves establishing the costs and evaluating whether they are affordable. As Rees (1985, p. 259) notes, although an economic perspective 'has no monopoly over the truth' it is commonly applied to the assessment of proposals and appraisals based on the goal of achieving economic efficiency. The latter is usually defined according to the Pareto criterion that an allocation of resources is efficient if there is no alternative allocation which simultaneously makes some people better off and no others worse off. The Pareto criterion may be relaxed, however, if nobody becomes worse off and some are better off, after the latter have compensated the former for any relative losses that they may have incurred (see Rees, 1985, pp. 118–120). Applying such a criterion involves the expression of all values in monetary units, so that a cost–benefit analysis can be undertaken. This can produce some bizarre consequences if taken to its logical conclusions (see Adams, 1970; 1974), and raises crucial issues with regard to the valuation of certain 'goods' that are not marketed (as with clean air and attractive landscapes, let alone human life) as well as the incorporation of spillover effects in time and space (some of which, as illustrated in Chapter 2, may be slow in developing and long-lasting in their impacts).

The application of cost–benefit analysis and other techniques of economic evaluation raises important political issues for those promoting pro-environmental viewpoints. To some the issues are not economic at all, but moral. Sagoff (1988), for example, presents a strong argument 'Why political questions are not all economic' and attacks those who argue that environmental problems can be solved through market mechanisms (his particular target is the economist Allen Kneese, author of several influential texts: see, for example, Kneese, 1964; Kneese and Bower, 1968). Sagoff (1988, p. 45) argues that the calculus of the market-place is inappropriate for issues such as environmental protection:

> They involve matters of knowledge, wisdom, morality, and taste that admit of better or worse, right or wrong, true or false – and these concepts differ from that of economic optimality. Surely environmental questions – the protection of wilderness, habitats, water, land, and air as well as policy toward environmental safety and health – involve moral and aesthetic principles and not just economic ones.

Those who control the state can and do impose policies which reflect moral and aesthetic concerns and can commit those subject to the state's sovereignty to pay for such policies. But they must be convinced of the desirability of such policies, of their 'rightness' in moral terms, and they must be able to convince those who will bear the costs that the burden is both necessary and tolerable. In particular, governments in capitalist states must be convinced that the economic base will not be substantially eroded by such expenditure and be able to persuade those who operate the economic base accordingly. It is not an easy task – and policies that are implemented reflect very much on the persuasive powers of those involved. For environmental groups this undoubtedly involves developing popular support for their actions, thereby indicating to politicians that electoral success may be conditional on accepting the arguments. And achieving such popular support may require substantial media campaigns and support, as Lowe and Goyder (1983) conclude from their analysis of the British situation.

Not all action by environmental groups need be directed either at or through the state apparatus, and situations may arise in which groups seek to influence other actors within society directly. Such actions can take a variety of forms, but usually involve challenging conventional methods of doing things – as by questioning a company's environmental policies at its annual shareholders' meeting. The challenges may be backed by actions which threaten the viability of those concerned – notably, in capitalist systems, by threatening markets and profits – and so put economic pressure on them to adopt an environmentally desirable policy.

A good example of such actions is provided by the issue of the obsolete Brent Spar oil platform in the North Sea. Its owners, Royal Dutch Shell, wished to dispose of it since it was no longer of use, and after considering various options decided to sink it in a deep trench in the North Atlantic.

Their research was challenged by Greenpeace, which claimed that the rig contained many tonnes of toxic chemicals which would be dangerous to marine life when released, through corrosion. They argued that the rig should be disassembled on-shore and the toxic materials disposed of safely. To prevent the rig being towed to the North Atlantic they boarded it and for a brief period prevented Shell occupying it. This won substantial media coverage, and was backed by a campaign aimed at getting Shell to change its mind by means of consumer boycotts of its products; governments were also asked to put pressure on Shell. The British government declined to, and argued that Shell's original decision was the correct one, backed by research findings. (Greenpeace later accepted this, indicating that its research materials were in error.) Other European governments did put pressure on Shell, however, and the consumer boycott had an impact. Thus the proposal to sink the platform was abandoned and it was towed to a Norwegian fjord to await a further review.

This success indicates the ability of campaigners to achieve victories on specific issues, especially if they can gain substantial media coverage and widespread public support for their campaigns. But such activities face many difficulties, not least that of sustaining consumer boycotts by continual mobilisation of public opinion. Occasional victories may be won, but the long-term campaign may be lost: some individual investors may put their savings in 'ethical companies' only, but most direct their savings through institutions such as pension funds and can have very little, if any, impact on investment decisions.

## INFLUENCE IN NON-DEMOCRATIC SOCIETIES

How can environmental pressure groups influence what happens in non-democratic societies? In the absence of a democratic process, there is no opportunity for them to seek either to influence the government through the electorate or to stand as candidates themselves. Thus the only option open is to apply pressure on those in charge of the state apparatus by other means.

Pressure groups associated with environmental concerns were by no means absent from the advanced communist/socialist states, especially those of Eastern Europe. Even more so than in the core countries of the liberal democratic world, the individuals involved in such groups were drawn from the more affluent members of society, especially those with a professional interest in the environment. For many, concern over environmental degradation stemmed directly from their scientific work, perhaps assisted by contacts with similar scientists in other parts of the world; their affluence meant that they were less keen for material advancement, and were prepared to put other goals first. They lacked access to the local media and the ability to mobilise the population to their cause, however, although some media became increasingly available to them during the years of *perestroika* and *glasnost*, when repression of 'underground literature' was relaxed.

Such organisations of committed environmentalists in the advanced communist/socialist countries operated in contexts of very serious environmental degradation; some of the worst effects of acid rain in the world can be found in parts of Slovakia, for example, and some Polish analysts argue that parts of their country are ecologically 'dead'. But the scientists who recognised the problems, and perceived the need for alternative policies if the environmental base to rapid industrialisation was to be sustained, were almost all members of the state apparatus, working in the academies of science and the universities (where the highest-ranking, most influential positions tended to be reserved for members of the Communist Party). Their influence was thus through those bodies and the scientific advice that they gave to the higher echelons of the party and the administration. It competed against that of others whose goal was to increase both production and productivity; quantitative measures of economic growth were important indicators of welfare to the senior bureaucrats, and many lost their positions because of failure to deliver the targeted volume of production.

Despite these difficulties faced by those committed to environmental policies, several of the countries concerned established offices to monitor environmental conditions, and supported the growth of relevant research institutes within the academies (Carter and Turnock, 1993a). But by being incorporated within the state apparatus, such institutions frequently found it difficult to promote their cause very far. They competed with other, generally stronger, parts of the bureaucracy for resources and standing, and though they made important gains in particular circumstances, their role did not have a very high general priority in most; their actions have been described by Gustafson (1981, p. 51) as 'not pressure-group politics, but the politics of waiting for the open window'.

To some extent, opening of windows through which environmentalists in advanced communist/socialist countries could advance their cause depended on the pressure brought to bear by the governments of other countries, both unilaterally and through multilateral international agencies. The Chernobyl incident of summer 1986, for example, allowed many eastern and western European governments to bring pressure on the Soviet Union and to demonstrate to it the ecological truth that natural environmental systems are no respecters of international boundaries. Such pressure is akin to that described in the Chicken/Assurance game scenarios. If the authorities in the people's democracies could have been led to value the public good of, say, pollution control sufficiently that they would contribute to it if others did, then their active participation in the development of international policies, and their willingness to allow monitoring of the implementation of such policies, might have led to altered attitudes, to the ultimate benefit of all. Of course, as the recent problems concerning the law of the sea illustrate, states may decline to participate in international collaboration: if they see major benefits from free-riding on the collaboration of others; if they are not convinced of the need for the collaboration in the general public good; or if there are no effective sanctions to stop them benefiting from free-riding.

The difficulties of promoting pro-environmental polices are even greater in the non-democratic countries of the periphery of the world economy, where parlous economic conditions make it difficult for governments to trade off possible economic benefits (and the assistance with legitimation and social consensus that these might bring) against protection of the environment, which reduces, if not removes, the value of some of their natural resources. Furthermore, the mobilisation of opinion in favour of policies that can be interpreted as negating economic growth is difficult in such countries, because of the small size of the educated, affluent population who might both appreciate and be sympathetic to the arguments; there are also problems of opposition to the autocratic rule in many of the countries. This is not to deny the existence of powerful, and sometimes successful, pressure groups there, and the occasional sympathetic reception that political leaders give to environmental causes, but only to note the structural difficulties faced. Given that many children in such countries are starving to death every year, it is difficult for governments to promote policies that seem to be reducing the food output, or at least not actively increasing it; arguments that such policies are conserving the environment for the ultimate good of all, including later generations, are hard to sustain when the alternative is death tomorrow for close relatives of those who are currently suffering.

Some of the best hopes for promoting environmental policies in such countries lie outside them. One way is through inter-governmental links in which advice and assistance with tackling environmental degradation are accompanied by aid that can only be used in 'environmentally friendly' ways. Unfortunately, the advice given often includes the case for rapid promotion of birth control in order to reduce the pressure on the land, a case that may be resisted because it is seen as a way of promoting the interests of those already powerful countries by containing the growth of others who might compete with them in a restructured world economy. The second way is not to influence the governments of the peripheral states directly, for they may be relatively powerless to act, but rather the agencies that are 'developing' the resources throughout much of the Third World. Many of these agencies are either multinational corporations, whose headquarters are in one of the core countries, or inter-governmental agencies, such as the International Bank for Reconstruction and Development. If their actions can be shown, via the media, to the population in the core as degrading the environment of the periphery in order to increase the profits of core companies, pressure might be brought upon them to change their practices in order to conserve rather than rape nature in other parts of the earth. As is so often the case with such issues, however, the conflict then involves the powerful economic interest groups against the much less powerful attitude groups. The latter can seek influence over the former by attacking their profits – i.e. by promoting the boycott of goods produced in 'unacceptable' ways – but few boycotts organised on an international basis have been successful for long periods of time, as other efforts to achieve political goals through interruptions to trade have shown.

Core country governments can also promote environmental causes through their aid and other programmes. Some do: the Australian government offered the Solomon Islands government an aid package if it banned logging by a Malaysian company in an environmentally sensitive area (*The Bulletin*, 16 August 1994). But Hayter (1989) concluded from a study of the effects of British aid on the world's forests that many aid programmes put pressure on Third World states to intensify their environmental exploitation and abuse. Thus:

> Current policies demanded by the West as a means of extracting continued debt servicing, together with big declines in the prices received for most exports, have meant that production, investment, imports and incomes per head have declined by substantial amounts in most of the Third World since the early 1980s.
> . . . Aid from the West . . . is concentrated in countries with 'friendly' governments. This means governments which welcome private investment from the West, allow the repatriation of profits, attempt to service their debts to Western banks, suppress dissent especially of the left-wing type which might threaten Western interests, and, increasingly, follow policies laid down by the World Bank and the IMF. Most Western governments, as well as the private commercial banks, now link the provision of aid and loans to compliance with the demands of those two institutions. The World Bank and the IMF require austerity policies which make possible transfers of financial resources to the West to service debt.

Third World countries are increasingly in thrall to Western creditors, and as a consequence are unable to prevent the destruction of their forests by commercial interests, whatever their rhetoric: financial survival depends on paying off debts, and this in turn depends on the royalties from logging. (See also O'Riordan, 1993.)

Somewhat similar are the 'debt-for-nature' swaps arranged with some commercial banks, whereby debts are written off in return for state policies to safeguard rainforests: Klinger (1994) reports 22 such 'swaps' in the period 1987–93, covering some $100 million and involving eight debtor countries. These are modest in the context of total debt owed by less developed countries ($1.3 trillion, with annual interest payments of $70 billion) and apply only to commercial debts (some 40 per cent of the total). Commercial banks negotiate such 'swaps' by selling debts to third parties, such as conservation groups, at a discount, and the purchasers then relieve the debtor countries of their obligations, in return for commitments to safeguard natural resources. The banks get some of the money they are owed – assuming that they are unlikely to get it all if they don't sell it on (in one case, a bank sold Peruvian debt at the rate of only 5 cents in the dollar), and conservation groups are able to promote their own goals. But those groups are almost entirely dependent on members' financial donations, and cannot expect to make major inroads into the enormous problems of Third World debt in this way; desirable though they are, therefore, they are very unlikely to be a major contributor to the solution of environmental problems in poor countries.

## THE STATE IN ACTION

Dryzek (1987) has suggested a range of actions available to states that wish to implement environmental policies (see p. 139), which can be reduced to three groups.

### EDUCATION

The role of education at a variety of levels is discussed in detail by Trudgill (1990), who identifies eight barriers to the introduction and implementation of environmental policies (Figure 6.3). The initial barrier is situation uncertainty; if people are not convinced that a problem exists, then they may call for more evidence (or better presentation of the existing evidence). Even so, they may then deny the problem's existence, which calls for better demonstrations – both of its present extent and, with greater difficulty, its likely future dimensions. Those two barriers may be overcome, but be followed by problem rejection; its existence is accepted, but its significance is not, again calling for more convincing demonstrations. The next barrier is problem dismissal; the extent and significance of a demonstrated problem are accepted, but not the suggested causes, and so calls to tackle it in a particular way are rejected. Alternatively, the proposed resolution may be rejected as intractable, but whatever the reason for dismissal, further clarification is needed if the problem is going to be fully recognised and tackled.

Convincing people that a problem exists is not always straightforward, especially if there are no immediate, concrete manifestations. Ungar (1992) illustrates this with reference to global warming. Scientists have been issuing warnings about this for at least two decades, but the media and public response in North America was weak until the very hot summer of 1988, when considerable media attention to the wider issue of warming initiated a major social scare. But the weather in later years (such as the cold December of 1989) rapidly erased the memory of that summer, and environmentalists

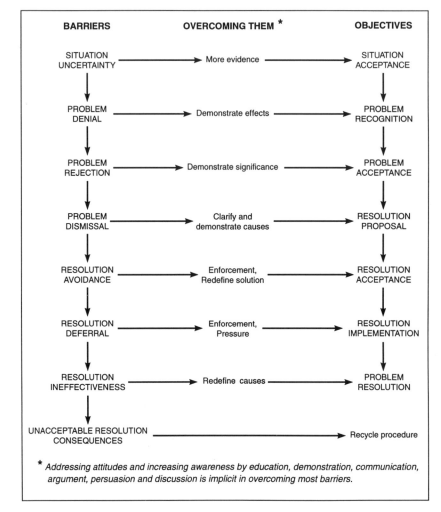

**Figure 6.3**   Barriers to the implementation of solutions to environmental problems (redrawn from Trudgill, 1990, p. 125).

were soon campaigning for measures to counter global warming, without much media attention or popular support. This enabled politicians to turn their attention elsewhere.

Widely publicised environmental problems put pressure on politicians to seek solutions, as with the hole in the ozone layer (Litkin, 1994), which became one of the 'mysterious technologies and hazards' identified by O'Riordan (1987). Much public fear was engendered by non-governmental pressure groups, preying on a combination of ignorance of the scientific causes and apprehension regarding the assumed link between the destruction of the ozone layer and increases in skin cancer. (Cancer is a much feared disease, which attracts a great volume of voluntary donations towards research into its causes and possible cures.) This suggests to Litkin (1994, p. 185) that:

> The importance of crises for catalyzing environmental regime formation [i.e. international solutions to problems] bodes poorly for problems that develop more gradually, such as a loss of biodiversity, tropical deforestation, and global climate change, even if the resulting damage may be huge and irreversible.

Problems with immediate potential consequences are also more pressing on politicians, because of their need to win popular support at elections.

These first four barriers all concern acceptance of a problem's existence, genesis and potential resolution (by any audience, but policy-makers and policy implementers are the most important). The final four refer to action. Resolution avoidance comes about when those with power to act decline to do so, perhaps because of fear of negatively affecting influential others, such as their electoral supporters; a proposed policy may be seen as too expensive, for example, so an alternative, more acceptable, solution is sought rather than implementing the one already agreed. At the next stage, the proposed action may be accepted and legislated for, but its implementation is then deferred, again possibly because of fears over the costs (as with the delay in meeting $CO_2$ emission targets); more pressure to make the government act decisively is needed. The policy may be implemented ineffectively – either because it has been badly drafted (which calls for a re-examination of the causes and how they can be tackled) or because of weak monitoring and sanctions (which calls for a tougher regime). Finally, all of the previous seven barriers may be overcome, and then the government finds it cannot accept the consequences and so aborts the policy – putting those pressing for action back at the beginning of the sequence.

Education and exhortation are necessary but not sufficient: unless people are aware of actual and potential problems they are likely to oppose state policies aimed at their removal. But calls to be 'environmentally friendly' are almost certainly not enough, because unless there is an already perceived need and requirement to act, some at least will probably choose to free-ride. Thus the state has to select one of the other two main options to achieve environmental goals: to regulate or to price.

## REGULATION

Regulation involves the state either passing laws to control behaviour that affects the environment or issuing directions (usually within the overall context provided by laws) aimed at the same goal. Much regulation is negative: it determines what cannot be done, and its effectiveness is based on the extent of monitoring of compliance and the use (and severity) of sanctions against offenders. Thus, as Rees (1985) argues, regulation neither reduces demand on environmental resources directly nor increases the capacity of the environment to meet societal needs.

Three types of regulatory instrument are available: laws and directives; licences; and voluntary agreements requested by the government. Countries vary in their relative use of these three. The US government makes much use of the first type, for example, as in its air pollution legislation which defines minimum air quality standards for different regions and fines polluters who breach the limits – the result is described by Rees (1985, p. 367) as 'a massive, cumbersome and expensive bureaucratic machine'. It has also been unsuccessful. Weale (1992, p.154) notes that the 1970 Clean Air Act's target was a 90 per cent reduction in certain emissions in urban areas by 1977. This was not achieved, so the target was put back, first to 1982 and then to 1987, and three cities were given a further 20 years' grace. The UK, on the other hand, relies much more on a consensus approach, within the overall goal of ending all noxious emissions rather than setting ambient standards, 'on the grounds that [the latter] are impracticable, too rigid and would not allow account to be taken of varying local physical and economic conditions' (Rees, 1985, p.367). The relevant inspectorate is required to take account of local conditions and circumstances, current technical knowledge, and the financial implications of requiring a change in behaviour when setting a 'consent standard' for a pollution source – a system which, compared to the American, is both flexible and relatively cheap.

Such forms of regulation are typical of the ameliorative problem-solving approach to planning identified above; they tackle individual problems pragmatically as they emerge rather than producing an overall blueprint for environmental standards. One exception to this is the Dutch National Environmental Policy Plan, published in 1989 (Weale, 1992, Chapter 5). This sets environmental policy objectives and targets for the year 2010 in terms of reductions (of the order of 50–70 per cent) in the volume of emissions from 1980 levels. The Plan is set in a theoretical framework of substance flow systems which are impeded by the emission of human-created pollutants, and the goal is to limit those emissions so that the systems can be returned to their 'natural cleansing state'. However, political difficulties within the ruling coalition prevented its full implementation, because of worries about costs and the implications of the needed transformation of economy and society for the country's economic health.

One form of regulation which became quite common from the 1960s on is the 'environmental impact assessment' (EIA), a concept introduced in the US National Environmental Policy Act. This requires any proposed federal project which might have an adverse environmental impact to be accompanied by an assessment of: what that impact would be; whether there are any unavoidable impacts, should the project go ahead; what alternatives are available; the relationship between the short-term costs and benefits and the long-term impacts; and any irreversible commitments of natural resources that would be involved. These are needed, according to the Act, to ensure that the federal government: acts as a trustee of the environment for future generations; ensures 'safe, healthful, productive, and aesthetically and culturally pleasing surroundings' for all Americans; attains the widest range of beneficial environmental uses without risking health or safety; preserves important historic, cultural and natural aspects of the national heritage, and wherever possible sustains an environment which supports diversity and individual choice; achieves a balance between population and resource use which will ensure high and widely shared standards of living; and enhances the quality of renewable resources and achieves the maximum possible recycling of depleted resources. Such extremely worthy goals are phrased in language which is not easily reduced to operational criteria. The intention was certainly not to achieve the radical changes to economy and society promoted by green activists (see p. 196). The role of EIA is to ensure that environmental concerns are taken into account when projects are being developed, and thereby to protect environmentally sensitive areas by providing evidence on which basis groups could challenge government proposals, but little more. Its introduction led to the creation of a large cadre of EIA specialists, both inside and outside government, whose presence ensured greater attention to environmental issues generally.

The use of EIA has spread very widely, and it has spawned much research on the techniques that can be used – 'many of which may be methodologically ingenious but of little practical relevance' (Rees, 1985, p. 329). Their use by decision-makers involves subjective judgement, as with other procedures, such as the large planning inquiries that have been held in the UK over major projects such as nuclear power stations (O'Riordan and Kemp, 1988). Such procedures have now been abandoned in New Zealand, where a more market-based approach under the 1991 Resource Management Act no longer requires the local governments which implement it to balance economic and environmental goals as long as externalities are properly controlled (Memon, 1993).

## PRICING

It is because of the perceived failings of the regulatory approach that considerable attention has been paid in recent years to one based on pricing – which is in line with the market-based ideology and the desire to reduce the role of the state prevalent in most capitalist countries during the 1980s and 1990s. The intention is to reduce environmental pollution by charging offenders, so that they use 'clean' technology, and to optimise resource use by eliminating waste. If people know the real cost of using the environment then their choices will be better informed and promote environmental protection; they will use less and treat it better. As one of the leading advocates expresses the issue:

> If the Earth's resources were available in infinite quantities, and if they could be deployed at zero cost, there would be no economic problem. Everyone could have everything they wanted without compromising each other's or later generations' wants and needs. It would not be necessary to *choose*. Choice becomes a necessity once it is recognised that resources are finite in terms of their absolute quantity, or in terms of the costs of extracting or using those resources. (Pearce, 1993a, p. 1)

Price mechanisms influence choices in markets, where customers weigh the relative quantity, quality and cost of what is on offer. The economist's goal is to implement such market-place practices to environmental policies. But how is, say, the atmosphere to be priced? How does one place a value on its pollution? (For a critique of the entire approach, see Harvey, 1993.)

Most environmental resources are unpriced goods, and so to bring them into the market-place it is necessary to impute their value. This involves transferring the concept of 'willingness to pay' from the markets for priced goods to those for unpriced goods by developing techniques which allow the value of the environment to be assessed. For example, when farmers grow crops they may well stimulate soil erosion, for which they do not pay – the future damage to soil productivity is a 'cost' to future generations. Proper pricing mechanisms would ensure that farmers met those costs, thereby encouraging them to alter their cropping methods so as to conserve the soil. But when proposals for their introduction were made within the British government they were blocked by the Treasury, which believed they would be inflationary (Weale, 1992, p. 160).

Economic valuation of the environment involves assessing people's 'willingness to pay' to use a resource (including its pollution). Where the resource is to be used to create products, this is relatively straightforward – as in the value of a forest relative to the proposed use(s) for the wood. But where the resource is more intangible – such as an attractive environment, or peace and quiet – the procedure is less easy and various estimation techniques of differing degrees of sophistication have been proposed; examples include the use of hedonic price methods to assess values, as in studies of housing prices which show how much people are prepared to pay for attractive environments. Even more difficult is the problem of bringing future use of a resource into the accounting equation. As Pearce notes with regard to such phenomena as global warming, either an inter-generational measure of sustainability has to be introduced to the pricing mechanism, so that users pay not only the current costs but also those of future users who are denied access (i.e. the opportunity costs of future use forgone), or a discounting mechanism has to be devised which incorporates inter-generational equity. In normal accounting for a project, a discount rate of about 10 per cent per annum is assumed, so that future costs are very much underestimated. (Pearce, 1993a, p. 55, notes that if a project to use a resource over 100 years was costed in this way, then its 'real impact' of $100 billion in a century's time would only be evaluated at $7.5 billion, so that the developer would pay very little of the full costs of the damage to be experienced in the future; see also Pearce et al, 1989, Chapter 6.) Finally, there is the problem of valuing human life. An attempt to estimate the cost of global warming for the 1995 'Climate Summit' at Berlin (see below, p. 229) valued the life of a Bangladeshi farmer killed by a cyclone at US$150 000 but that of a contemporary in the USA or western Europe as $1 500 000 (*The Times*, 5 April 1995): if used in cost–benefit analyses of project options, such a lower valuation of life in the developing world (seen there as a further example of 'Western imperialism') would involve it carrying a disproportionate portion of the total burden of environmental costs!

Many estimates of the environmental costs of particular actions have been produced (a series of case studies is provided in Barde and Pearce, 1991a). Estimates for the Federal Republic of Germany, for example (Schulz and Schulz, 1991), show that air pollution cost the country DM48 billion per annum in 1985, water pollution DM17.6 billion, soil contamination DM5.2 billion, and noise DM32.7 billion. (The last is made up of DM29.3 billion in 'decline of value of residences', DM3.0 billion in decline in productivity, and DM0.4 billion in noise compensation; Germans would have been prepared to pay a lot more for noise-free homes.) This total of DM103.5 billion in 'calculable damages' – which Schulz and Schulz (1991, p. 35) call the 'bottom line', based on 'the most conservative estimates' and omitting a whole range of intangible costs that could not be evaluated – amounted to about 6 per cent of the country's 1985 GDP, a very substantial sum which could have been better spent (directly or indirectly) on welfare rather than on illfare. But how are these costs to be removed, or at least reduced? Schulz and Schulz recommend the use of cost–benefit analysis, for five reasons:

(1) By making the costs of any project explicit, the issue of pollution is clarified.
(2) By putting the costs into an accepted metric, they are made objective.
(3) By showing how scarce resources can best be directed, the best returns (in terms of environmental damage) are achieved.
(4) Polluters are made fully aware of the costs of what they do.
(5) The overall welfare of the country can be better determined.

To be successful, a cost–benefit analysis has to focus on feasible options, such as a tax which will reduce pollution without necessarily harming overall prosperity. One such is a 'carbon tax' imposed to reduce the amount of $CO_2$ emitted and so cut the amount of global warming (Nordhaus, 1991). Its consequences, according to Barrett (1991), could include: the substitution of lower–polluting fuels for those currently used (gas rather than coal, for example); the replacement of fossil by non-fossil fuels (nuclear for coal, oil and gas); and energy conservation (through technological improvements). Such measures may reduce expenditure in some parts of the economy (the coal industry especially), with consequent loss of jobs, but stimulate activity and growth elsewhere. Unlike income taxes, it is argued, the carbon tax would not reduce consumption by creating a disincentive to work, rather it would transfer expenditure to more environmentally friendly activities and, assuming similar labour–capital ratios, maintain overall levels of employment and prosperity.

Such a tax may have undesirable consequences, however: Pearce (1991) quotes a report by the Institute for Fiscal Studies which said that an energy tax would be regressive in its incidence (the poor would pay relatively more) and, because of the inelasticity of demand for energy, the fall in demand for household fuel consequent on a 15 per cent value-added tax (VAT) imposition would be only 4 per cent. (These arguments were used in 1993–5 when the British government proposed to impose VAT at 17½ per cent on fuel; eventually it was forced politically to limit it to 8.5 per cent only, and to make substantial rebates to lower-income households, thus showing how difficult it is to act in an environmentally friendly way when some groups of citizens, in this case the old and infirm, are negatively affected by the policy shift.)

A major feature of environmental system operations identified in Chapter 2 is the spillover or externality effect. In terms of human interference with those systems, this means that many others than those involved in their pollution may be impacted. Proper market-based approaches to environmental issues require externalities to be costed and charged for. But since the spillovers are uneven in both time and space, this is a further extremely difficult task.

Pearce (1993b, p. 93) recognises that economic valuation methods cannot account for intrinsic values, which are parts of a society's cultural inheritance. They merely measure individuals' preferences for different types of environmental change – what they are prepared to pay to protect and what they are not. They provide an economic case to go alongside ethical and practical concerns (Barde and Pearce, 1991b). The ethical concerns are of particular interest to 'deep greens' who claim that natural resources, human life and health cannot be reduced to an economic calculus. Their radical programmes are partly outside the ambit of a capitalist system but, as public arguments over funding of the British National Health Service increasingly show, with constrained resources decisions are being made on whether action to try to save a human life can be afforded. These are political issues too, and politicians prefer flexibility in which to make their judgements rather than the constraints which certain economic decision-making methodologies may impose.

The pricing approach to environmental conservation calls for even more radical shifts in the way national accounts are compiled (Pearce et al, 1989). Most countries measure their standards of living through calculation of the gross domestic product (GDP) per capita; if this increases in real terms (i.e. after allowing for inflation), then it is assumed standards have improved. But the additional volume of activity may not have been involved in creating welfare but rather in cleaning up the results of illfare. For example, because of pollution from car exhausts leading to greater rates of asthma suffering among children, health-care costs may have been increased and GDP per capita grows accordingly. But the quality of life has not been improved; its deterioration has had to be tackled by additional spending. If the extra expenditure had gone on either better control of car exhausts or reducing car use by promoting public transport, then welfare would have been increased directly. (For other examples, see Johnston 1976; 1977.)

Pearce et al (1989, Chapter 4) propose two alternative measures of welfare. One is current welfare, defined as

Current Welfare    = Measured Consumption (i.e. GDP)
                   − Household Defensive Expenditures
                   − Monetary Value of Pollution Damage

This identifies the costs of 'cleaning up illfare' (insurance policies etc.) by the current generation and the inter-generational transfer of such costs as reductions in welfare. The other, sustainable income, is more future-oriented, and is defined as

Sustainable Income = Measured Consumption
                   − Household Defensive Expenditures
                   − Monetary Value of Pollution Damage
                   − Depreciation of Human-Created Capital
                   − Depreciation of Environmental Capital

This definition calls for much more detailed evaluation of the costs of activities in and on the environment; it brings inter-generational transfers explicitly into the accounts, and penalises those societies which run down their capital, including environmental, stocks (i.e. those which 'sell off the family silver'). Application of this approach to the Japanese national accounts suggests that 'real' GNP per capita increased at a compound rate of 5.8 per cent rather than 8.5 per cent between 1955 and 1985, while for Indonesia the comparable figures for 1971–1984 were 4.0 and 7.1 per cent.

Restructuring national accounts in this way allows environmental costs to be introduced into a framework which not only measures increased welfare and illfare more accurately but also allows alternative projects to be evaluated in terms of their overall contribution to 'real' increases in living standards. This was done in a report produced by Jackson and Marks (1994), which showed that from 1950 to 1990 although GNP increased by 230 per cent in the UK, the overall quality of life did not (indeed, it declined after 1970) because of the costs of commuting, pollution and other environmental damage, and policing. Detailed analyses of the environmental impacts of various policy proposals can also be conducted, as with Breheny's (1995) critical analysis of urban containment policies – the so-called 'compact city' designed to counter decentralisation and sprawl – which suggests that 'disappointingly low' energy savings will result.

## INTERNATIONAL ACTION

A fundamental barrier to the resolution of many environmental problems, and certainly many of the most pressing, is that they are global in their scope and as a consequence must be tackled through international agreement. We lack effective mechanisms, however. Furthermore, the current political structuring of more than 150 separate states militates against their creation.

This last point is readily illustrated by reference back to the issue of a carbon tax to reduce global warming. Taxes are imposed by individual states. Within any one state such a tax may be neutral in its effects on the overall performance of the national economy (though it may have distributional consequences within it), but it may be far from neutral in its effects on the state which imposes the tax relative to others which do not. In an increasingly global economy, if one country's costs of production increase relative to those of its competitors, then producers in the former are likely to lose market share, with obvious consequences for local prosperity. Such concerns led the British government to decline to sign the Social Chapter of the 1992 European Union Maastricht Treaty, because it believed that accepting the conditions (such as minimum wages) would harm the competitiveness of British industry. Similar concerns have been used to justify national action (and sometimes inaction) regarding global environmental issues.

Many attempts have been made to tackle environmental issues internationally and globally (see, for example, the comprehensive lists in Kiss, 1983; Rummel-Bulska and Osafo, 1991; Susskind, 1994). Some have had considerable success, such as those regarding the use of inner space discussed above (p. 161) and regional agreements on pollution of marine environments. But many have not.

A good example of substantial difficulties with an attempted global solution to a major environmental problem is the Vienna Convention on the Ozone Layer. This was signed by 28 states in 1985, and followed by further protocols agreed in Montreal in 1987 (signed by 46 states, though ratified by only 15 – none of them in the rapidly developing economies of east Asia: O'Riordan, 1993) and 1990. The impetus for this Convention was the discovery in the 1970s that CFCs (used in some aerosol propellants and refrigerators, including air-conditioning equipment, since their reported discovery in 1930: Litkin, 1994, p. 59) were destroying the ozone layer over the Antarctic and (later) the Arctic and accordingly threatening human and other life. There was initial disagreement over both the extent of the problem and how it should be tackled, and the Vienna Convention included no obligation on the signatory states to act in any way. Later meetings produced few advances, and few states co-operated with the attempts of the United Nations Environment Programme to assemble data on production and consumption levels. Scientific developments provided further evidence of the cause and extent of the problem, however, which convinced leading American politicians and bureaucrats of the need for urgent action. The Montreal Protocols led to general agreement on global phasing out of CFC production and use. (The effect of the protocols was to change access to the upper atmosphere from free to limited: it was no longer REC – see p. 161.)

There was much initial resistance to the Montreal Protocols, however, because they 'sounded the death knell for an important part of the international chemical industry, with implications for billions of dollars in investment and hundreds of thousands of jobs in related sectors' (Benedick, 1991, p. 1). The UK government's resistance was bolstered by the strong influence of the chemical giant ICI, and for some time

> some governments allowed commercial self-interest to influence their scientific positions and used the scientific uncertainty as an excuse for delaying difficult decisions. Many political leaders were long prepared to accept future environmental risks rather than to impose the certain short-term costs entailed in limiting use of products seen as necessary to modern standards of living. (Benedick, 1991, p 64)

Indeed, as Susskind (1994; see also Litkin, 1994) notes, it was only when scientists developed viable alternatives to CFCs that political resistance ended and governments such as the British were prepared to sign the Montreal Protocols which set timetables for eliminating their production and use. A follow-up conference at Copenhagen in 1992 brought the phasing-out date forward from 2000 to 1996 and agreed a US$500 million aid package (over three years) to assist developing countries in the replacement of CFC-producing technologies. The replacements for CFCs (HCFCs) are not believed to be entirely safe either, but moves to phase out their production and use were not agreed, and instead of a target date of 2004 for their elimination the year 2030 was set, 'allowing chemical companies a return on their investment' (*The Guardian*, 26 November 1992): as *The Guardian*'s leader writer expressed it then:

> Stand by for a bigger hole in the ozone layer. The chemical industry won its confrontation with the green lobby in Copenhagen yesterday. Delegates from the 95 nations who signed the Montreal Protocol protecting the ozone layer have turned a blind eye to the newest chemical threats by setting phase-out dates that ignore science and put the world at renewed risk.

The timetable was not the only issue under dispute in Montreal. The economically powerful states were very concerned that they may be relatively uninfluential over the Protocols' implementation. The US government, for example, successfully pressed for a clause which meant that the Protocol would only come into effect when it had been ratified by at least 11 states which were together responsible for two-thirds of the world production of CFCs. This effectively gave the USA a veto that it exercised until it ratified the Protocols in 1989. Furthermore, those same powerful states were concerned about the costs of implementation globally. It was generally recognised that developing countries, which make much use of CFCs in refrigeration and other technology, would need aid (subsidies, credits and guarantees) in order to meet the targets for reduced use, and a fund was proposed, under the auspices of the World Bank, to be operated by a committee drawn from 14 countries, seven each from the developing and developed worlds. The USA demanded (and was accorded) a permanent place on that committee, which adopted a two-thirds majority voting rule, thereby giving veto power to either group of seven. It was determined that states should contribute to the fund according to their 1986 production levels, with none asked to provide more than 25 per cent of the total, set at US$250 million for the first three years. The USA insisted on a principle of 'additionality' being included, whereby its contribution (US$21 million per annum) did not have to be in addition to its foreign aid budget but could merely be diverted from other causes then being supported.

This example illustrates the difficulty of achieving international agreement on effective means of tackling serious global environmental problems: individual states are more concerned about short-term local economic self-interest than they are about long-term global issues. In the absence of a global authority which can ensure compliance, as is the case within national state territories, the problems are likely to continue. There is no global government to manage the global commons, so although major environmental issues continue to be raised and discussed, progress is usually painfully slow.

The much-publicised 'Earth Summit' (the United Nations Conference on Environment and Development) held at Rio de Janeiro in 1992 provides further illustration of that fundamental point. It produced five major agreements (Grubb et al, 1993):

(1) The *Framework Convention on Climatic Change*, which accepted the seriousness of the problem and the need to tackle it immediately despite the continuing scientific uncertainties about its extent. It required developed countries to take the lead in reducing the emissions of greenhouse gases to 1990 levels by the year 2000 (though in a non-binding way).

(2) The *Convention on Biological Diversity*, which promotes the protection of species and ecosystems.

(3)  *Agenda 21*, which is an 'action plan' for sustainable development.
(4)  The *Rio Declaration of 27 Principles* to guide action on environment and development.
(5)  The *Forest Principles*, which are the residual from a failure to get a convention on the sustainable development of timber resources.

Each of these was accepted by the United Nations General Assembly three months later; it established a Commission on Sustainable Development to oversee their implementation, which is proving difficult. The US government refused to sign the Biodiversity Convention because of feared threats to its biotechnology industry from safety and patenting requirements and because of concerns (shared by other countries) over the financial arrangements (every country is required to contribute to the costs 'according to its capabilities' and 'developed country Parties shall provide new and additional financial resources to enable developing country Parties to meet the full incremental costs of implementing measures': Grubb et al, 1993, pp. 80–1). The US President (George Bush, then running for re-election) said that he would not sign because the Convention threatened 'American jobs and American families', and 'we cannot permit the extreme in the environmental movement to shut down the United States' (quoted in Pepper, 1993b, p. 219); in a televised news conference before going to Rio, President Bush said:

> I am the one that is burdened with the responsibility to find a balance between sound environmental practice on the one hand and jobs for American families on the other . . . If they don't understand it in Rio, too bad. (Quoted in *The Independent*, 6 June 1992)

The Convention on Climate Change (ratified by 118 countries) is similarly causing concern to many governments, as illustrated by their attitudes at a major follow-up conference held in Berlin in March–April 1995. Many, though by no means all, accept the scientific evidence for global warming (though whether it has as high a priority as water pollution or soil erosion is questioned), but few of the developed world countries are likely to meet the targets set for reducing carbon emissions. The UK may meet its targets serendipitously as a consequence of the major switch from coal- to gas-burning power stations following the privatisation of the electricity industry. The costs of such a switch on a global scale may be prohibitive, however, and there is little evidence of the developed world being prepared to make major contributions to those costs; indeed, the issue of voting rights on the oversight committee was not considered at Berlin.

Some governments have proposed meeting their part of the costs of an international programme by agreeing 'joint implementation' agreements with developing countries. The richer countries would pay for emission-reducing policies in poorer contemporaries (by, for example, pollution control or tree planting) and count the savings against their own targets, thereby avoiding difficult problems 'at home' and, in effect, exporting the problem to the developing world. These proposals are similar to the 'tradable emission rights' introduced in the 1977 amendments to the US Clean Air Act (Weale, 1992). The Act sets an overall air quality standard for a locality, and requires each polluter to meet a maximum level of emissions. Some polluters find that it will cost more to meet their levels than do others, and so 'trade' their levels with others who find them cheaper. The overall standard is met, and a market mechanism is used to produce the optimal distribution of individual achievements, while reducing the total cost to the economy because those who can most readily reduce their emissions do so.

The costs of global warming, relative to those of controlling it, concern many economists and others, some of whom have undoubtedly been influential in advising governments. Beckerman (1992) provides a good illustration. Even if we accept the argument that sea levels will rise appreciably as a result of global warming (which is far from certain), the costs may be negligible, he says. If sea walls in the USA have to be increased in height by 1 metre over the next century, this would cost only 0.43 per cent of the country's estimated GNP in 2090, and as a cost to be met over a full century the amount involved would be 'totally trivial' (1992, p. 265). Globally, similar works would cost only 2 per cent of GNP in 2090 – and 'as a fraction of cumulative world GNP over the whole period [1990–2090] it would still be negligible' (1992, p. 266). Furthermore

> given that (a) the latest predictions of the rise in sea level are about half those assumed in these estimates and (b) a given reduction in the estimated sea-level rise implies a more than proportionate reduction in the costs of adaptation or the damage done through land loss, the costs of adaptation and land loss for the world as a whole would be negligible even allowing for a generous margin of error in the above estimates.

Beckerman accepts that the impact of sea-level rises will be spatially variable – Bangladesh will suffer much more than the USA – but argues that it will be much cheaper for the less affected countries to make a contribution to necessary measures in those that will be most affected than for all countries to take what he clearly sees as extreme precautions. Hence his conclusion that,

> according to the latest scientific consensus, such as it is, the damage done by the predicted climate change will be nothing like as great as is widely believed and certainly not the inevitable global catastrophe scenario hawked around by most environmentalist movements, politicians trying to get some mileage out of the environmental bandwagon, or sections of the media that love scare stories of any kind. (Beckerman, 1992, p. 288)

There is plenty of time still to work out the costs and benefits of various amelioration schemes, which will undoubtedly prove to be much cheaper than feared, especially if mechanisms are put in place to ensure that the emission of greenhouse gases is fully priced and paid for.

Such examples encourage free-riding. Weale (1992, p.135) reports that the cost of the Netherlands National Environmental Policy Plan (see above, p.220) was estimated as a cumulative loss of 2.6 per cent of GNP by the year 2010, covering both the direct costs of achieving the required reduction in emissions and the indirect effect on the relative costs of Dutch products in international markets. If all other countries implemented similar measures, the cumulative loss would be only 0.9 per cent. A difference of 1.7 per cent of GNP is a very substantial cost for taking action that others might decline to take – and was undoubtedly an important influence on the decision not to implement the plan.

These examples show the relevance of the tragedy of the commons and Prisoner's Dilemma metaphors to the problems of tackling global environmental problems. In the absence of a global power which can require compliance, too many states will put local economic self-interest first; they may sign the various conventions but will then be reluctant to implement them. (Some countries may benefit from global warming if their agricultural lands become more productive.) International environmental diplomacy may facilitate long-term agreements (Susskind, 1994), perhaps not soon enough according to some environmentalists, but in plenty of time if the views of optimists such as Beckerman are valid.

Such analyses have led Hurrell (1994, p.146) to conclude that 'in relation to the environment . . . the national-state as a political form is either already in crisis, or else heading towards a crisis'. Three arguments lead him to this reasoning. First, the fragmented system of states is to a considerable extent anarchic, with relatively little co-operation and a great deal of war and conflict; it cannot address issues of global management. Second, states are becoming weaker within their own territories, with less authority and ability to ensure sensible environmental management. Finally, the global nature of environmental problems means that increasingly people do not look to the territorially circumscribed nation-state for resolutions to perceived problems. Thus:

> First . . . the state is caught between two contradictory processes: fusion, globalization, and integration on the one hand; and fragmentation, fission and disintegration on the other. Second, . . . processes of globalization (economic, technological, environmental, cultural) force us to reopen questions about both the nature and limits of state sovereignty and the solidity of established identities. And third, there is the pervasive sense that the pace and scope of change have undermined the established spatial and temporal categories around which global politics has been traditionally conceived and analysed. (Hurrell, 1994, pp.147–8)

But no alternative is available, there is no 'world community in waiting'. States are involved in the production of environmental problems, but must also be involved in their resolution ('the state system may well be part of the problem but it is also an essential part of the solution': Hurrell, 1994, p. 165). The salient issue, Hurrell concludes, is that people and their leaders are as yet unprepared to admit the nature and seriousness of environmental threats; until they are, they will not look constructively for viable political mechanisms which will ensure that such threats are tackled and removed.

## SUCCESSES

The arguments presented in this chapter suggest that the state may not be very receptive to environmental causes, for a variety of reasons linked to its basic functions, particularly that concerned with the promotion of accumulation. And yet, much environmental legislation has been passed, and continues to be passed, especially in the core states of the world economy. A great deal of that legislation is of the ameliorative problem-solving type, and no state has an operational, viable blueprint for living in relative equilibrium with nature. Many environmental policies have been put in place, and an outline of the reasons why will assist in understanding how collective action has been determined. This is in two parts. The first looks at the ability of the state to act; the second at the contexts within which it acts.

### COLLECTIVE POWER AND INDIVIDUAL FREEDOM

Control of individual and corporate action within the environment frequently involves limiting (if not removing altogether) the rights of individuals and other bodies to use their property as they wish. Capitalism is built on the institution of private property, and the rights of individuals to do what they wish with it. Thus if the state restricts those rights, it will be eroding one of the foundations of the mode of production that it exists to defend and promote. On what grounds does it do that?

The placing of collective interests above those of the individual involves the state implementing what is known as the 'police power', the ability to act in ways that limit individual freedoms in order to promote the general good. It is defined by Witt (1979, p. 358) as 'the authority of the state to govern its citizens, its land and its resources, and to restrict individual freedom to protect or promote the public good'. This is enacted in a large variety of ways, as in the restrictions of the freedom to drive as one wishes by laws determining what side of the road one must occupy, making it a crime to drive with more than a minimum level of alcohol in the blood and faster than a certain speed, and so forth. Such laws restrict individual freedoms, but are accepted because they benefit society as a whole; everybody is safer on the roads as a consequence of those restraints.

Can the general principles underlying the above example be applied to the use and disposal of land? Land differs somewhat from most forms of private property (see Laver, 1986, p. 360). Commodities have two values in capitalist societies: their *use value* is a measure of their utility, based on their importance to consumers, or their ability to satisfy a need; their *exchange value* is a measure of their relative use value, and is thus an evaluation of the utility of one commodity compared to that of another. The relationship between the use value and exchange value of commodities varies considerably, depending on how much people are prepared to pay for something in order to be able to use it. In this context, as Harvey (1973) makes clear, land is a special case; compared to most commodities it is immobile, is necessary to all (because it is the source of food and other commodities), is infrequently traded, is permanent and relatively indestructible, and once bought is then usable for long periods of time and so is relatively expensive (most commodities are purchased for either immediate consumption or use over only a few years), and can be used in a variety of ways. As such, it has not only high use value but also very high exchange value, because in buying it you are buying the right to use it *ad infinitum*, and thus reap its use values for ever; further, you may be able to sell it with its use value unchanged (see also Pearce et al, 1989, p. 62). Thus if the state is to restrain the use of land for the public good, it is undertaking a major erosion of the rights to use and exchange private property freely, including its inter-generational transmission.

The justification for state actions which constitute such erosion varies from country to country. The US Constitution protects private property rights, for example, with the following statement in the Fourteenth Amendment (ratified in 1868):

> No State shall make or enforce any law which shall abridge the privileges or immunities of citizens of the United States; nor shall any State deprive any person of life, liberty, or property, without due process of law . . .

Thus the state can only restrict individuals' use of their property if what it does can be legally justified, and the courts provide protection against any illegal restraints of individual freedom by the state apparatus.

A key case which illustrates the justification of the 'police power' is a 1926 judgment of the US Supreme Court which upheld the validity of land-use zoning by local governments. The municipal council in the village of Euclid, in the suburbs of Cleveland, Ohio, proposed a zoning scheme. One landowner, Ambler Realty Company, had recently assembled several blocks of land which it intended to develop for industrial use, and which it valued at $10 000 per acre. Most of that land was zoned for residential use, however, which Ambler argued reduced its value to $2500 per acre. The company claimed that it had been deprived of its property rights, without due process, and would lose several hundred thousand dollars as a consequence. The Supreme Court judgment found in favour of the municipality. The zoning plan had been passed by a properly elected municipal council, 'presumably representing a majority of the inhabitants and voicing their will', and was acting on their behalf 'so that the public welfare may be secure'. Thus the justification accepted by the Court, and providing the basis on which all zoning is deemed constitutional in the United States, was that it was a democratic act undertaken for the general good, and thus a proper exercise of the police power. Further cases established that a zoning plan had to be clearly phrased as promoting the public good, in order to justify a serious invasion of property rights, and was not to be an 'arbitrary whim'; people affected by zoning decisions could thus contest whether the zoning was arbitrary, but if they failed to prove that it was they could not claim compensation for an act undertaken for the public good. The state has to define what is in the public good, so its defence of zoning is that it creates a pattern of land use that is generally beneficial, even if the exchange value of some people's land is depressed as a consequence. (For fuller details, see Johnston, 1984.)

The police power has been used in a variety of other ways to promote environmental policies in the USA, and in general the power has gone unchallenged. For example, the 1970 Water Quality Improvement Act, through which water pollution is controlled, begins with the declaration that it is enacted in

> connection with the exercise of jurisdiction over the waterways of the Nation and in consequence of the benefits resulting to the public health and welfare by the prevention and control of water pollution . . .

The 1967 Air Quality Act has as its primary purpose 'to promote health and welfare and the productive capacity of [the] population'. The police power is justified not only in the context of the state's legitimation functions but also with respect to the promotion of accumulation; an Act limiting air pollution improves people's health, and makes them a better workforce as a consequence.

The United Kingdom lacks a written constitution and a Bill of Rights; Parliament is sovereign, so its definition of the public welfare, and hence justification of the use of the police power, holds. The main challenges are through the electoral system, which can return a government pledged to rescind an Act that it argues is an unjustified infringement of individual freedoms. Should the British state choose to exercise the police power over the use of land, and have the support of Parliament, then this is entirely justified. It has been done on many occasions.

Elsewhere, the police power over the use of land may be somewhat irrelevant, since the land is owned by the state. Common land rapidly disappeared in most of western Europe in recent centuries, as rights of individual use were granted, exemplified by the more than 5000 Acts of Parliament in Great Britain which permitted its enclosure. But in some parts of the world, including much of the western half of the United States, the land has remained in state hands and its use is thus determined by what the state deems to be in the public good – which may involve the state as the land user itself, but more likely involves it leasing the land to individuals, with clear constraints on what they can and cannot do with it. That may be governed by the desire for profit alone, or it may involve restraints introduced to protect the land from abuse and the creation of degradation – as happened in New Zealand after clear evidence that sheep farming in much of the state-owned High Country was leading to rapid soil erosion. In advanced communist/socialist states, of course, most of the land is state-owned, and land-use policies are promoted for the public good, irrespective of any individual desire for gain, but the demand for increased material welfare in those societies puts great pressure on the state to increase land productivity, with the inherent dangers of degradation that this can bring.

Land is a common resource in some societies and not in others. Air and water are common resources everywhere, so that state action to control their use is more readily promoted without facing the issues of invading individual property. There are contests over the location of boundaries between private and public property. Is the air within a family's home private property, so that they can pollute it, and ultimately pollute the air outside? And how far below the surface of the earth do individual property rights extend, an important issue with regard to the exploitation of both mineral and water resources? Different states have taken different attitudes to these boundary issues, as illustrated by Wescoat's (1985) analysis of Colorado water law and State Court decisions.

## THE PROMOTION OF THE PUBLIC GOOD THROUGH ENVIRONMENTAL LEGISLATION

Even where land is treated as private property, therefore, the exercise of individual freedom to use (and abuse) it is constrained by the police power; the use of land is thus contingent on state definitions of the wider public interest. How and why do those controlling the state apparatus choose to exercise that power?

Most restrictions on individual freedoms have been introduced after agitation from interest and pressure groups for legislation or similar action. They have been justified as promoting the general welfare, in many cases by appealing to the morality of the proposed action; part of the justification for campaigns for environmental causes is ensuring that the environment can sustain life in the future, and thus leaving it in a condition that we would like to receive it in. (This argument characterises Rawls's, 1971, theory of justice.) The state has to be convinced, first, that the proposed action would have general support (or at least would not be widely and strongly opposed), and thus would not contribute towards a legitimation crisis; and second, that it would not seriously damage accumulation, and thus lead to a rationality crisis. The latter may be the more difficult to argue, since in many cases a proposal will either increase the costs of production or reduce the potential productivity of land. But with many pieces of environmental legislation, as long as all are subject to them and the costs are equitably shared, the benefits to profit-seekers may be substantial too; as the quotation from the US Air Quality Act showed, anti-pollution legislation can be justified in terms of producing a healthier, and so more productive, workforce. Thus much environmental legislation can be justified in terms that in effect imply solving the Prisoner's Dilemma. The main problem, which has increased recently, is that environmental legislation in one state alone may affect the competitiveness of its producers relative to those in states with fewer restrictions, and may make it difficult for the state to attract external investment. For this reason, it is difficult to insist on strict constraints in many of the countries of the periphery of the world economy.

The history of environmental legislation is therefore a history of struggle to convince the state of the desirability, if not necessity, of exercising the police power to control the use of both land, as an item of personal property, and other 'commons', such as air and water. That struggle is depicted in the title of Sidney Plotkin's (1988) book *Keep Out: The Struggle for Land Use Control*, which he introduces as follows:

> Domination and resistance form the central themes of this book, which is an examination of some of the high-level controls of capitalist society and of the ability of human beings to say no. (Plotkin, 1988, p. xi)

The issue which he discusses is whether local communities can continue to operate exclusionary zoning, whereby the land-use planning power vested in American municipalities is employed to exclude certain unwanted uses from their territories, or whether those policies can be overridden by a federal agency set up to further the goals of capitalist enterprises (in this case, the oil industry). Similarly, Hays (1987) reviewed the struggles and achievements of environmentalists, notably the 1969 National Environmental Policy Act which extended the evaluation of major federal projects beyond the traditional parameters of cost–benefit analysis to incorporate the 'unquantifiable' (see also Garner and O'Riordan, 1982, on the difference between the technical procedure of environmental impact assessment and the wider process of environmental assessment). As Hays (1987, pp. 287–8) notes, those successes generated opposition

> that was continuous, increasingly vocal and determined, accelerating through the 1970s, and rising to a peak in the early 1980s. A coherent anti-environmental movement emerged with an over-riding goal of restraining environmental political influence . . . Environmentalists presented a serious challenge to agriculture, labor and business, which turned on them with alarm. Although these groups made opportunistic adjustments to environmental objectives, their overall political strategy was one of maximum feasible resistance and minimum feasible retreat.

The successes resulted from the demands of affluent Americans; they were countered by the pessimistic managers of the economy who argued that the world could not be made as healthy, clean, safe and beautiful as those people wanted, and they would have to settle for less (1987, p. 542). So the contemporary struggle within American capitalism is not, as Marx predicted, between the proletariat and the bourgeoisie, but between sections of the latter and

> the growing mass middle class, [which] in seeking to shape a newer world revolving around its values and conceptions about the good life, gave expression to precisely the rising standard of living the managerial and technical leadership professed to extol. (Hays, 1987, p. 542)

The issue is the legitimacy of the claims made by the 'technical intelligentsia' against those of the 'humanistic intelligentsia' (p. 191), and their relative success in the political fora.

Very similar conclusions can be drawn in Britain. Sheail's (1976; 1981) outline of the introduction of various pieces of environmental legislation illustrates the importance of 'well-connected' pressure groups, whose members appear to come from the same backgrounds as those described by Hays; according to Lowe and Goyder (1983, p. 181), the growth of such groups

> derives from intrinsic changes in public consciousness and is not simply a result of encouragement by political elites and the media attention given to environmental issues . . . Many of the groups springing up questioned the direction of society and tended to view individual environmental problems as having a common cause in economic and population growth.

Relative affluence and security, plus the absence in many cases of any direct link between their work and the production of goods, provided the context within which concern for the environment could be stimulated among such people. For those not as fortunate, whose daily survival depended on jobs in the production of goods, the ecological movement was less attractive, as it also was to those whose wealth derived directly from the profitability of producing and selling goods and services. The state was left in the middle, facing potential rationality and legitimation crises if it accepted the environmental case too readily, and yet increasingly convinced by the scientific evidence.

The degree of influence pressure groups have reflects how those controlling the state apparatus are advised as they weigh up the pros and cons of complex arguments. In this, the nature of the policy communities with which they interact is crucial, as illustrated by Weale's (1992, p. 72) comparison of anti-pollution legislation in the United Kingdom and the Federal Republic of Germany:

during the 1970s and 1980s in the UK, the clean air coalition comprised a wide range of environmental and public health groups, some elements of the Labour Party, and some members of the policy elite including influential members of the scientific advisory system. On the other side was a coalition of groups who stressed the uncertainties attached to the benefits supposedly flowing from costly investments in acid rain abatement policies, including the Central Electricity Generating Board, the industrial emitters, the Confederation of British Industry, most of the Conservative Party and some members of the policy advisory elite. The debate between these two coalitions was essentially framed in terms of costs and benefits, with much attention being paid to the question of how far the putative benefits had to be discounted in light of the scientific uncertainties that attached to them. A similar constellation of interests formed around competing belief systems in the Federal Republic of Germany. In the clean air coalition could be found the environmental movement, pollution control officials, some parts of the Social Democrats and members of the policy elite. In the economic feasibility coalition could be found the power generating companies, the industrial emitters, the Christian Democrats, some Social Democrats particularly from North-Rhine Westphalia, the German Industrial Federation (BDI) and some members of the policy elite. But in Germany, unlike Britain, the balance of advantage shifted to the clean air coalition.

Overcoming the barriers (p. 217) thus depended on the relative weight of the arguments.

The nature of the policy introduced also reflects the local cultural context. In the UK, this tends to be based on what Weale (1992, p. 81) terms the 'principle of the scientific burden of proof'. There is no general programme or principles, but instead a preparedness to act pragmatically when this is clearly required – the British style (in most areas of policy and not just in environmental issues) involves

> an absence of explicit and medium- or long-term objectives on the one hand and unplanned and incremental decision-making in which policies are arrived at by a continuous process of mutual adjustment between a plurality of actors on the other.

Thus anti-pollution legislation was introduced only as and when the balance of opinion among the government's advisors/influencers favoured it; it was ameliorative problem-solving only. In the Federal Republic, on the other hand, the 'principle of precaution' was employed once the government was convinced of the need to act. Legislation was preceded by a statement of general principles which identified the possible consequences of continued pollution and, despite the costs involved, determined that actions should be taken to limit potential problems even while scientific controversy about their likelihood raged. And so the British and the German responses to pressure for anti-pollution legislation differed, because of the relative weight of arguments for and against and the general policy styles adopted by their two governments. The British prefer 'the particular over the general, the concrete over the abstract and the commonsensical over the principled' (Weale, 1992, p. 81) whereas the Germans are more prepared to stress the anticipation of problems, with the state taking the lead in actions designed to protect the economy in the long term.

The 'principle of precaution' was also adopted by the US government in its approach to the Montreal meetings regarding the destruction of the ozone layer (see p. 227). Several EU countries argued against that position, claiming that the scientific uncertainties meant that more research was needed: they contended in 1986 that significant destruction of the layer would not occur for decades, and distrusted the American position, which they interpreted as meaning that 'U.S. industry had secretly developed CFC substitutes' (Litkin, 1994, p. 106). Thus the availability of scientific evidence is a necessary condition for the adoption of policies designed to counter perceived environmental problems, but it is not sufficient. Powerful interest groups and influential individuals/governments must accept that evidence and be prepared to campaign strongly with it – which may involve (as Thomas and Middleton, 1994, show) the creation of a 'myth' regarding the intensity of the problem in order to mobilise public support and, where necessary, inter-governmental action.

## CONCLUSIONS

States have immense powers to act, economically, militarily, politically and ideologically. Those powers present those controlling the state apparatus with myriad opportunities. Which opportunities they perceive and act upon, and why, is a matter of local determination, reflecting both the immediate context of any decision-making and the cultural matrix within which that is set. There are also many constraints on the exercise of those powers, because of the various demands on the state and its accountability to its citizens; how those exercising the powers do so is thus also influenced by the constraints and how they are perceived. The scope to act is substantial, but so are the limits to action.

Environmental issues illustrate the scope and limits very clearly. Pressure is put on the state to act in a variety of ways to protect the environment for present and future generations; there are also pressures not to act, because to do so might harm the immediate interests of some, if not all, of its citizens. Thus the struggle continues, between the momentum of the dominant mode of production, on the one hand, and the claims that it is destroying the earth, on the other.

# 7 And the Future?

> Without a theory of how the world economy works, and without theories about the relations between people, capital and state power, sustainable development thinking – and most conservation action – is locked within a limited compass. (Adams, 1990, p. 200)
>
> It is better to be a pessimist and be proved wrong, than to be an optimist and be wrong.

This book has focused on the economic and political constraints to the resolution of environmental problems, and has implicitly reached the same conclusion as Adams: that a sustainable relationship between people and nature is very unlikely to be achieved within the political economy which now predominates in almost all of the world. Others are not as pessimistic, however, so what alternative futures are available?

According to Falk (1972) – writing before environmental issues reached their current prominence in academic analysis, media coverage and political attention – once the carrying capacity of the earth is realised there are only two possible ways forward. Each takes about four decades to complete. The first is the pathway to degenerative strife, proceeding from the politics of despair in the 1970s through the politics of degeneration and then catastrophe in the next two decades, and ending with the era of annihilation at the start of the twenty-first century. The alternative is the pathway to progressive egalitarianism and justice, which proceeds through decades of awareness (the 1970s), mobilisation (1980s) and transformation (1990s) to an era of world harmony after the year 2000. We are now more than half-way through one of those sequences, and there is little evidence of substantial transformation. Capitalism has continued to evolve (Lash and Urry, 1987), but its transformation has incorporated relatively little change in the relationships involving people and nature. We are more likely to be in the decade of catastrophe, leading to annihilation, than of transformation, leading to egalitarianism and justice, therefore. But the time-scale may be wrong. There may still be time to change the trajectory.

This conclusion assumes that it is not too late to avoid the pessimistic scenario: if that is so, how can change be achieved? O'Riordan (1981a, p. i) examined possible institutional reforms which might deliver a satisfactory resolution, all of them (following Pirages and Ehrlich, 1974) based on the argument that 'the present system of liberal-pluralist politics cannot be sustained' (O'Riordan, 1981a, p. 302) because: special interest groups (representing capital in this case) tend to undermine resolute governments, which then use short-term expediency to override long-term commitments; political leaders prevaricate in the face of conflicting proposals and contradictory evidence and advice; the authority of legislatures is eroded by the ability of special interest groups to avoid regulation; citizens are weak when confronted by the power of the neo-corporate state; and 'pluralism is predicated upon compromise, but the fear of scarcity encourages confrontation and irresolution. In such circumstances, only the powerful are satisfied' (1981a, p. 302). The liberal-democratic state is largely oriented to the resolution of immediate problems (the ameliorative mode of 'planning': see above, p. 203), and a potential environmental catastrophe requires a solution of the type that it cannot deliver: whereas liberal politics is about means (the defence of democracy), much of green politics is about ends (saving the earth, in whatever way possible).

If, as the neo-corporatist case holds, the people do not really rule in liberal democracies and politicians only serve their electorates in a very general sense, and if we accept the view of O'Riordan (1981a, 302–3) that:

> Voters are neither concerned nor humane, they are alienated, frustrated, and confused, and are often forced to elect politicians from a group of candidates not of their choosing. Urbanisation, bureaucratic centralisation, mobility, and the dominance of technology, combined with the monotony and impersonalisation of most occupations, breed a collective disinterest in the affairs of others, an almost inhuman lack of compassion for the weaker in distress

then there is a clear need for a revolution in the organisation of human society. O'Riordan identifies four possible outcomes from such a revolution.

(1) *A new global order*, in which the current system of states is dissolved and replaced by a single, global organisation. Its proponents, O'Riordan (1981a, p. 303) suggests,

> appear to believe that global order can be achieved by transferring the funds currently deployed as military expenditures to the institutions of peace and goodwill, through the recognition of mutual dependence between rich and poor nations, and the wise realisation that life-support systems can only be protected through a coercive common government.

Frankel (1987) calls such protagonists ecopacificists. Whether their goal can be attained depends on global recognition that the tragedy of the commons is upon us (we are playing Prisoner's Dilemma games when we should be playing Assurance/Chicken) and a willingness to yield sovereignty in order to avert the tragedy. It also begs the question of whether ecological equilibrium can be achieved within the capitalist mode of production founded on ever-increasing material welfare, whatever the nature of the state.

(2) *Centralised authoritarianism*, which goes further than the first outcome (in which democracy is retained) and sees the replacement of liberal-democratic structures by a totalitarian state which has global ecological equilibrium as the predominant element of its mission.

(3) *The authoritarian commune*, which involves blending the religious orientation and military-style discipline characteristic of a monastery with the recent policy orientation of the Chinese (Heilbroner, 1974). If all people are guaranteed the basic minima for existence, live in communal social systems where all are cared for by kin and friends, and economic organisation is based on collectivisation and regional self-sufficiency, then the drive for unending material progress that characterised some advanced communist/socialist societies (let alone the capitalist) would be removed, and harmony with nature could be accomplished.

(4) *The anarchist solution*, which goes further than the third outcome because it promotes a society without any state; instead, self-sufficient and self-sustaining (almost certainly small-scale) communities, in harmony with their environments, are the structures for social organisation.

Are any of these solutions attainable – or are they utopian idealism? The second, for example, could only be brought about if the state apparatus in the current liberal democracies were taken over by promoters of an authoritarian mode of government which is 'pro-environment'. It would have to legitimate that action, in the long term especially, and would probably need to be backed by coercive force, at least initially. Its policies would be against the interests of many powerful groups of both producers and consumers; in the long term, these may be convinced through emancipatory education of the need for the new state form (Johnston, 1988), but in the short term they would be strongly opposed. Elsewhere, in the countries without liberal democratic structures, those currently in power would either have to be convinced of the need for change (which would pit them against the special interests there) or replaced – again needing coercion. The costs of coercion are great – as illustrated by the failure of the advanced communist/socialist regimes in the late 1980s.

The third scenario faces the same difficulties as the second, and the fourth calls for people to renounce the institutions of private property, to accept collective ownership, and to accept clear limits to their material conditions of life. Again, these are unlikely to be achieved voluntarily, except on a very small scale involving an insignificant proportion of the world's population. They would have to be imposed, with the implication that a state is necessary to achieve anarchy before withering away.

The likelihood of any of these three eventualities emerging from the current economic and political world order is extremely remote, therefore. One or more could be created *de novo* by the survivors of a major ecological catastrophe, but to accept that as the only way forward is both defeatist and unethical – letting many die in order to achieve change. Furthermore, it may well be that the earth cannot be reclaimed after such a catastrophe: if we do not want to take that chance, then action must be taken earlier.

This only leaves the first solution. The likelihood of a global state taking over the 180 or more countries that now exist is extremely remote, and many will be unwilling to yield sovereignty (as British resistance to developments within the European Union illustrates). But there may be potential for movements towards a more globally organised world order that will protect the environment and leave it in a usable condition for future generations.

## ACHIEVABLE EQUILIBRIUM

The fundamental question that we face is whether equilibrium with the environment is possible within the capitalist mode of production. Its achievement would undoubtedly require major changes to the nature of politics and economics within capitalism.

### POLITICAL CHANGE?

To date, little political success has been achieved by those promoting the green agenda – either by working through existing parties or by creating new ones. Indeed, although there have been local, limited successes, proponents of green views are not especially enamoured of green politics at present (as dissension within the German and British green parties illustrates: see also Porritt and Winner, 1988).

Green politics is associated in many minds with left-wing ideas and attitudes on a range on other issues, as illustrated by a leader writer for the right-wing British newspaper, *The Daily Telegraph* (quoted by Porritt and Winner, 1988, p. 81):

> for most Conservatives the word 'green' conjures up most disagreeable images. Legions of eccentric, muesli-crunching peace fanatics in open-toed sandals are hardly the stuff of which Conservative Party majorities are made.

That image reflects the commitment of most greens to radical social change, and according to Pepper (1985, p. 15),

> the socialist, too, seeks radical social change and the liberation of the masses from the tyranny of material want, from capitalist economic 'laws' and from the inter-human and human-to-nature relationships which are predicated by the capitalist mode of production. Furthermore, following Marx, he believes that such change is possible, and that human societies have freedom of will to shape themselves – to 'make their own history'

according to their own desires . . . the socialist argues that there is nothing inevitable, 'natural' or predetermined about capitalism, neither should any ultimate limits set by nature be invoked to suggest that there are constraints against achieving a truly socialist future . . . a socialist society is not thought to be so free in relation to nature that it can dominate, exploit or destroy it for its own immediate gain (a crude materialist interpretation of Marx which has been applied in the Soviet Union to such disastrous effect) . . . a socialist society's relationship to nature will be more of a balanced and mutually reciprocal one.

Pepper argues for an alliance (if not integration) of green and socialist politics, promoting a realistic 'red-green' political, social and economic scenario rather than the 'green–green' one favoured by most environmental idealists.

Is such an alliance feasible, especially given the focus of support for green causes among the professional classes, most of whom do not also favour radical social, economic and political change on other issues (as illustrated by Cotgrove's, 1982, findings that middle-class 'nature conservationists' are also economic individualists), whereas support for socialism has traditionally come from the working class (most of whom do not support radical change either)? Pepper (1986) argued that Labour and the greens should unite in common cause in the UK because both base their analysis of contemporary society on the destructive nature of capitalism. He identified three barriers to such a move within Labour: the party's 'clientist' orientation, with much negotiation with special interest groups to obtain their electoral endorsement; its continued commitment to economic growth as a fundamental policy objective; and the power of the trade unions, which are really only interested in changing the balance of the share-out of the proceeds from capitalism. Nevertheless, Pepper believed in 1986 (p. 132) that Labour was more likely to create a socialist Britain, and that

the Labour movement has that breadth of vision which can set green policies in the context of broader social and political policies, therefore, in the long run, making them appeal beyond a middle-class clique.

He is unlikely to be as optimistic now. After the 1987 general election, Porritt and Winner (1988, pp. 63-71) wrote that:

Even at the most superficial level, green politics was a complete irrelevance to the Labour party at the time . . . The message for Greens intent on taking their politics into the heartland of socialism is surely clear: there is a long, long way to go.

A decade later, Pepper would undoubtedly be even more pessimistic about the Labour Party's orientation.

Pepper's (1993a, p. 56) current pessimism focuses on many supporters of the greens, however, whom he clearly considers unrealistic. Ecologism, he claims, is not only 'suffused by faith in the power of ideas to change society' but also antagonistic to the mode of production:

> ecologism . . . fosters the view that developments in the productive forces and material wealth are the enemy, rather than being part of the bedrock on which ecological consciousness will ultimately develop. (p. 57)

It is characterised by a postmodern, anarchist view of society as self-sufficient communities in complete control, characterised by '. . . personal freedom, and an end to state domination. Most things will be allowed, but not for money making' (p.58), except that they will have to conform to the 'ecological imperatives' – there are scientific laws to be obeyed, but not social ones, which he finds to be an '. . . ultimately incoherent and distasteful melange of ideas' (p.59).

And so, it seems, green politics is likely to fail.

## CHANGING CAPITALISM?

Green politics is mainly practised in the countries at the core of the capitalist world economy where, as Pepper (1993a, p.57) notes, there have been some attempts to work within the capitalist framework to achieve desirable environmental change. This involves convincing both the consumers and the producers of material goods and services that the threats posed to the environment by current production and consumption processes must be tackled if material living standards are to be sustained for those for whom they are already high and are to be improved for everybody else. Consumers have to be convinced that they should focus their purchases on products that can be provided and disposed of without major harm to the earth's fragile ecosystems, and producers have to be persuaded that they should alter their manufacturing processes accordingly. This is green consumerism, which assumes (as do many classical views of capitalism's operations) that producers respond to market signals, so that if consumers demand certain types of product the market will react accordingly and environmental goals will be fulfilled. Alternatively, there are those whose view of the operations of the economy sees consumers manipulated by producers and marketers: they call for a green producerism which involves convincing producers that consumers will prefer to be sold 'ecologically sound' goods and services.

In a number of cases both sides see the benefits and act accordingly: manufacturers who produce fuel-efficient cars will be selling products which are not only environmentally friendly but also cheaper to run – their market share should increase, customers should be happy, and green goals will be advanced. Such strategies are illustrated in Porritt and Winner's (1988) chapter on 'Consuming Interests'. Some retail chains refuse to stock certain lines because of the ways in which they are produced, and financial institutions are promoting 'ethical investment portfolios' through funds which exclude perceived 'unethical' industries (tobacco companies and armaments producers, for example), whatever their profitability. Britain's most successful supermarket chain, J. Sainsbury, produced a 12-page booklet in 1989 (on recycled paper) entitled *Sainsbury's Living Today. You and the Environment: It's Your Responsibility Too.* Six pages identified major current environmental concerns, and four covered 'Action by Sainsbury's', including the following:

(1) For every tree cut down to provide timber for sale in a Sainsbury's store, 'at least four saplings are planted or up to 20 sown and the forest is tended for at least 10 years'.
(2) More than half the new stores built since 1984 have occupied formerly derelict sites, thereby improving urban environments.
(3) All Sainsbury's own-brand aerosols are CFC-free and all new refrigeration equipment in the stores will similarly be CFC-free.
(4) Sainsbury's stocks organically grown fruit and vegetables.
(5) None of Sainsbury's own-brand cosmetics are tested on animals.

The leaflet concludes with 13 actions that all consumers can take, and the firm's slogan: 'Sainsbury's: Helping to Care for the Environment'.

Porritt and Winner (1988, p.193) recognise the substantial advances that these and similar programmes offer, but also indicate that they pose a dilemma:

> capitalism itself continues to put Greens in a moral dilemma. If consumption is the name of the game, then at least let it be green. But how does that square with the basic green critique of the consumer-driven economy, in which success is measured by quantitative increases in production and consumption, regardless of its impact on the environment?

Furthermore, corporate altruism is only sustainable by profitable firms, plus the individuals who benefit from shares in their ownership, which are profitable. Unless all firms conform, in the end the altruistic may well lose out; consumers may stay with them in times of plenty (even if purchasing environmentally friendly goods is slightly more expensive), but desert them in times of relative hardship – and permanent times of plenty are not a characteristic of capitalism. Similarly, a state may be able to promote some environmentally friendly policies, such as paying farmers not to use some of their land (especially if it is ecologically significant) or not to use intensive farming methods in order to protect the local environment (as in the English Broadland). But it can only sustain them if the society is relatively affluent and profits are being made elsewhere, not necessarily within its territory;

when a squeeze on profitability comes, as analysis of capitalism says it must, and the state's budget is under pressure, will it still be able to afford such environmentally desirable policies?

Dobson (1990, pp. 141–2) goes further in his critique of 'green consumerism':

> The positive aspect of this strategy is that some individuals do indeed end up living sounder, more ecological lives. More bottles and newspapers are recycled, more lead-free petrol is bought, and less harmful detergents are washed down the plughole. The disadvantage, though, is that the world around goes on much as before, unGreened and unsustainable. . . . It is evidently hard to predict just how far the message will spread, and how many people will act on it, but it seems unlikely that a massive number of individuals will experience the conversion that will lead to the necessary changes in their daily behaviour.

In any case, he continues:

> There is nothing inherently Green . . . in green consumerism . . . It is true that consumer pressure helped bring about a reduction in the use of CFCs in aerosol sprays. It is true that the Body Shop will supply you with exotic perfumes and shampoos in reusable bottles and that have not been tested on animals. It is true that we help extend the life of tropical rainforests by resisting the temptation to buy mahogany toilet seats.

But none of this tackles the underlying problems of the capitalist dynamic. The green case is that the earth cannot sustain unlimited production and consumption, however environmentally friendly; people must consume less if that is to happen. In other words, green consumerism is consistent with environmentalism, but not with ecologism (see p. 196).

Nor does it face up to the global problem, for green consumerism in the core of the world economy can only involve a small proportion of the global population, most of them relatively affluent and able to afford small financial sacrifices to salve their 'green consciences'. This takes little account of the large mass of exploited poor in the periphery; how can they be mobilised behind 'green consumerism' when they have few resources and little choice over what they consume? Why should they pay more for material prosperity because they are achieving it later than the developed world, whose residents have belatedly discovered that their prosperity threatens the environment? The global North–South divide between the developed and developing worlds is the focus of much stress at international conferences, such as the Rio 'Earth Summit' in 1992, the Cairo World Population Conference in 1994, and the 1995 Climate Conference in Berlin. To the political elites of many developing countries, 'green consumerism' and related strategies promoted by developed world states are merely a new round of Western imperialism, while its enterprises use the developing world as the dumping ground for products they are unable to sell at home because they are not environmentally friendly.

And what can states do? There are many examples of those, especially in the developed world, which have successfully implemented policies that produce environmental improvements. The UK government responded to the campaign for lead-free petrol, for example, by introducing a tax differential in its 1989 budget. (Interestingly, the government expected the oil companies to reduce the price of unleaded petrol by 0.9p per litre in order to achieve an overall differential of 2.2p, but instead they increased the price of leaded petrol by 0.9p!) But this involves reacting to problems rather than preventing their occurrence. More investment in scientific research might achieve the latter – but such investment might be seen as counter-productive by the government's supporters!

## SUSTAINABLE DEVELOPMENT

A way forward increasingly pressed on all sides is that encompassed by the term 'sustainable development'. This is not susceptible to easy definition, and Moffat (1992, p.35) describes it as a 'slippery concept' which is difficult to translate into a 'useful tool'. (Pearce et al, 1989, have a 13-page appendix to their *Blueprint* volume entitled, 'Sustainable Development – A Gallery of Definitions'.) But it is now so much part of the language of development that it must be taken into account. As O'Riordan (1993, 37) puts it:

> It is tempting to dismiss the term 'sustainable development' as an impossible ideal that serves to mask the continuation of the exploitation and brutality that have characterised much of human endeavour over millennia.

But, he continues:

> The staying power of the concept is understandable, if not forgivable. No public figure or private corporation can afford to speak any other language. The greening of society may still be essentially cosmetic but it does have political force and powerful public relations and marketing implications.

There may indeed be strong latent wishes for a sustainable future, at least among the populations of the core of the world economy.

The concept of sustainable development emerged from the sequence of reports and conferences that have attacked the issues of global inequalities and impending environmental disaster over the last three decades (for a history, see Adams, 1990). Simon (1989, p.43) quotes the World Commission on Environment and Development's (1987) definition:

Sustainable development is development that meets the needs of the present without compromising the ability of future generations to meet their own needs.

Meeting needs, especially those of the world's poor, is an overriding priority, but that is restricted by social organisation, technology and environmental constraints. It is, according to Turner (1993, p. 5), 'economic development that endures over the long run' and, as discussed below, the meaning of development is crucial to ideas about the concept's implementation.

Fundamental to the concept is the view that no generation should deplete the earth's stock of resources and so constrain the life chances of future generations. To many, this means that the environment should not be allowed to deteriorate, but Turner shows that this is inconsistent with at least some views of sustainable development. The stock of capital assets is split into four components: natural capital (i.e. the environment); human capital; capital created by humans, which is basically the built environment; and moral and cultural capital. Different definitions of sustainability approach maintenance of these stocks in different ways.

(1) *Very weak sustainability.* According to this view, the overall capital stock should remain constant over time, but its composition can change: reductions in the volume of some components can be countered by increases in others. Thus natural capital can be allowed to deteriorate if either or both of human and human-created capital increase in compensation: very weak sustainable development does not necessarily involve sustaining natural capital, and if technology allows the environment can deteriorate.

(2) *Weak sustainability.* This view, unlike the previous one, does not allow for unlimited replacement of one type of capital by another, notably natural by human-created. The necessity of a basic minimum of environmental resources is recognised, along with the bounds on replacements produced by technological innovations. This is, in part, an argument for biodiversity to retain an agreed minimum of natural resources. Nevertheless this approach, like the other 'weak' version of sustainability, allows decline in environmental quality and natural resource availability as long as other forms of capital can be substituted.

(3) *Strong sustainability.* This accepts that at least some of the natural capital cannot be substituted. As a consequence, some available natural resources must be conserved and the overall structure of ecosystems not radically changed.

(4) *Very strong sustainability.* This recognises severe constraints on three of the four capitals (the exception is moral and cultural capital), and so leads to calls for a steady-state economy, defined by Daly (1977a, p. 17) as 'an economy with constant stocks of people and artifacts, maintained at some desired, sufficient levels by low rates of maintenance throughout': not only

are natural resources conserved but also population growth must be ended and the limits to technological developments recognised.

Those promoting sustainability thus have to decide which of the four approaches is necessary. Turner (1993) (following Chambers and Conway, 1992, pp. 27–8) suggests the following criterion, based on the concept of 'livelihood', which comprises

> the capabilities, assets (stores, resources, claims and access) and activities required for a means of living: a livelihood is sustainable which can cope with and recover from stresses and shocks, maintain or enhance its capabilities and assets and provide sustainable livelihood opportunities for the next generation: and which contributes net benefits to other livelihoods at the local and global levels in the short and long term.

With regard to natural capital, he suggests five rules that should govern utilisation within this definition – roughly ordered from that which will ensure very weak sustainability to that which will generate very strong sustainability:

(1) All market and (state) intervention failures relating to resource prices and property rights should be corrected.
(2) The regenerative capacity of renewable natural resources should be maintained and excessive pollution which threatens the environment should be avoided.
(3) Technological change should be steered towards the use of renewable rather than non-renewable natural resources, and the efficiency of their use should be increased.
(4) Renewable natural resources should be exploited, but only at a rate equal to the creation of substitutes (including recycling).
(5) The scale of economic activity should be restrained so that it remains within the carrying capacity of the available natural resources, with a built-in margin for error.

These involve the use of both economic incentives and regulations.

This approach to sustainable development is clearly set in the market-economy paradigm illustrated in Chapter 6, whereby pricing and other instruments are used to value and manipulate natural resource use. It is illustrated by Pearce's (1993b) work, which is set in the context of a belief that whereas in the 1970s analysts thought environmental growth and environmental conservation to be incompatible, they are now seen as potentially compatible. He argues that per-capita welfare levels can be increased while reducing the rate of natural resource usage, and bolsters this with examples from OECD countries which show that since 1970 energy requirements and sulphur dioxide emissions have declined per unit of GDP.

He claims that 'technological change can substantially alter the coefficients between real income and environmental impact . . . [and] this technological change . . . holds out the greatest promise for sustainable development' (1993b, p. 78) especially in the developing world where energy consumption per unit of GNP has been rising. His thesis is that economic growth can be decoupled from negative environmental impacts, and that growth in real incomes can be achieved without environmental degradation.

That decoupling requires information and incentives, thereby reducing uncertainty, ensuring that the correct price and quality signals are given, and allowing an appraisal of potential investments which incorporates environmental impacts. In the past, he argues, producers have selected the wrong trade-off among productivity, stability, sustainability and equitability. Highly productive exploitation – as of tropical forests – may not be sustainable; equitable systems may not be very productive (feudal England is his example); biological pest control may create sustainability, but at the costs of instability (fluctuating yields) and productivity. He concludes that: 'Uncertainty about the future tends to bias the trade-off towards productive but unsustainable systems. Ensuring sustainability therefore requires efforts to reduce uncertainty' (1993b, p. 91). Much uncertainty results from insecurity, especially over rights to use resources: if people were secure in their long-term access to land, for example, they may be less concerned to 'mine' it to obtain its productivity immediately, so land-tenure reforms may be sufficient to ensure improved resource management. Other strategies include resource pricing:

> Prices are powerful incentives. If resource prices are set too low, excessive use will be made of the resource . . . and overuse can readily contribute to environmental degradation. To secure an efficient use of resources, outputs should be priced at their marginal social cost, which comprises the marginal cost of production and the 'external costs' of pollution or resource degradation caused by producing the good. (1993b, p. 94)

But, as discussed in Chapter 6, there are problems with pricing the use of resources, especially the social costs; hence the need for state taxation policies to ensure that resource users (large corporations as well as individual farmers) meet the full social as well as private costs of their actions. To achieve this, governments must be better informed. This is illustrated by his case studies from the developing world (Pearce et al, 1990), which call for more research, better information, altered land-tenure rights, and pricing policies which reflect the full costs.

The implementation of sustainable development strategies on a global scale calls for a new political order – in order to implement Pearce's proposals, for example. Even under the weak sustainability strategies there is likely to be a need for both population control and the redistribution of human-made capital. As the Duke of Edinburgh (1989, p.7) put it in his Dimbleby Lecture:

> it is up to us as procreators, predators, manipulators, exploiters and consumers to realise that we have to live off the limited land of our planet. We`have to learn to accept that any further growth in the human population, any further increase in the exploitation of the Earth's limited natural and mineral resources, and any further degradation of the physical and biological systems of our planet, are bound to cause very serious problems for the generations that we have every reason to believe will come after us.

If world society is not to grow, in terms of either its material content or its numbers, then three types of institution are needed (Daly, 1977b): one for stabilising population (perhaps by marketing licences to have children?); one for stabilising physical wealth; and one for ensuring its equitable distribution. If the physical resource base is not to be depleted further, then four precepts must be satisfied (O'Riordan, 1989): first, that it is possible to know scientifically the rate at which resources are renewed, so that their management can be organised accordingly; second, that resource systems must be homoeostatic (see p. 26), so that if well managed they will remain in equilibrium; third, that the implications of drawing on a resource must be restricted to the tight ecosystem of which it is a part; and fourth, that using a resource up to its level of renewability can be ethically justified. O'Riordan (1989, p.30) argues that 'none of these principles is realistic, practicable or justifiable'. The first two are statements of scientific possibilities (or would be if it were feasible to make them), and are thus necessary, though insufficient, conditions for sustainable development. But sustainability

> is a much broader phenomenon, embracing ethical norms pertaining to the survival of living matter, to the rights of future generations and to institutions responsible for ensuring that such rights are fully taken into account in policies and actions. (1989, p.30)

It involves subjective judgements as well as objective assessments.

One of the biggest difficulties with the implementation of sustainable development for many commentators relates to the uneven distribution of power within the core–periphery structure of the world economy (see, for example, O'Connor, 1989). Thus Redclift (1984, p.130) argues that:

> The challenge, then, is not to seek to protect the natural environment from man, but to alter the global economy in which our appetites press on the 'outer limits' of resources. This can only be done by altering the entitlements of the poor in the South [the periphery] so that the environmental discourse becomes a development discourse.

Similarly, Adams (1990, p.202) concludes that: 'Green development is not about the way the environment is managed, but who has the power to decide how it is managed.' Most of the proposals for sustainable development based on market forces are likely to benefit the residents of the world's core and not the great mass who live in the periphery (at all spatial scales). Even within the core, many sustainable development policies will undoubtedly harm the material standards and prospects of many people – not least farmers – and coping with such impacts will call for sensitive economic and social policies.

Nevertheless, 'sustainable development' is firmly placed on the global agenda, in part, according to O'Riordan (1989, p.30), because it is 'safely ambiguous'. When carefully analysed, however, it is clear that it is 'politically treacherous because it challenges the status quo'. Furthermore, he argues (O'Riordan, 1993, p.39), it is not achievable:

> The trouble is that sustainable development needs much more than shirtsleeve greenery and the latent guilt of what are charmingly referred to as 'couch potatoes' for its survival. It confronts modern society at the very heart of its purpose. Humankind is still a colonising species. It has no institutional or intellectual capacity for equilibrium. Like it or not, true sustainability requires five conditions that are still far from any political consensus.

Those five conditions are:

(1) a form of democracy that transcends the nation-state and the next election, bringing 'sacrifice' to the fore and relegating 'self-interest';
(2) guarantees of rights and justice to peoples throughout the world, so that they are allowed to consume resources in an equilibrium manner;
(3) the commitments of technology, intellectual property and money to impoverished and environmentally vulnerable places, where they can be used by stable and uncorrupt governments;
(4) elimination of debt which results from core–periphery exploitation;
(5) the creation of mechanisms which will deliver training, resources and management to communities in need in ways that are socially acceptable and democratic.

These challenge the foundations of the capitalist world economy and, despite the efforts of non-governmental organisations, are unlikely to be achieved: according to O'Riordan (1993, p.39), 'the world is still in a desperately sorry state and is growing worse'. Milbrath et al (1994) illustrate the sorts of changes necessary if an implicit policy of maximising economic growth, at the cost of pollution, is to be replaced by one with a focus on reducing waste and avoiding pollution, even at economic cost. Public policy would have to: discourage conspicuous consumption; emphasise fulfilment in work, rather than work being the means to meeting material needs; conserve resource stocks; emphasise the use of renewable, as against non-renewable, resources;

plan for resource shortages; critically evaluate and, if necessary, restrict the deployment of science and technology; phase out nuclear energy; protect other species, rather than sacrificing them for economic gain; preserve biodiversity; limit population growth; emphasise particular forms of non-intrusive agriculture; and rely more on planning and less on markets. The likelihood of such major changes in lifestyles, including restrictions on what are now widely defined as individual freedoms, seems remote.

In sum, however attractive it is as a concept, sustainable development is not a feasible strategy within the economic and political constraints of the contemporary world economy. The problems which face its implementation summarise the basic theme of this whole book: the creation of environmental problems is a necessary outcome of the dominant mode of production, and their resolution is difficult because the only institutions which might be mobilised to promote sustainable development exist to promote the interests of those who benefit most from the status quo. Removal of the mechanisms generating the problems, other than through a major catastrophe, is extremely remote. As Harvey (1993, p. 28) puts it:

> it is pure idealism . . . to suggest that we can somehow abandon in a relatively costless way the immense existing ecosystemic structures of, say, contemporary capitalistic urbanization in order to 'get back close to nature'. Such systems are a reworked form of 'second nature' that cannot be allowed to deteriorate or collapse without courting ecological disaster for our own species. Their proper management (and in this I include their long-term socialistic or ecological transformation into something completely different) may require transitional political institutions, hierarchies of power relations and systems of governance that could well be anathema to both socialists and ecologists alike. But this occurs because there is nothing *unnatural* about New York City and sustaining such an ecosystem even in transition entails an inevitable compromise with the forms of social organisation and social relations which produced it.

## CONCLUSIONS

This book was not written to provide a blueprint for the future but rather to indicate the gaps in understanding which characterise much of the debate about environmental problems – though I take Simmons's (1993, p. 16) point that the term 'environmental problems' implies that the environment is behaving badly, when all of the evidence suggests that the bad behaviour is committed by humans! Tackling those problems requires much more than scientific understanding of environmental processes – this is a necessary but far from sufficient condition for progress to be made in ensuring equilibrium between human society and nature. It demands an understanding of how human societies work – especially their political economy.

The dominant ideology in contemporary world society with regard to environmental issues is what Cotgrove (1982, p.120) terms 'cornucopian'; there is an overriding belief in human ability to dominate nature, involving the application of science and technology (especially through the marketplace), with the necessary support of the state. Whether that vision is correct is probably best not put to the test, since if it fails it may be too late to design an alternative and thereby save the earth. It is extremely difficult to design a scenario that might be attainable through the political and economic processes that now permeate the whole world. Radical economic, social and political change is unlikely to occur; instead, we will continue with attempts to keep environmental damage within reasonable bounds, listening to the optimists who are confident of human ability to enhance material conditions of life unendingly, through a mode of production which encourages overproduction and waste. Until it is too late . . . always assuming that we believe that the pace of resource depletion and/or environmental degradation is threatening long-term human survival.

What are the options? Pearce et al (1989, p.11) set out a 'payoff matrix' (derived from Costanza, 1989) which simplifies them to four:

|  | **Actual State of the World** | |
| --- | --- | --- |
| **Policy Type** | *Optimists Right* | *Pessimists Right* |
| *Optimistic* | High | Disaster |
| *Pessimistic* | Moderate | Tolerable |

If the optimists are correct about environmental resilience and human technological abilities, then optimistic policies (which involve relative indifference to environmental issues) should lead to high material gains – economic development will continue untrammelled. But if such policies are followed and the pessimists are right, then ecological disaster is the likely consequence. 'Prudent pessimism' – following sustainable development policies even if the optimists are largely correct – could lead to moderate gains, whereas implementing those policies in a context when the pessimists are right could result in a tolerable future, if no more. The implication, to all but the largest risk-takers (and they would be taking many more risks with the life chances of future generations than with their own), is that optimistic policy programmes carry very substantial risks unless we are absolutely sure that the optimistic case regarding environmental resilience is correct. It is better to implement pessimistic policies, which will ensure at worst a tolerable future and at best moderate economic growth. This should be a price worth paying, but will it be?

# References

Abel, N.O.J. et al (1985) 'The problems and possibilities of communal land management in Ngwaketse District – a case study'. Summary Report, International Livestock Centre for Africa.

Abler, R.F., Adams, J.S. and Gould, P.R. (1971) *Spatial Organisation*. Prentice Hall, Englewood Cliffs, NJ.

Adams, J.G.U. (1970) 'Westminster: the fourth London airport', *Area*, 2: 1–9.

Adams, J.G.U. (1974) '. . . and how much for your grandmother?', *Environment and Planning*, 6: 619–26.

Adams, W.M. (1990) *Green Development: Environment and Sustainability in the Third World*. Routledge, London.

Agnew, J. and Corbridge, S. (1989) 'The new geopolitics: the dynamics of geopolitical disorder', in R.J. Johnston and P.J. Taylor (eds) *A World in Crisis? Geographical Perspectives* (2nd edn). Blackwell Publishers, Oxford, pp. 266–88.

Akehurst, M. (1977) *A Modern Introduction to International Law* (3rd edn). George Allen & Unwin, London.

Alford, R.R. and Friedland, R. (1985) *Powers of Theory*. Cambridge University Press, Cambridge.

Allen, B.J. and Crittenden, R.F. (1987) 'Degradation and a pre-capitalist political economy: the case of the New Guinea highlands', in P. Blaikie and H. Brookfield, *Land Degradation and Society*. Methuen, London, pp. 145–56.

Archer, J.C. and Taylor, P.J. (1981) *Section and Party*. John Wiley, Chichester.

Aubert, J.-F. (1978) 'Switzerland', in D. Butler and A. Ranney (eds) *Referendums*. American Enterprise Institute, Washington, pp. 39–66.

Ball, A.R. and Millard, F. (1986) *Pressure Politics in Industrial Societies*. Macmillan, London.

Barbier, E. B., Burgess, J. C. and Folke, C. (1994) *Paradise Lost: The Ecological Economics of Biodiversity*. Earthscan, London.

Barde, J.-P. and Pearce, D. (eds) (1991a) *Valuing the Environment: Six Case Studies*. Earthscan, London.

Barde, J.-P. and Pearce, D.W. (1991b) 'Introduction', in J.-P. Barde and D. W. Pearce (eds) *Valuing the Environment: Six Case Studies*. Earthscan, London, pp. 1–8.

Barlow, J. (1988a) 'A note on biotechnology and the food production chain', *International Journal of Urban and Regional Research*, 12: 229–46.

Barlow, J. (1988b) 'The politics of land into the 1990s', *Policy and Politics*, 16: 111–21.

Barrett, S. (1991) 'Global warming: economics of a carbon tax', in D. Pearce (ed.) *Blueprint 2: Greening the World Economy*. Earthscan, London, pp. 31–62.

Bayliss-Smith, T.P. and Feachem, R.G. (eds) (1977) *Subsistence and Survival: Rural Ecology in the Pacific*. Academic Press, London.

Beckerman, W. (1992) 'Global warming and international action: an economic perspective', in A. Hurrell and B. Kingsbury (eds) *The International Politics of the Environment*. Oxford University Press, Oxford, pp. 253–89.

Beckerman, W. (1995) *Small is Stupid*. Duckworth, London.

Beckerman, W. and Malkin, J. (1994) 'How much does global warming matter?' *The Public Interest*, 114: 3–16.

Benedick, R. E. (1991) *Ozone Diplomacy*. Unwin Hyman, Boston.

Bennett, R.J. and Chorley, R.J. (1978) *Environmental Systems: Philosophy, Analysis and Control.* Methuen, London.

Benton, T. (1992) 'Animal rights and wrongs: prolegomena to a debate', *Capitalism, Nature, Socialism*, 3(2): 79–127.

Berg, E. (1978) 'Democracy and self-determination', in P. Birnbaum, J. Lively and G. Parry (eds) *Democracy, Consensus and Social Contract.* Sage Publications, London, pp.149–72.

Berry, B.J.L. (1972) *The Human Consequences of Urbanization.* Macmillan, New York.

Binder, P. (1977) *Treasure Islands.* Blond and Briggs, London.

Binns, T. (1990) 'Is desertification a myth?', *Geography*, 75: 106–13.

Blaikie, P. (1985) *The Political Economy of Soil Erosion in Developing Countries.* Longman, London.

Blaikie, P. (1989) 'Natural resource use', in R.J. Johnston and P.J. Taylor (eds) *A World in Crisis?* (2nd edn). Basil Blackwell, Oxford, pp.125–50.

Blaikie, P. and Brookfield, H. (1987a) 'Approaches to the study of land degradation', in P. Blaikie and H. Brookfield, *Land Degradation and Society.* Methuen, London, pp.27–48.

Blaikie, P. and Brookfield, H. (1987b) 'Questions from history in the Mediterranean and Western Europe', in P. Blaikie and H. Brookfield, *Land Degradation and Society.* Methuen, London, pp.122–42.

Blaikie, P. and Brookfield, H. (1987c) 'Common property resources and degradation worldwide', in P. Blaikie and H. Brookfield, *Land Degradation and Society.* Methuen, London, pp.186–95.

Blaikie, P. and Brookfield, H. (1987d) 'Socialism and the environment', in P. Blaikie and H. Brookfield, *Land Degradation and Society.* Methuen, London, pp.208–13.

Bloch, M. (1961) *Feudal Society.* Routledge & Kegan Paul, London.

Blowers, A.T. and Leroy, P. (1994) 'Power, politics and environmental inequality: a theoretical analysis of the process of "peripheralization". *Environmental Politics*, 3: 197–228.

Bluestone, B. and Harrison, B. (1982) *The Deindustrialization of America.* Basic Books, New York

Bogdanor, V. and Butler,: D. (eds) (1983) *Democracy and Elections.* Cambridge University Press, Cambridge.

Bollen, K.A. (1983) 'World system position, dependency and democracy: the cross-national evidence', *American Sociological Review*, 48: 458–79.

Bradley, P.N. and Carter, S.E. (1989) 'Food production and distribution – and hunger', in R.J. Johnston and P.J. Taylor (eds) *A World in Crisis?* (2nd edn). Basil Blackwell, Oxford, pp.101–24.

Brams, S.J. (1975) *Game Theory and Politics.* The Free Press, New York.

Brandt, W. (1980) *North–South: A Programme for Survival.* Pan, London.

Brandt, W. (1983) *Common Crisis, North–South: Cooperation for World Recovery.* Pan, London.

Brechin, S. R. and Kempton, W. (1994) 'Global environmentalism: a challenge to the postmaterialism thesis', *Social Science Quarterly*, 75: 245–69.

Breheny, M. (1995) 'The compact city and transport energy consumption', *Transactions, Institute of British Geographers*, NS 20. 81–101.

Brotherton, D.I. (1986) 'Party political approaches to rural conservation in Britain', *Environment and Planning A*, 18: 151–60.

Burton, I., Kates, R.W. and White, G.F. (1978) *The Environment as Hazard.* Oxford University Press, New York.

Butler, D. (1960) 'The paradox of party difference', *The American Behavioral Scientist*, 3: 3–5.

Butler, D., Penniman, H.R. and Ranney, A. (eds) (1981) *Democracy at the Polls*. American Enterprise Institute, Washington.

Butlin, R.A. and Dodgshon, R.A. (eds) (1989) *An Historical Geography of England and Wales* (2nd edn). Academic Press, London.

Carroll, J.E. (1986) 'Water resources management as an issue in environmental diplomacy', *Natural Resources Journal*, 26: 207–20.

Carter, F.W. (1993a) 'Bulgaria' in F.W. Carter and D. Turnock, (eds) *Environmental Problems in Eastern Europe*. Routledge, London, pp. 38–62.

Carter, F.W. (1993b) 'Poland' in F.W. Carter and D. Turnock, (eds) *Environmental Problems in Eastern Europe*. Routledge, London, pp. 107–34.

Carter, F.W. and Turnock, D. (1993a) 'Introduction' in F.W. Carter and D. Turnock (eds) *Environmental Problems in Eastern Europe*. Routledge, London, pp. 1–6.

Carter, F.W. and Turnock, D. (eds) (1993b) 'Problems of the pollution scenario' in F.W. Carter and D. Turnock (eds) *Environmental Problems in Eastern Europe*. Routledge, London, pp. 188–219 .

Carter, F.W. and Turnock D. (eds) (1993c) *Environmental Problems in Eastern Europe*. Routledge, London.

Catton, W.R. (1978) 'Carrying capacity, overshoot, and the quality of life', in J.M. Yinger and S.J. Cutler (eds) *Major Social Issues: A Multidisciplinary View*. The Free Press, New York, pp. 233–49.

Catton, W.R. (1983) 'Social and behavioral aspects of the carrying capacity of natural environments', in I. Altman and J.F. Wohlwill (eds) *Behavior and the Natural Environment*, Volume 6. Plenum Press, New York, pp. 269–306.

Catton, W.R. (1985) 'On the dire destiny of human lemmings', in M. Tobias (ed.) *Deep Ecology*. Avant Books, San Diego, CA, pp. 74–89.

Catton, W.R. (1987) 'The world's most polymorphic species: carrying capacity transgressed two ways', *BioScience*, 37: 413–19.

Catton, W.R. and Dunlap, R.E. (1980) 'A new ecological paradigm for post-exuberant sociology', *The American Behavioral Scientist*, 24: 15–47.

Catton, W.R., Lenski, G. and Buttel, F.H. (1986) 'To what degree is a social system dependent on its resource base?', in J.F. Short (ed.) *The Social Fabric: Dimensions and Issues*. Sage Publications, Beverly Hills, CA, pp. 165–86.

Cawson, A. (1987a) 'Corporatism', in V. Bogdanor (ed.) *The Blackwell Encyclopaedia of Political Institutions*. Basil Blackwell, Oxford, pp. 154–6.

Cawson, A. (1987b) 'Corporatism', in D. Miller, J. Coleman, W. Connolly and A. Ryan (eds) *The Blackwell Encyclopaedia of Political Thought*. Basil Blackwell, Oxford, pp. 104–6.

Chambers, R. and Conway, G. (1992) *Sustainable Rural Livelihoods: Practical Concepts for the 21st Century*. Discussion Paper 296. Institute of Development Studies, University of Sussex, Brighton.

Chandler, T.J. (1965) *The Climate of London*. Hutchinson, London.

Chisholm, M. (1962) *Rural Settlement and Land Use*. Hutchinson, London.

Chorley, R.J. and Kennedy, B.A. (1971) *Physical Geography: A Systems Approach*. Prentice Hall, Englewood Cliffs, NJ.

Chorley, R.J., Beckinsale, R.P. and Dunn, A.J. (1973) *The History of the Study of Landforms: Volume III. The Life of William Morris Davis*. Methuen, London.

Churchill, R. R. (1991) 'International environmental law and the United Kingdom', in R.R. Churchill, L. Warren and J. Gibson (eds) *Law, Policy and the Environment*. Basil Blackwell, Oxford, pp. 155–73.

Clark, A.H. (1949) *The Invasion of New Zealand by People, Plants and Animals*. Rutgers University Press, New Brunswick, NJ.

Clark, G.L. (1982) 'Instrumental reason and policy analysis', in D.T. Herbert and R.J.

Johnston (eds) *Geography and the Urban Environment, Vol. 5.* John Wiley, Chichester, pp. 41–62.

Clark, G.L. and Dear, M.J. (1984) *State Apparatus.* Allen & Unwin, Boston.

Clingan, T.A. (1986) 'The United States and the Law of the Sea Conference', in G. Pontecorvo (ed.) *The New Order of the Oceans.* Columbia University Press, New York, pp. 219–37.

Cooke, R.U. (1984) *Geomorphological Hazards in Los Angeles.* Allen & Unwin, London.

Cooke, R.U. and Reeves, R.W. (1976) *Arroyos and Environmental Change in the American South-West.* Clarendon Press, Oxford.

Costanza, R. (1989) 'What is ecological economics?', *Ecological Economics*, 1: 1–7.

Cotgrove, S. (1982) *Catastrophe or Cornucopia: The Environment and the Future.* John Wiley, Chichester.

Coulter, P. (1975) *Social Mobilization and Liberal Democracy.* Lexington Books, Lexington, MA.

Council on Environmental Quality (1982) *The Global 2000 Report for the President.* Penguin Books, London.

Crocombe, R.G. (1972) 'Land tenure in the South Pacific', in R.G. Ward (ed.) *Man in the Pacific Islands.* Clarendon Press, Oxford, pp. 219–51.

Crosby, A.W. (1986) *Ecological Imperialism: The Biological Expansion of Europe, 900–1900.* Cambridge University Press, Cambridge.

Crosland, C.A.R. (1956) *The Future of Socialism.* Jonathan Cape, London.

Cumberland, K.B. (1947) *Soil Erosion in New Zealand.* Whitcombe and Tombs, Christchurch.

Curry, L. (1962) 'Climatic change as a random series', *Annals of the Association of American Geographers*, 52: 21–31.

Dahl, R.A. (1978) 'Democracy as polyarchy', in R.D. Gastil (ed.) *Freedom in the World.* G.K. Hall, Boston, pp. 134–46.

Daly, H.E. (1977a) *Steady-State Economics.* W.H. Freeman, San Francisco.

Daly, H.E. (1977b) 'The steady-state economy: what, why and how', in D.C. Pirages (ed.) *The Sustainable Society.* Praeger, New York, pp. 107–30.

Department of the Environment (1990) *The Common Inheritance.* HMSO, London.

Department of the Environment (1992) *The UK Environment.* HMSO, London.

Desai, M. (1983) 'Capitalism', in T. Bottomore, L. Harris, V.G. Kiernan and R. Miliband (eds) *A Dictionary of Marxist Thought.* Basil Blackwell, Oxford, pp. 64–7.

Dobson, A, (1990) *Green Political Thought: An Introduction.* Unwin Hyman, London.

Douglas, I. (1983) *The Urban Environment.* Edward Arnold, London.

Douglas, I. (1986) 'The unity of geography is obvious . . .', *Transactions, Institute of British Geographers*, NS 11: 459–63.

Downs, A. (1957) *An Economic Theory of Democracy.* Harper and Row, New York.

Dreze, J. and Sen, A. (1989) *Hunger and Political Action.* Oxford University Press, Oxford.

Dryzek, J.A. (1987) *Rational Ecology.* Basil Blackwell, Oxford.

Dubs, M. (1986) 'Minerals of the deep sea: myth and reality', in G. Pontecorvo (ed.) *The New Order of the Oceans.* Columbia University Press, New York, pp. 85–124.

Dufournaud, C. and Harrington, J. (1989) 'Temporal and spatial distribution of benefits and costs of basin schemes', *Environment and Planning A*, 22: 1517–22.

Duke of Edinburgh (1989) 'Living off the land', *The Listener*, 121 (3104): 4–7.

Dunleavy, P. and Husbands, C.T. (1985) *British Democracy at the Crossroads.* Allen & Unwin, London.

Dunleavy, P. and O'Leary, B. (1987) *Theories of the State.* Macmillan, London.

Eckersley, R. (1992) *Environmentalism and Political Theory: Toward an Ecocentric Approach.* UCL Press, London.

Elliott, L. (1994) 'Environmental protection in the Antarctic: problems and prospects', *Environmental Politics*, 3: 247–72.

Emel, J. and Bridge, G. (1995) 'The earth as input', in R.J. Johnston, P.J. Taylor and M.J. Watts (eds) *Geographies of Global Change: Remapping the World in the Late Twentieth Century.* Blackwell Publishers, Oxford, pp. 318–32.

Eyles, J. and Lee, R. (1982) 'Human geography in explanation', *Transactions, Institute of British Geographers*, NS, 7: 117–22.

Falk, R.A. (1972) *This Endangered Planet.* Vintage Books, New York.

Ferejohn, J.A. (1974) *Pork-Barrel Politics.* Stanford University Press, Stanford, CA.

Fernie, J. and Pitkethly, A.S. (1985) *Resources: Environment and Policy.* Harper and Row, London.

Finley, N.I. (1983) 'Slavery', in T. Bottomore, L. Harris, V.G. Kiernan and R. Miliband (eds) *A Dictionary of Marxist Thought.* Basil Blackwell, Oxford, pp. 440–1.

Frankel, B. (1987) *The Post-industrial Utopians.* Polity Press, Cambridge.

Fukuyama, F. (1992) *The End of History, and the Last Man.* Penguin Books, London.

Gardiner, V. (1990) 'Pollution of air, land, rivers and coasts', in R.J. Johnston and V. Gardiner (eds) *The Changing Geography of the United Kingdom* (2nd edn). Routledge, London.

Garner, J.F. and O'Riordan, T. (1982) 'Environmental impact at a time of financial restraint', *The Geographical Journal*, 148: 343–61.

GER UK (1995) 'Climate change special', *The Globe* (issue 24). UK GER Office, Swindon.

Giddens, A. (1989) *The Nation State and Violence.* Polity Press, Cambridge.

Glacken, C.J. (1967) *Traces on the Rhodian Shore.* University of California Press, Berkeley.

Glantz, J. (1995) 'Erosion study finds high price for forgotten menace', *Science*, 267: 1088.

Gleick, J. (1988) *Chaos: Making a New Science.* Cardinal Books, London.

Glick, T.C. (1987) 'History and philosophy of geography', *Progress in Human Geography*, 11: 405–16.

Gore, A. (1992) *Earth in the Balance: Forging a New Common Purpose.* Earthscan, London.

Goudie, A.S. (1986a) *The Human Impact on the Natural Environment* (2nd edn). Basil Blackwell, Oxford.

Goudie, A.S. (1986b) 'The integration of human and physical geography', *Transactions, Institute of British Geographers*, NS 11: 454–8.

Gould, P.C. (1988) *Early Green Politics.* Harvester Press, Brighton.

Gould, P.R. (1963) 'Man against his environment: a game theoretic framework', *Annals of the Association of American Geographers*, 53: 290–7.

Gouldner, A. (1979) *The Future of Intellectuals and the Rise of the New Middle Class.* Macmillan, London.

Grainger, A. (1990) *The Threatening Desert: Controlling Desertification.* Earthscan, London.

Gregory, D. (1980) 'The ideology of control', *Tijdschrift voor Economische en Sociale Geografie*, 71: 327–42.

Gregory, K.J. (1985) *The Nature of Physical Geography.* Edward Arnold, London.

Griffiths, M.J. and Johnston, R.J. (1990) 'What's in a place?' *Antipode*, 23: 185–213.

Grove, J.M. (1988) *The Little Ice Age.* Methuen, London.

Grubb, M., Koch, M., Munson, A., Sullivan, F. and Thomson, K. (1993) *The Earth Summit Agreements: A Guide and Assessment.* Earthscan, London.

Gudgin, G. and Taylor, P.J. (1980) *Seats, Votes and the Spatial Organisation of Elections*. Pion, London.

Gustafson, T. (1981) *Reform in Soviet Politics*. Cambridge University Press, Cambridge.

Haines-Young, R.H. and Petch, J.R. (1985) *Physical Geography: Its Nature and Methods*. Harper and Row, London.

Hall, P. (1988) *Cities of Tomorrow*. Basil Blackwell, Oxford.

Hardin, G. (1968) 'The tragedy of the commons: The population problem has no technical solution; it requires a fundamental extension in morality', *Science*, 162: 1243–8.

Hardin, G. (1974) 'Living on a lifeboat', *Bioscience*, 24: 561–8.

Hare, F.K., Kates, R.W. and Warren, A. (1977) 'The making of deserts: climate, ecology and society', *Economic Geography*, 53: 332–46.

Harrop, M. and Miller, W.L. (1987) *Elections and Voters*. Macmillan, London.

Harvey, D. (1973) *Social Justice and the City*. Edward Arnold, London.

Harvey, D. (1974) 'Population, resources, and the ideology of science', *Economic Geography*, 50: 256–77.

Harvey, D. (1982) *The Limits to Capital*. Basil Blackwell, Oxford.

Harvey, D. (1985a) *The Urbanization of Capital*. Basil Blackwell, Oxford.

Harvey, D. (1985b) 'The geopolitics of capitalism', in D. Gregory and J. Urry (eds) *Social Relations and Spatial Structures*. Macmillan, London, pp.128–63.

Harvey, D. (1993) 'The nature of environment: the dialectics of social and environmental change', in R. Miliband and L. Panitch (eds) *Real Problems, False Solutions: The Socialist Register 1993*. Merlin Press, London, pp.1–51.

Hay, P.R. and Haward, M.G. (1988) 'Comparative green politics: beyond the European context?' *Political Studies*, 36: 433–48.

Hays, S.P. (1987) *Beauty, Health and Permanence: Environmental Politics in the United States, 1955–1985*. Cambridge University Press, Cambridge.

Hayter, T. (1989) *Exploited Earth: Britain's Aid and the Environment*. Earthscan, London.

Hechter, M. (1975) *Internal Colonialism*. Routledge & Kegan Paul, London.

Hechter, M. and Brustein, W. (1980) 'Regional modes of production and patterns of state formation in Western Europe', *American Journal of Sociology*, 85: 1061–94.

Heilbroner, R.L. (1974) *An Inquiry into the Human Prospect*. Harper and Row, New York.

Hilton, R.H. (1983) 'Feudal society', in T. Bottomore, L. Harris, V.G. Kiernan and R. Miliband (eds) *A Dictionary of Marxist Thought*. Basil Blackwell, Oxford, pp.166–71.

Hirsch, F. (1977) *Social Limits to Growth*. Routledge & Kegan Paul, London.

Hobbes, T. (1968) *Leviathan*. Penguin Books, London.

Hodge, D. and Staeheli, L.A. (1989) 'Social transformation and changing urban electoral behaviour', in R.J. Johnston, F.M. Shelley and P.J. Taylor (eds) *Developments in Electoral Geography*. Routledge, London.

Huggett, R.J. (1980) *Systems Analysis in Geography*. Clarendon Press, Oxford.

Hulme, M. (1989) 'Is environmental degradation causing drought in the Sahel?' *Geography*, 74: 38–46.

Hurrell, A. (1994) 'A crisis of ecological viability? Global environmental change and the nation state', *Political Studies*, 42: 146–65.

Inglehart, R. (1977) *The Silent Revolution: Changing Values and Political Styles*. Princeton University Press, Princeton, NJ.

Inglehart, R. (1995) 'Public support for environmental protection: objective problems and subjective values in 43 societies', *PS: Political Science and Politics*, 28: 57–72.

Ionescu, G. (1975) *Centripetal Politics.* Hart-Davies, London.

Jackson, T. and Marks, N. (1994) *Measuring Sustainable Economic Welfare – A Pilot Index.* New Economics Foundation, London.

James, C. (1992) *New Territory.* Bridget Williams Books, Wellington.

Johnston, R.J. (1976) 'Observations on accounting procedures and urban size policies', *Environment and Planning A,* 8: 327–40.

Johnston, R.J. (1977) 'Novel and eccentric . . . but valuable? Some response to Richardson', *Environment and Planning A,* 9: 357–60.

Johnston, R.J. (1979a) *Political, Electoral and Spatial Systems.* Oxford University Press, Oxford.

Johnston, R.J. (1979b) *Geography and Geographers: Anglo-American Human Geography since 1945.* Edward Arnold, London.

Johnston, R.J. (1980a) *The Geography of Federal Spending in the United States of America.* John Wiley, Chichester, Sussex.

Johnston, R.J. (1980b) 'On the nature of explanation in human geography', *Transactions, Institute of British Geographers,* NS 5: 402–12.

Johnston, R.J. (1982a) *Geography and the State.* Macmillan, London.

Johnston, R.J. (1982b) 'On the nature of human geography', *Transactions, Institute of British Geographers,* NS 7: 123–5.

Johnston, R.J. (1982c) 'Political geography and political power', in M.J. Holler (ed.) *Power, Voting and Voting Power.* Physica-Verlag, Vienna, pp. 289–306.

Johnston, R.J. (1983) 'Resource analysis, resource management and the integration of physical and human geography', *Progress in Physical Geography,* 7: 127–46.

Johnston, R.J. (1984) *Residential Segregation, the State and Constitutional Conflict in American Urban Areas.* Academic Press, London.

Johnston, R.J. (1986a) *On Human Geography.* Basil Blackwell, Oxford.

Johnston, R.J. (1986b) 'The state, the region and the division of labor', in A.J. Scott and M. Storper (eds) *Production, Work, Territory.* Allen Unwin, Boston, MA, pp. 265–80.

Johnston, R.J. (1986c) 'Four fixations and the unity of geography', *Transactions, Institute of British Geographers,* NS 11: 449–53.

Johnston, R.J. (1988) 'There's a place for us', *New Zealand Geographer,* 44: 8–13.

Johnston, R.J. (1989) 'The individual in the world-economy', in R.J. Johnston and P.J. Taylor (eds) *A World in Crisis?* (2nd edn). Basil Blackwell, Oxford, pp. 200–28.

Johnston, R.J. (1992) 'Laws, states and super-states: international law and the environment', *Applied Geography,* 12: 211–28.

Johnston, R.J. (1993) 'The rise and decline of the corporate welfare state: a comparative analysis in global context', in P.J. Taylor (ed.) *Political Geography of the Twentieth Century: A Global Analysis.* Belhaven Press, London, pp. 115–69.

Johnston, R.J. (1995) 'Proportional representation and proportional power', *Politics Review,* 4(4): 28–33.

Johnston, R.J. and Honey, R.D. (1988) 'Political geography of contemporary events X: The 1987 general election in New Zealand', *Political Geography Quarterly,* 7: 363–9.

Johnston, R.J. and Pattie, C.J. (1989) 'A nation dividing? Economic well-being, voter response and the changing electoral geography of Great Britain', *Parliamentary Affairs,* 42: 37–57.

Johnston, R.J. and Pattie, C.J. (1995) 'People, place and the economic theory of voting: the 1992 British general election', *Politics,* 15: 9–18.

Johnston, R.J., O'Loughlin, J. and Taylor, P.J. (1987) 'The geography of violence and premature death', in R. Vayrynen (ed.) *The Quest for Peace.* Sage Publications, London, pp. 241–59.

Johnston, R.J., Pattie, C.J. and Allsopp, J.G. (1988) *A Nation Dividing?* Longman, London.

Johnston, R.J., Taylor, P.J. and Watts, M.J. (eds) (1995) *Geographies of Global Change: Remapping the World in the Late Twentieth Century.* Blackwell Publishers, Oxford.

Jones, D.K.C. (1983) 'Environments of concern', *Transactions, Institute of British Geographers,* NS 8: 429–57.

Jones, D.K.C. (1990) 'Human occupance and the physical environment', in R.J. Johnston and V. Gardiner (eds) *The Changing Geography of the United Kingdom* (2nd edn). Routledge, London, 382–428.

Kennedy, P. (1988) *The Rise and Fall of the Great Powers: Economic Change and Military Conflict from 1500 to 2000.* Fontana Books, London.

Kiss, A. C. (ed.) (1983) *Selected Multilateral Treaties in the Field of the Environment.* United Nations Environment Programme, Nairobi.

Klinger, J. (1994) 'Debt-for-nature swaps and the limits to international cooperation on behalf of the environment', *Environmental Politics,* 3: 229–46.

Kneese, A.V. (1964) *The Economics of Regional Water Quality.* Johns Hopkins University Press, Baltimore, MD.

Kneese, A.V. and Bower, B.T. (1968) *Managing Water Quality.* Johns Hopkins University Press, Baltimore, MD.

Kolakowski, L. (1978) *Main Currents of Marxist Though* (3 vols). Oxford University Press, Oxford.

Komarov, B. (1981) *The Destruction of Nature in the Soviet Union.* Pluto Press, London.

Lamprey, H. (1978) 'The integrated project on arid lands', *Nature and Resources,* 14: 2–11.

Landsberg, H.H. (1981) *The Urban Climate.* Academic Press, New York.

Lane, S. (1995) 'The dynamics of river channels', *Geography,* 80: 147–62.

Lash, S. and Urry, J. (1987) *The End of Organized Capitalism.* Polity Press, Cambridge.

Laver, M. (1981) *The Politics of Private Desires.* Penguin Books, London.

Laver, M. (1984) 'The politics of inner space: tragedies of three commons', *European Journal of Political Research,* 12: 59–71.

Laver, M. (1986) 'Public, private and common in outer space', *Political Studies,* 34: 359–73.

Lawson, S. (1988) 'Fiji's communal electoral system', *Politics,* 23(2): 35–47.

Lee, E.C. (1978) 'California', in D. Butler and A. Ranney (eds) *Referendums.* American Enterprise Institute, Washington, pp. 87–122.

Leifer, M. (1995) 'Tigers, tigers spurning rights'. *The Times Higher Education Supplement,* 21 April, 16.

le Marquand, D. (1986) 'Pre-conditions to cooperation in Canada–U.S. boundary waters', *Natural Resources Journal,* 26: 221–42.

Lipset, S.M. and Rokkan, S.E. (1967) 'Cleavage structures, party systems and voter alignments: an introduction', in S.M. Lipset and S.E. Rokkan (eds) *Party Systems and Voter Alignments.* The Free Press, New York, pp. 3–64.

Litkin, K. (1994) *Ozone Discourses: Science and Politics in Global Environmental Cooperation.* Columbia University Press, New York.

Lloyd, W.F. (1833) *Two Lectures on the Checks to Population.* Oxford University Press, Oxford.

Lorenz, E.N. (1963) 'Deterministic nonperiodic flow', *Journal of the Atmospheric Sciences,* 20: 130–41.

Lovelock, J. (1988) *The Ages of Gaia: A Biography of Our Living Earth.* Oxford University Press, New York.

Lowe, P. and Goyder, J. (1983) *Environmental Groups in Politics.* Allen & Unwin, London.

Lowenthal, D. (ed.) (1965) *George Perkins Marsh: Man and Nature.* Harvard University Press, Cambridge, MA.

McCaskill, L. (1969) *Molesworth.* A.H. and A.W. Reed, Wellington.

McCaskill, L. (1973) *Hold This Land: A History of Soil Conservation in New Zealand.* A.H. and A.W. Reed, Wellington.

McKibben, W. (1990) *The end of Nature.* Penguin, London.

Macpherson, C.B. (1968) 'Introduction' to T. Hobbes, *Leviathan.* Penguin Books, London, pp. 9–63.

Mann, M. (1984) 'The autonomous power of the state', *European Journal of Sociology,* 25: 185–213.

Mann, M. (1986) *The Sources of Social Power.* Cambridge University Press, Cambridge.

Markusen, A. (1985) *Profit Cycles, Oligopoly and Regional Development.* MIT Press, Cambridge, MA.

Marx, K. (1970) *A Contribution to the Critique of Political Economy,* International Publishers, New York.

Marx, K. (1977) *Capital* (Vol. 1). Lawrence and Wishart, London.

May, R.J. (1976) 'Simple mathematical models with very complicated dynamics', *Nature,* 261: 459–67.

Meadows, D.H., Meadows, D.L., Randers, J. and Behrens, W.W. (1972) *The Limits to Growth.* Universe Books, New York.

Meinig, D.W. (1962) *On the Margins of the Good Earth.* Rand McNally, Chicago.

Memon, P. A. (1993) *Keeping New Zealand Green: Recent Environmental Reforms.* University of Otago Press, Dunedin.

Middlemass, K. (1979) *Politics in Industrial Society.* André Deutsch, London.

Mikesell, M.W. (1969) 'The deforestation of Mount Lebanon', *Geographical Review,* 59: 1–28.

Milbrath, L., Downes, Y. and Miller, K. (1994) 'Sustainable living: framework of an environmentally grounded political theory', *Environmental Politics,* 3: 421–44.

Millington, A.C., Mutiso, S.K., Kirby, J. and O'Keefe, P. (1989) 'African soil erosion – nature undone and the limits of technology'. *Land Degradation and Rehabilitation,* 1: 279– 90.

Milner, C. (1972) 'The use of computer simulation in conservation management', in J.N.R. Jeffers (ed.) *Mathematical Models in Ecology.* Basil Blackwell, Oxford, pp. 249–75.

Moffat, I. (1992) 'The evolution of the sustainable development concept: a perspective from Australia', *Australian Geographical Studies,* 30: 27–42.

More, R.J. (1967) 'Hydrological models and geography', in R.J. Chorley and P. Haggett (eds) *Models in Geography.* Methuen, London, pp. 145–85.

Myers, N. (1979) *The Sinking Ark: A New Look at the Problem of Disappearing Species.* Pergamon Press, Oxford.

Nordhaus, W. (1991) 'A sketch of the economics of the greenhouse effect', *American Economic Review,* 81: 146–50.

O'Connor, J. (1972) *The Fiscal Crisis of the State.* St Martin's Press, New York.

O'Connor, J. (1989) 'Uneven and combined development and ecological crisis', *Race and Class,* 30(3): 1–11.

Odell, P.R. (1989) 'Draining the world of energy', in R.J. Johnston and P.J. Taylor (eds) *A World in Crisis?* (2nd edn). Basil Blackwell, Oxford, pp. 79–100.

O'Loughlin, J. (1989) 'World power competition and local conflicts in the Third World', in R.J. Johnston and P.J. Taylor (eds) *A World in Crisis?* (2nd edn). Blackwell Publishers, Oxford, pp. 289–332.

O'Loughlin, J. and Parker, A.J. (1989) 'Tradition contra change: the political geography of Irish referenda', in R.J. Johnston, F.M. Shelley and P.J. Taylor (eds) *Developments in Electoral Geography*. Routledge, London, pp. 60–85.

Olson, M. (1965) *The Logic of Collective Action*. Harvard University Press, Cambridge, MA.

Openshaw, S., Steadman, P. and Greene, O. (1983) *Domesday*. Basil Blackwell, Oxford.

O'Riordan, T. (1981a) *Environmentalism*. Pion, London.

O'Riordan, T. (1981b) 'Environmentalism and education', *Journal of Geography in Higher Education*, 5: 3–18.

O'Riordan, T. (1987) 'The public and nuclear matters', in N. Geary (ed.) *Nuclear Technology International*. Sterling Publications, London, pp. 257–63.

O'Riordan, T. (1989) 'The politics of sustainability', in R.K. Turner (ed.) *Sustainable Environmental Development*. Belhaven Press, London, pp. 29–50.

O'Riordan, T. (1993) 'The politics of sustainability', in R. K. Turner (ed) *Sustainable Environmental Economics and Management: Principles and Practice*. Belhaven Press, London, pp. 37–69.

O'Riordan, T. and Kemp, R. (1988) *Sizewell B: Anatomy of an Inquiry*. Macmillan, London.

Ostrom, E. (1990) *Governing the Commons: The Evolution of Institutions for Collective Action*. Cambridge University Press, New York.

Ostrom, E. (1995) 'Constituting social capital and collective action', in R. O. Keohane and E. Ostrom (eds) *Local Commons and Global Interdependence: Heterogeneity and Cooperation in Two Domains*. Sage Publications, London, pp. 125–60.

O'Sullivan, N. (1988) 'The political theory of neo-corporatism', in A. Cox and N. O'Sullivan (eds) *The Corporate State*. Edward Elgar, London, pp. 3–26.

Owens, S. (1986) 'Environmental politics in Britain: new paradigm or placebo?' *Area*, 18: 195–201.

Packard, V. (1961) *The Waste Makers*. Longman, London.

Pahl, R.E. (1985) *Divisions of Labour*. Basil Blackwell, Oxford.

Painter, J. (1995) 'The regulatory state: the corporate welfare state and beyond' in R.J. Johnston, P.J. Taylor and M.J. Watts (eds) *Geographies of Global Change: Remapping the World in the Late twentieth Century*. Blackwell Publishers, Oxford, pp. 127–44.

Papadakis, E. (1988) 'Social movements, self-limiting radicalism and the Green Party in West Germany', *Sociology*, 22: 433–54.

Park, C.C. (1987) *Acid Rain: Rhetoric and Reality*. Methuen, London.

Pattie, C.J., Russell, A.T. and Johnston, R.J. (1991) 'Going green in Britain? Votes for the Green Party and attitudes to green issues in the late 1980s' *Journal of Rural Studies*, 7: 285–97.

Pearce, D. (1991) 'Introduction' in D. Pearce (ed.) *Blueprint 2: Greening the World Economy*. Earthscan, London.

Pearce, D. (1993a) *Economic Values and the Natural World*. Earthscan, London.

Pearce, D. (1993b) 'Sustainable development and developing country economies', in R.K. Turner (ed.) *Sustainable Environmental Economics and Management: Principles and Practice*. Belhaven Press, London, pp. 70–105.

Pearce, D., Markandya, A. and Barbier, E. (1989) *Blueprint for a Green Economy*. Earthscan, London.

Pearce, D., Barbier, E. and Markandya, A. (1990) *Sustainable Development: Economics and Environment in the Third World*. Earthscan, London.

Peet, J.R. (1969) 'The spatial expansion of commercial agriculture in the nineteenth century', *Economic Geography*, 45: 283–301.

Pepper, D. (1984) *The Roots of Modern Environmentalism*. Croom Helm, London.

Pepper, D. (1985) 'Determinism, idealism and the politics of environmentalism: a viewpoint', *International Journal of Environmental Studies*, 26: 11–19.

Pepper, D. (1986) 'Radical environmentalism and the labour movement', in J. Weston (ed.) *Red and Green: The New Politics of the Environment*. Pluto Press, London, pp. 115–39.

Pepper, D. (1993a) 'Political philosophy and environmentalism in Britain', *Capitalism, Nature, Socialism*, 4(3): 41–60.

Pepper, D. (1993b) *Eco-Socialism: From Deep Ecology to Social Justice*. Routledge, London.

Perry, A.H. (1981) *Environmental Hazards in the British Isles*. Allen & Unwin, London.

Peters, R.L. and Lovejoy, T.E. (1990) 'Terrestrial fauna', in B.L. Turner II, Clark, W.C, Kates, R.W., Richards, J.F., Matthews, J.T. and Meyer, W.B. (eds) *The Earth as Transformed by Human Action: Global and Regional Change in the Biosphere over the Past 300 Years*. Cambridge University Press, Cambridge, pp. 353–70.

Pimental, D., Harvey, C., Resoudarmo, P., Sinclair, K., Kurz, D., McNair, M., Crist, S., Shpritz, L., Fitton, L., Saffouri, R. and Blair, R. (1995) 'Environmental and economic costs of soil erosion and conservation benefits ', *Science*, 267: 1117–23.

Pirages, D.C. and Ehrlich, P.R. (1974) *Ark II: Social Response to Environmental Imperatives*. W.H. Freeman, San Francisco.

Plotkin, S. (1987) *Keep Out: The Struggle for Land Use Control*. University of California Press, Berkeley.

Polanyi, K. (1971) *Primitive, Archaic and Modern Economies: Essays of Karl Polanyi* (edited by G. Dalton). Beacon Press, Boston.

Porritt, J. and Winner, D. (1988) *The Coming of the Greens*. Collins Fontana, London.

Postan, M.M. (1973) *Essays on Medieval Agriculture and General Problems of the Medieval Economy*. Cambridge University Press, Cambridge.

Powell, J.M. (1970) *The Public Lands of Australia Felix*. Oxford University Press, Melbourne.

Powell, J.M. (1977) *Mirrors of the New World*. Dawson, Folkestone.

Prescott, J.R.V. (1985) *The Maritime Political Boundaries of the World*. Methuen, London

Rae, D.W. (1971) *The Political Consequences of Electoral Laws*. Yale University Press, New Haven, CT.

Ranney, A. (1978) 'United States of America', in D. Butler and A. Ranney (eds) *Referendums*. American Enterprise Institute, Washington, pp. 67–86.

Rawls, J. (1971) *A Theory of Justice*. Harvard University Press, Cambridge, MA.

Redclift, M. (1984) *Development and the Environmental Crisis*. Methuen, London.

Rees, J. (1985) *Natural Resources: Allocation, Economics and Policy*. Methuen, London.

Richards, J.F. (1990) 'Land transformation', in B.L. Turner et al (eds) *The Earth as Transformed by Human Action: Global and Regional Changes in the Biosphere over the Past 300 Years*. Cambridge University Press, Cambridge.

Roberts, R.S., Ufkes, F. and Shelley, F.M. (1989) 'Populism and agrarian ideology: the 1982 Nebraska corporate farming referendum', in R.J. Johnston, F.M. Shelley and P.J. Taylor, (eds) *Developments in Electoral Geography*. Routledge, London. pp. 153–75.

Rohrschneider, R. (1991) 'Public opinion towards environmental groups in Western Europe: one movement or two?', *Social Science Quarterly*, 72: 251–66.

Rostow, W.W. (1971) *The Stages of Economic Growth*. Cambridge University Press, Cambridge.

Rudig, W. and Lowe, P. (1986) 'The "withered" greening of British politics: a study of the Ecology Party', *Political Studies*, 34: 262–84.

Rummel-Bulska, I. and Osafo, S. (1991) *Selected Multilateral Treaties in the Field of the Environment.* United Nations Environment Programme, Nairobi.

Rykiel, E.J. and Kuenzel, N.T. (1971) 'Analog computer models of "The wolves of Isle Royale"', in B.C. Patten (ed.) *Systems Analysis and Simulation in Ecology,* Vol. 1. Academic Press, London, pp. 513–41.

Ryle, M. (1988) *Ecology and Socialism.* Radial Books, London.

Sack, R.D. (1983) 'Human territoriality: a theory', *Annals of the Association of American Geographers,* 73: 55–74.

Sack, R.D. (1988) 'The consumer's world: place as context', *Annals of the Association of American Geographers,* 78: 642–64.

Sagoff, M. (1988) *The Economy of the Earth: Philosophy, Law and the Environment.* Cambridge University Press, Cambridge.

Sanders, D. (1994) 'Economic influences on the vote: modelling electoral decisions', in I. Budge and D. Mackay (eds) *Developing Democracy.* Sage Publications, London, pp. 79–97.

Sarlvik, B. and Crewe, I. (1983) *Decade of Dealignment.* Cambridge University Press, Cambridge.

Schachter, O. (1986) 'Concepts and realities in the new Law of the Sea', in G. Pontecorvo (ed.) *The New Order of the Oceans.* Columbia University Press, New York, pp. 29–59.

Schulz, W. and Schulz, E. (1991) 'Germany', in J.-P. Barde and D. W. Pearce (eds) *Valuing the Environment: Six Case Studies.* Earthscan, London, pp. 9–63.

Schumacher, E.F. (1973) *Small is Beautiful.* Harper Torchbooks, New York.

Scott, A.J. (1988) *Metropolis.* University of California Press, Los Angeles.

Sen, A. (1981) *Poverty and Famines: An Essay on Entitlement and Deprivation.* Oxford University Press, Oxford.

Sewell, W.R.D. and Utton, A.E. (1986) 'Getting to yes in United States–Canadian water disputes', *Natural Resources Journal,* 26: 213–20.

Shaw, B.D. (1981) 'Climate, environment and history: the case of Roman North Africa', in T.M.L. Wigley, M.J. Ingram and G. Farmer (eds) *Climate and History.* Cambridge University Press, Cambridge, pp. 379–403.

Sheail, J. (1976) *Nature in Trust.* Blackie, Glasgow.

Sheail, J. (1981) *Rural Conservation in Inter-War Britain.* Clarendon Press, Oxford.

Simmons, I. G. (1991) *Earth, Air and Water: Resources and Environment in the Late 20th Century.* Edward Arnold, London.

Simmons, I. G. (1993) *Interpreting Nature: Cultural Constructions of the Environment.* Routledge, London.

Simon, D. (1989) 'Sustainable development: theoretical construct or attainable goal?', *Environmental Conservation,* 16: 41–8.

Simon, J.L. and Kahn, H. 1984: *The Resourceful Earth – a Response to Global 2000.* Basil Blackwell, Oxford.

Smil, V. (1987) 'Land degradation in China', in P. Blaikie and H. Brookfield, *Land Degradation and Society.* Methuen, London, pp. 214–22.

Snidal, D. (1995) 'The politics of scope: endogenous actors, heterogeneity and institutions', in R.O. Keohane and E. Ostrom (eds) *Local Commons and Global Interdependence: Heterogeneity and Cooperation in Two Domains.* Sage Publications, London, pp. 47–70.

Spoehr, A. (1956) 'Cultural differences in the interpretation of natural resources' in W.L. Thomas (ed.) *Man's Role in Changing the Face of the Earth.* University of Chicago Press, Chicago, pp. 93–102.

Stoddart, D.R. (1987) 'To claim the high ground', *Transactions, Institute of British Geographers,* NS 12: 327–36.

Susskind, L.E. (1994) *Environmental Diplomacy: Negotiating More Effective Global Agreements.* Oxford University Press, New York.

Swann, J.F. (1966) 'Acclimatisation of animals', *Encyclopaedia of New Zealand* (Vol. 1). Government Printer, Wellington, pp. 2–5.

Taagepera, R. and Shugart, M. (1989) *Seats and Votes: The Effects and Determinants of Electoral Outcomes.* Yale University Press, New Haven, CT.

Taylor, M. (1976) *Anarchy and Cooperation.* John Wiley, Chichester.

Taylor, M. (1988) *The Possibility of Cooperation.* Cambridge University Press, Cambridge.

Taylor, M. and Ward, H. (1982) 'Chickens, whales and lumpy goods', *Political Studies,* 30: 350–70.

Taylor, P.J. (1989a) *Political Geography* (2nd edn). Longman, London.

Taylor, P.J. (1989b) 'The error of developmentalism', in D. Gregory and R. Walford (eds) *Horizons in Human Geography.* Macmillan, London, pp. 303–19.

Taylor, P.J. (1989c) 'Extending the world of electoral geography', in R.J. Johnston, F.M. Shelley and P.J. Taylor (eds) *Developments in Electoral Geography.* Routledge, London.

Taylor, P. J. (1994) 'The state as container: territoriality in the modern world-system', *Progress in Human Geography,* 18: 151–62.

Taylor, P. J. (1995) 'Beyond containers: internationality, interstateness, interterritoriality ', *Progress in Human Geography,* 19: 1–15.

Taylor, P.J. and Johnston, R.J. (1979) *Geography of Elections.* Penguin Books, London.

Taylor, P. J. and Johnston, R. J. (1993) '1989 and all that: a reply to Michalak and Gibb'. *Area,* 25: 300–5.

Thomas, D. S. G. and Middleton, N. J. (1994) *Desertification: Exploding the Myth.* John Wiley, Chichester.

Thomas, K. (1984) *Man and the Natural World.* Penguin Books, London.

Thompson, C. (1989) 'The geography of venture capital', *Progress in Human Geography,* 13: 62–98.

Thornes, J.B. (1987) 'Environmental systems', in M.J. Clark, K.J. Gregory and A.M. Gurnell (eds) *Horizons in Physical Geography.* Macmillan, London, pp. 27–46.

Thrift, N.J. (1989) 'The geography of international economic disorder', in R.J. Johnston and P.J. Taylor (eds) *A World in Crisis?* (2nd edn). Basil Blackwell, Oxford, pp. 16–78.

Timberlake, L. (1981) 'Poland – the most polluted country in the world'. *New Scientist,* 92 (1276): 248–50.

Todd, E. (1985) *The Explanation of Ideology: Family Structures and Social Systems.* Basil Blackwell, Oxford.

Todd, E. (1987) *The Cause of Progress: Culture, Authority and Change.* Basil Blackwell, Oxford.

Trudgill, S.T. (1988) *Soil and Vegetation Systems* (2nd edn). Clarendon Press, Oxford.

Trudgill, S.T. (1990) *Barriers to a Better Environment: What Stops Us Solving Environmental Problems?* Belhaven, London.

Turner, B.L. II, Clark, W.C., Kates, R.W., Richards, J.F., Matthews, J.T. and Meyer, W.B. (eds) (1990) *The Earth as Transformed by Human Action: Global and Regional Changes in the Biosphere over the past 300 Years.* Cambridge University Press, Cambridge.

Turner, R.K. (1993) 'Sustainability: principles and practice', in R.K. Turner (ed.) *Sustainable Environmental Economics and Management: Principles and Practice.* Belhaven Press, London, pp. 3–36.

Turnock, D. (1993) 'Romania' in F.W. Carter and D. Turnock (eds) *Environmental Problems in Eastern Europe.* Routledge, London, pp. 135–63.

Ungar, S. (1992) 'The rise and (relative) decline of global warming as a social problem', *Social Science Quarterly*, 33: 483–94.

Urry, J. (1981) *The Anatomy of Capitalist Societies.* Macmillan, London.

Walker, R.A. and Williams, M.J. (1982) 'Water from power: water supply and regional growth in the Santa Clara Valley', *Economic Geography*, 58: 95–119.

Ward, H. (1987) 'The risks of a reputation for toughness', *British Journal of Political Science*, 17: 23–52.

Ward, H. (1989) 'Testing the waters: taking risks to gain reassurance in public goods games', *Journal of Conflict Resolution*, 33: 274–308.

Watts, M. (1983) *Silent Violence.* University of California Press, Berkeley.

Watts, M. (1989) 'The agrarian question in Africa', *Progress in Human Geography*, 13: 1–41.

Weale, A. (1992) *The New Politics of Pollution.* Manchester University Press, Manchester.

Weatherford, M.S. (1986) 'Economic determinants of voting', in S. Long (ed.) *Research in Micro-Politics*, Volume 1. Greenwood Press, New York, pp. 219–69.

Wescoat, J.L. (1985) 'On water conservation and reform of the prior appropriation doctrine in Colorado', *Economic Geography*, 61: 3–24.

Whatmore, S., Munton, R., Little, J. and Marsden, T. (1987a) 'Towards a typology of farm businesses in contemporary British agriculture', *Sociologia Ruralis*, 27: 21–37.

Whatmore, S., Munton, R., Little, J. and Marsden, T. (1987b) 'Interpreting a relational typology of farm businesses in southern England', *Sociologia Ruralis*, 27: 103–22.

Wheatley, P. (1971) *The Pivot of the Four Quarters.* Aldine Press, Chicago.

Williams, M. (1989) 'Deforestation: past and present', *Progress in Human Geography*, 13: 176–208.

Williams, W.T. (1963) 'The social study of family farming', *The Geographical Journal*, 129: 63–74.

Wilson, A.G. (1981a) *Geography and the Environment: Systems Analytical Methods.* John Wiley, Chichester.

Wilson, A.G. (1981b) *Catastrophe Theory and Bifurcation.* Croom Helm, London.

Witt, E. (1979) *Guide to the U.S. Supreme Court.* Congressional Quarterly Inc., Washington.

Wittfogel, K.A. (1956) 'The hydraulic civilizations', in W.L. Thomas (ed.) *Man's Role in Changing the Face of the Earth.* University of Chicago Press, Chicago, pp. 152–64.

Wittfogel, K.A. (1957) *Oriental Despotism.* Yale University Press, New Haven, CT.

Woods, R.I. (1989) 'Malthus, Marx and population crises', in R.J. Johnston and P.J. Taylor (eds) *A World in Crisis?* (2nd edn). Basil Blackwell, Oxford, pp. 151–74.

World Commission on Environment and Development (1987) *Our Common Future.* Oxford University Press, Oxford.

Worster, D. (1979) *Dust Bowl.* Oxford University Press, New York.

Young, O. R. (1995) 'The problem of scale in human/environment relationships', in R.O. Keohane and E. Ostrom (eds) *Local Commons and Global Interdependence: Heterogeneity and Cooperation in Two Domains.* Sage Publications, London, pp. 27–46.

# Index